NATURE
AND
CULTURE
IN THE
ILIAD

James M. Redfield

NATURE

AND

CULTURE

IN THE

ILIAD:

THE

TRAGEDY

OF

HECTOR

E tu onore di pianto, Ettore, avrai
ove fia santo e lagrimato il sangue
per la patria versato, e finchè il Sole
risplenderà su le sciagure umane.
Ugo Foscolo: *Sepolcri*

The University of Chicago Press
Chicago & London

THE UNIVERSITY OF CHICAGO PRESS, CHICAGO 60637
The University of Chicago Press, Ltd., London

© 1975 by The University of Chicago
All rights reserved. Published 1975
Phoenix Edition 1978
Printed in the United States of America

82 81 80 79 78   98765432

Library of Congress Cataloging in Publication Data
Redfield, James M.   1935–
    Nature and culture in the Iliad: The tragedy of Hector.

    Bibliography: p.
    Includes index.
    I. Homerus. Ilias. I. Title.
PA4037.R38   883'.01   74–33511
ISBN 0–226–70652–4 pbk.

DEDICATORY EPISTLE

In an earlier time scholars often dedicated their work to past or pro-spective patrons. Today the scholar perhaps believes that he has no patrons and requires none; he is of course deluded. It is only that his patrons have become more numerous, anonymous, and removed from his view, mediated by such agencies as the universities, the foundations, and the state. Patrons do not now support individual scholars but rather the enterprise of science and scholarship in general; the indi-vidual scholar will be wrong if he concludes that he has therefore no one to thank.

Certainly the present book would not have been written if the Joseph Regenstein Library had not existed; I returned to America after a year abroad to find that this library had opened in my absence, and for the first time I knew how the physicists feel when someone gives them an accelerator. The Regenstein Library is very large, very expensive, and it works. Probably no environment better adapted to the activity of scholarship has ever been created. In this library much that had been impossible becomes possible, and much that had been difficult becomes easy.

One theme of the present book is that men are more dependent on their circumstances than they can know or care to admit. It seems appropriate at the beginning of the book to acknowledge some of the resources which made possible its composition. I therefore dedicate this volume to Helen Regenstein, whose foresight and thoughtfulness, exercised through the Joseph and Helen Regenstein Foundation, have made her a benefactress of scholars—as the poet says: essomenoisi pu-thesthai, *"for men-to-come to inquire about."*

CONTENTS

PREFACE

WILAMOWITZ' BOOK ON HOMER grew out of the First World War; mine (to compare small things with great) out of two weeks' jury service in the Cook County Criminal Court building. Like him I felt the need to "submerge myself in the depths of a true masterpiece"; every day I took with me to Twenty-sixth and California an india-paper Homer. There were no cases to hear and nothing to do; we spent our days sitting at long tables, a room full of silent men. It was like being in prison, except that they let us go home at night. I was thrown, as they say, "on my own resources"; I went back to the book I knew best. There I slowly read and considered, not the entire *Iliad*, but the story of Hector, which I saw for the first time as a self-contained and partly detachable whole.

As I thought about Hector, my affection for him grew. I found in him a martyr to loyalties, a witness to the things of this world, a hero ready to die for the precious imperfections of ordinary life. I became Hector's partisan; I felt he had been neglected by the critics, unjustly shaded by the glamour of Achilles.[1] I saw his story as that of an admirable man who falls into error without ceasing to be admirable and who dies a death which is tragic because we find it inevitable and in some sense his own fault, but undeserved. For the first time I thought that I understood Aristotle's praise of the story of such a hero as the best kind of tragic plot. I determined to write something about, and in praise of, Hector and Homer.

The present book thus grew out of an interest in, and even perhaps an identification with, one hero. As the book has grown, it has become less personal. I found myself working from part to whole and from text to context. As I worked outward from the center, I found that around Hector's story I could cluster and sort impressions and observations accumulated through the years. I have avoided involvement in the Homeric Question. My premises are broadly Unitarian;[2] for me, as for others, the Homeric Question has become the question of Homer's sources, and if compelled to commit myself I should be inclined to favor the conception of the monumental composer as a dictating oral poet, but I have not argued these premises.[3]

The book has developed, broadly, in two directions: toward a picture of the *Iliad* as a unified work of art and toward a picture of

Homeric society as a functioning cultural system. To some extent I have allowed these two lines of argument to appear parallel, yet they must in fact be closely intertwined. Social analysis is the necessary precondition of literary criticism, because poetry implies culture just as *parole* implies *langue*. As long as we work with literature close to us, we remain unaware of this dimension; when we read Milton or Shakespeare—even Dante or Virgil—we more or less have the culture already and seldom have to think about it. Of course this is a matter of degree; the more exotic the text, the more contextual reconstruction is required. For me, the *Iliad* is a text almost as exotic as the *Mahabharata*, reflecting social conditions almost, but not quite, unimaginable by us. Perhaps I overstress this point; if so, it is in reaction to those who conclude (by no means cogently) that because the *Iliad* is a classic of our tradition, we therefore understand it. To some degree the very familiarity of the text gets in our way; we may have to set it at some distance before we can recover it.

Homer does not speak to us when we assign our meanings to his words[4] or when we allow ourselves to be guided by our immediate response to his scenes. We are all charmed when Hector fondles his little boy; we are less charmed when he prays that the boy may someday come back from the battle carrying a dead enemy's armor, "that his mother may joy in her heart." We wonder why Hector, who has just spoken so forcefully of the horrors of war, should not wish for his son a life of peace. But in Hector's ethic—the ethic of the *Iliad*—there is no complete manhood without war. War is thus both terrible and also necessary to happiness.

Culture is, like language, a "system of differences." When a hero acts or responds in a way we would not have expected, we should not only record our surprise but also ask ourselves what alternatives the hero had before him. No element of culture has meaning except in contrast to the other elements which might have become actual in that place. Therefore, no part can be interpreted without some reference to the whole system. We understand Homer's meaning only when we interpret him in relation to the whole system of potential meanings he presumes. Thus is defined for us—to follow the analogy with language—the task of translation; we must know the culture in order to interpret the story, just as we must know the language to translate the text.

On the other hand, we are translating from a dead language. We cannot interview the Homeric Greeks and elicit new data. The poem does not protest against misinterpretation; it maintains, in Socrates' phrase, "a very dignified silence." Homeric culture, further, is transmitted to us only in poetic imitation. We should not speak of the "background" of the poems, as though we could reconstruct Homeric society and then apply this reconstruction to interpretation of the poems. On the contrary: we discover the society by interpreting the poems, just as we learn Homeric Greek, not in order to read Homer, but by reading Homer.

Our view of Homeric society, like our view of Homeric language, has been shaped by accidents of representation within a small body of evidence. No doubt we often go wrong. Yet I allow myself one hypothesis which establishes an important control: I assume that the poem is a success. The poem can serve to interpret the culture if we assume that the poem is successfully founded on exactly that culture, so that any understanding of the implicit system of meanings will enable us to see this particular poem as more of a poem. I assume that Hector's prayer for his son was, for Homer's audience, the "right" prayer for Hector to make at that point—right in the sense that it best condenses the themes of Hector's story as they are at the moment. As we make such assumptions, we become able to interpret one passage in the light of another; gradually the poem makes more sense.

But this way of working has compelled me to ask what kind of sense a poem makes. I was thus drawn into the general question of the relation between poetry and culture. Clearly a poet gives us some kind of picture of his culture, but the picture is by no means literal. Clearly the poem is some kind of product of its culture, but the cause cannot be directly inferred from the effect. Both relations between poetry and culture must be interpreted, I came to think, in the light of a third relation: the poet as a maker of culture. We can understand the way in which the poem is a true picture of culture, and a characteristic product of culture, when we understand what the poem is for.

In order to reach these questions I found myself writing about Aristotle's *Poetics*. That section is almost accidentally about Aristotle; I began with the intention of setting out my own notions. The more I thought about the relation between poetry and culture, the more I thought I understood what Aristotle meant and the more I thought he was right. Furthermore, I suspect that for Aristotle also the *Iliad* is the work of art par excellence; he in fact says as much. I found Aristotle congenial, I think, precisely because so often we have the same poem before us. Once I had gone this far, Aristotle's terms came so neatly to hand that it would have seemed artificial not to quote him. But the treatment of Aristotle is intended as an introduction to the treatment of Homer; I would stand by my treatment of Aristotle in its own terms, but I have not attempted to argue it in those terms, in the sense that I have not attempted to respond to the very numerous body of critics who read Aristotle very differently from the way I read him.

I have drawn on other, more recent, theorists as well. The distinction that most pervades these pages is the distinction between nature and culture, and my essay may seem to be haunted by the spirit of Claude Lévi-Strauss, of whom it could well be said that "he has become a specter in his own time." It is true that I have read some works of Lévi-Strauss with enormous pleasure, but I do not declare myself a structuralist. The distinction between nature and culture is not the property of any school; it is already present in Aristotle's remark that "of things, some are by nature and some by other causes."

Aristotle and Lévi-Strauss I take to be appropriate figures for an essay which stands between the humanities and the social sciences. As between the two, Lévi-Strauss is perhaps more the humanist—since for him social artifacts and structures are primarily expressive and come to exist by clarifying acts of the human intelligence—while Aristotle is more thoroughly the scientist—since for him the form of anything, including a work of art, is the manner of its functioning, both internally, as an organized thing, and externally, as a thing with specifiable sources and uses.

My own work also is a human thing, having a history, a form, and a purpose. I have given the reader this personal, genetic, developmental account of the book before him in order to make clear what is primary. I did not choose the *Iliad* because I thought it a convenient object for analysis; rather, I developed the analysis because I care about the *Iliad*.

I thus remind the reader of a puzzle, a puzzle which is central to this book. It is this: Why do we care about these stories, which are so far from us and which are anyway not true? This, like many central puzzles, seems most of the time no puzzle at all; yet at times, when one is in the proper mood, it can appear to be an absolutely baffling mystery. We carry with us in our solitude these fictions the poets have left us, we brood over their meanings, feel joy and sorrow at the events, make of the characters our friends and enemies, and find ourselves somehow nourished by the experience. These unreal worlds become at certain moments more real to us than reality itself; that is the puzzle. I have found this puzzle engrossing. I have not been able to write this book without asking myself why I was writing it. The book is thus to a certain degree reflexive, aware of itself. I have tried to show the reader what I find in Homer and why I find him worth reading.

The things we read, I think, are worth reading only to the extent that we find them in some sense true. But this truth is of various kinds.

In the first place I find much truth in the Homeric way of seeing the world, a way of seeing which cannot have been personal to the monumental poet himself but must have been derived, partly from his society, partly from his poetic tradition. There is in Homer an implicit but systematic understanding of the relations of man with nature, man with man, man with god: a psychology, an ethics, a theology. All these, perhaps because they were created largely by poets, seem to me uniquely true to the phenomena of experience, including my own experience. The Homeric gods, for instance, provide me with a language for describing the world as it actually appears to me, full of irrational purposes and erratic interventions. I have lived with these Homeric heroes so long that I have come to think of them the way an ethnographer thinks of his tribe: as "my people"; and I find much wisdom among them. So in describing the Homeric world view, I have also intended to praise it.

Then there is a truth in the story. Insofar as it unfolds "in accordance with probability or necessity," it is—however unfamiliar its premises and exotic its locale—true to life. In order to speak of this kind of truth, I have found myself saying that fiction is the outcome of an inquiry into the causes of action and that we learn from fiction something about the conditions of action. Of course it must be understood that the result of the inquiry is a story, not a report, and that what we learn (one could almost say "appreciate") is the probability of this particular story, not some general propositional truth.

Finally, there is the truth achieved by the poet vis-à-vis his material as he brings it to a formal intelligibility. This truth is not much like the truth of science; it is more the kind of truth we mean when we say that a man is true to himself or to his vocation. In order to be master of his material, the poet must adopt a certain stance toward it, must be observant yet detached, personal but not self-indulgent. Every work of fiction is both a criticism of a society and a comprehension of it; the grander the conception, the more difficult the synthesis. To the degree that the poet achieves this synthesis he acquires a kind of dignity; he becomes a figure we admire and whose company we value. It is this kind of truth that I value in the author of the *Iliad*; his poem seems to me, more than any other, to embody the mature understanding a true man should have of his world.

Dignity of bearing we associate particularly with the tragic poets, perhaps because tragedy deals not only in truth but in harsh, uncomfortable truth. The tragic poet sets before us an unblinking vision of the world as it is, not according to our wish; he shows us those "inconvenient facts" which, according to Max Weber, are the special responsibility of the teacher. Thus the tragic poet, like the teacher, calls us to mature intelligence and shows us what demands that call makes upon us.

In our own time the tragic vision has been most associated with certain scientists—with Weber himself, for instance, and with Sigmund Freud, who wrote, in *Civilization and Its Discontents*: "People tell us that if life has no purpose it will have no value to them. But such threats alter nothing." We call this vision "tragic" for two reasons, which have to do with the harshness of the truth stated and with the dignity of the man who states it. Man, in the vision of a Weber or a Freud, is confined by the conditions of his nature and his history, irremediably subject to the contradictions of his own existence. He has, however, the power to reflect upon these conditions and to understand them, and he has the power to teach this understanding. He is "a reed, but a thinking reed"—and a speaking reed. Thus men, as they come to knowledge, find in their confrontation with their own weakness a certain heroic strength.

The wise men of the archaic age—the *sophoi*—were poets, and Homer was the wisest of the poets. In this essay I have tried to show what wisdom I find in Homer and how I find that wisdom expressed. Partly the poet is a magician—an enchanter and a seer; he shows us unreal and impossible worlds and with his spell makes us believe in them. But then it is also true that we believe in his unreality because we find it a way of seeing reality and of coming to terms with reality. After all, as W. H. Auden put it: "Nothing is lovely, not even in poetry, which is not the case."

ACKNOWLEDGMENTS

My chief thanks must go to Paul Friedrich; we have been collaborators in the field of Homeric studies for the past several years. Friedrich encouraged me to write the book in the first place and helped give it direction by his response to the first painful sketches. In so close a collaboration it is often impossible to remember who first conceived a notion or a line of inquiry, and I have not been able to acknowledge my intellectual debts to him in detail. The present book, in fact, has a kind of first cousin in Friedrich's "Defilement and Honor in the *Iliad*" (Friedrich 1973). The two manuscripts, however, while they have grown up together, have developed independently, and Friedrich should not be held to approve everything that is here.

Another manuscript which was being composed contemporaneously with this one is Wendy Olmsted's dissertation, "An Examination of the Relations between Thought and Perception with Reference to Homer, the Pythagoreans, Heraclitus, Plato, and Aristotle." This work obviously extends far beyond Homer; but to the extent that she concerned herself with Homer, I must acknowledge another collaborator whose thought I can no longer, in detail, disentangle from my own.

Yet another dissertation was being written during this time under my (in this case, largely nominal) supervision: Robert Vacca's "The Development of Sophrosyne in Homer and Aeschylus." Vacca and I did not read each other's manuscripts until they were largely done; if at certain points we seem to be proceeding on parallel tracks (although nearly always in opposite directions), this must be ascribed, not to collaboration, but to a friendship founded on many years of sympathetic intellectual contention.

Those who read the manuscript as a whole or in part at some stage in its composition and made valuable comments, too many of which I ignored, include Wayne C. Booth, Hoda Brigman, Eugene Gendlin, David Grene, Arthur Heiserman, Leonard Meyer, Roger Michener, Victor Turner, Edward Wasiolek, Karl J. Weintraub, James White, and Anthony Yu.

Special thanks are due to Stanley Gwynn for help at a crucial moment, to the Social Sciences Division of The University of Chicago for two small but timely grants, to Stephen Kane and Mary Redfield for reviewing the references and quotations, and to Mary Ann Fordyce for prodigies with the typewriter.

All translations (with one exception, noted on p. 240) are my own. Greek words have been transliterated, not rendered in phonemic transcription; I have not attempted to represent quantity except as it is represented in the Greek spelling. Proper names have been given in the form which, it was thought, would seem most familiar to the common reader. Uppercase roman numerals refer to books of the *Iliad*; lowercase, to books of the *Odyssey*.

J. M. R.

NATURE
AND
CULTURE
IN THE
ILIAD

INTRODUCTION:

ACHILLES AND HECTOR

ACHILLES AND THE CRITICS

In Book Nine of the *Iliad*, lines 308–429, Achilles responds to the embassy which brings Agamemnon's offer of restitution. This speech is the longest in the poem up to this point, and the moment of its giving has been long anticipated.[1] In Book One Achilles and Agamemnon quarrel; Achilles is about to kill Agamemnon when Athena appears and restrains him; in exchange for Agamemnon's *hubris*, she says, Achilles will receive "threefold gifts" (I.213–14). This promise sets the program for the books that follow. Achilles accepts Athena's instruction; he tells Agamemnon that he will allow the girl Briseis to be taken from him, as Agamemnon had demanded, but that "someday the longing for Achilles will overtake the Achaeans . . . when many fall in death at the hands of man-slaying Hector" (I.240–43). Achilles retires from the battle and asks his mother, Thetis, to appeal to Zeus for a Trojan victory so that the Achaeans

> should all appreciate their king
> And Atreus' son should come to know, wide-ruling Agamemnon,
> His error [*atē*], that he honored not the best of the Achaeans.
> (I.410–12)

Thetis goes to Olympus and makes her appeal:

> You, at least, give him honor, Olympian-ruling Zeus:
> So long give power to the Trojans, until the Achaeans
> Repay my son and advantage him with honor.
> (I.508–10)

Zeus promises that he will do as she asks, and the promise is kept, although with some delay. Already in Book Two the Greeks are fearful that Achilles' rage will harm them; Thersites blames Agamemnon (II.235–42), and Agamemnon is willing to admit that he was most in the wrong (II.375–78). We are told that Achilles is soon to return to battle (II.694). Later Apollo tells the Trojans that Achilles' absence is their opportunity (IV.509–13), and Hera warns the Greeks of their weakness without him (V.787–91). For a moment it looks as though Diomedes (VI.99–101) or Ajax (VII.226–32) might replace Achilles, but in Book Eight the Trojans press their advantage—in fulfillment, as a

3

speech of Athena's reminds us, of Zeus's promise to Thetis (VIII.358–72).

By the beginning of Book Nine the Greeks have been pushed back into their camp, the Trojan watchfires fill the plain, and Agamemnon is in tears (IX.14). Everything has happened as Achilles had threatened and Zeus had promised. Nestor takes charge and arranges a council, at which he puts all the blame on Agamemnon and says they must now pay Achilles back with gifts and soothing words (IX.103–13). Agamemnon accepts full responsibility and promises full restitution, setting forth an enormous catalogue of gifts (IX.115–61). Nestor responds: "These are no longer to be scorned, these gifts you offer prince Achilles" (IX.164). Nestor organizes an embassy, which Achilles receives kindly: "These men are my best friends here under my roof" (IX.204). Odysseus makes a careful speech, in which he describes the desperate position of the Greeks, sets out the catalogue of gifts all over again, makes a personal appeal to Achilles, and promises him the chance at last to kill Hector (IX.225–306). It is to this speech that Achilles responds.

Nothing in all this (except perhaps one phrase of Odysseus': IX.300–301) prepares us for Achilles' reply: Achilles refuses the gifts. I here set out the entire speech.

> Noble son of Laertes, crafty Odysseus,
> My speech will come straight through, forgetting tact,
> Just what I think—and I'll see it happen so.
> No need to sit there muttering each to each;
> I hate that man like to the gates of Hell
> Who hides one thing in his heart and says another.
> I'll say it straight, the way I see it best.
> I'm not for Agamemnon. He'll not sway me,
> Nor all the rest of you. There's no thanks in it
> To broil with killers without a pause forever.
> The same share comes however well you fight;
> There is one price for the brave man and the coward;
> They die together, doing little or much.
> Nothing I've got from it but heart's pain,
> Forever risking my life in the battle line.
> Like a nesting bird that brings, to featherless young,
> Morsels, whatever she gets, and herself goes short,
> So I have passed sleepless nights at my post
> And wasted bloody days in endless war,
> Fighting with men for other people's wives.
> Twelve cities I have sacked with strength of ships
> And eleven by land I count, near fertile Troy;

And out of them all, the spoil, plenty and choice,
I got, and gave it all to Agamemnon,
Atreus' son. He stays behind in camp,
Takes it, shares a little, and keeps the rest.
The other prizes given to princes and kings,
They can keep them, but from me alone
He took my lovely wife. Let him sleep with her
And enjoy her. Why did we come to fight
In Troy? Why did he have to call the army?
Or wasn't it for the sake of fair-haired Helen?
Do they alone among mortals love their wives,
These sons of Atreus? Any man of courage and sense
Values his own and cares for her, as I
Loved mine from the heart, spear prize though she was.
Now since he snatched my prize and cheated me,
Let him not try me. I know him; he won't persuade me.
Go on, Odysseus, you and the other lords;
Plot how to keep the fire away from your ships.
A lot of trouble he's taken while I was away.
He built a wall and drove a trench around it,
A great broad trench, and filled it full of stakes;
But it's not enough for the strength of man-killing Hector,
To hold him. While *I* was at war among the Achaeans,
He'd hardly leave the shade of the wall, this Hector;
Only as far as the gates and the oak he'd come;
There once he stood, and there I almost caught him.
No more do I wish to fight with noble Hector;
Tomorrow I'll pray to Zeus and the other gods
While I load my ships; when I put them in the water
You'll see—if you like, and if these things concern you—
At dawn on the fish-full Hellespont, sailing away,
My ships, and the sailors in them pulling the oars.
And if the lord of earthquakes give fair winds,
On the third day I'll come to fertile Phthia.
There's plenty I left when I came this cursed journey.
There's more I got here, gold and russet bronze,
Deep-waisted women, and ingots of gray iron;
I'll take my allotted share. But the prize he gave me
His arrogance took back, strong Agamemnon,
Atreus' son. Report me just as I tell you,
Openly, so the other Greeks will hate him.
Perhaps he hopes to cheat still another Danaid,
Cloaked in his shamelessness. But not to me
Would he come with his bitch's eyes and look in my face.
Not a bit will I join his council or do his work.

5

He cheated me and wronged me. Never again
Will he cozen me with his words. It's enough. At ease
Let him perish, for Zeus has snatched from him his wits.
Hateful his gifts—I count them a hair's worth;
Not if he offered me ten or twenty times
As much as now, if he could get it someplace,
Not so much as Orchomenus holds, or Thebes
In Egypt, where the houses bulge with goods—
There are a hundred gates, two hundred men
Ride out at each with chariots and horse—
Not if his gifts were numbered like sand or dust,
Not even so can the king persuade my heart
Until he has given me back the whole outrage.
I will not marry his girl, Agamemnon's daughter,
Not if she strives with Aphrodite in beauty
And her crafts are rivals even to owl Athena.
She's not for me. Some other Greek can have her,
Someone more to his heart, and more of a king.
But if the gods preserve me and I come home,
My father Peleus will find me a proper wife.
There are many women in my country, in Phthia,
Daughters of princes who rule their castle walls;
I can have whichever I want for a wife.
That is the way I am called by my strong-willed heart,
To marry a wedded wife, a fitting companion,
And enjoy in peace the wealth of my aged father.
No, it is not a life's worth, not all they say
Troy once possessed, that well-provided castle,
Before, in peace, before the Achaeans came here—
No, not so much as guards the stony lintel
Of Phoebus Apollo, high in rocky Pytho.
These can be stolen: cattle and fat flocks;
These can be won: tripods and red-maned horses,
But the life, to come back to the man—it cannot be stolen
Or grasped, when once it has passed the fence of his teeth.
My goddess mother tells me, bright-shod Thetis,
A double death-bringer bears me to the end:
If I stay here and fight by the walls of Troy,
I lose my return, but my fame will be immortal;
If I go home to the lovely land of my fathers,
I lose my noble fame, but long my life
Will be, nor soon the end of death will seek me.
And so to all you others, this my counsel:
Go, turn back home, for the end is not at hand
Of steep-walled Troy. For Zeus who sees it all

Has set on her his hand; her men take heart.
Go, turn back to the princes of the Achaeans.
Give them my message—that is the privilege of elders—
Let them contrive another plan, and a better,
To save their ships and the army of the Greeks,
Trapped in the camp, since this one wouldn't work,
This plan of yours, responding to my wrath.
Phoenix, though, can pass the night with us
So he can come in the ships to his own country
Tomorrow, if he like. But I would not force him.

(IX.308–429)

Obviously this speech is one of the great moments of the *Iliad*. It is full of rhetorical virtuosity, with its use of simile, analogy, and irony, its repeated ascending series, its mixture of long and short sentences, its gnomic formulations, even the hammerfall of the four-times repeated line-opening *Atreidēs/ēi/ai*: "Atreus' son(s)." Achilles, furthermore, responds to every point in Odysseus' speech; he rejects the gifts, rejects Agamemnon's friendship, tells his friends they must look elsewhere, restates the dangers of their position, and asserts that Hector no longer interests him. Yet where Odysseus' speech was organized and pointed, Achilles' speech comes through with blunt, obsessive power. He leaves each topic only to return to it, as though his mind were prowling within the closed circle of his rage. Odysseus' speech was composed with a careful view to his ends; Achilles begins with a claim to simple truth, and he explodes with the raw truth of his mental condition. It is as if he were talking to himself.

This speech is so powerful, and so unexpected, that the poem clearly opens out at this point into some previously unexplored territory. Achilles is himself the explorer, and he explores alone; from this point onward the other characters in the poem find him baffling and speak to him in protest and incomprehension. The embassy is utterly defeated by him; as Diomedes says, it is clear that the Greeks can do nothing with him and had better leave him alone (IX.697–703). Patroclus later says he is not acting like a human being at all:

Pitiless, your father was not the horseman Peleus,
Nor Thetis your mother, but the gray sea bore you,
And steep rocks, since your mind is harsh.

(XVI.33–35)

In different ways Phoenix (IX.515–26), Odysseus (XIX.216–29), and Apollo (XXIV.39–54) all say that Achilles is not behaving as human beings behave; he is not like a man, says Apollo, but a lion. The other

7

characters of the *Iliad*, in fact, do not interpret Achilles but confront him. The poet leaves the interpretation to us.

The critics have been, to say the least, divided. For Maurice Bowra the *Iliad* is a "profoundly moral story" held together by a scheme of "sin and punishment." For Bowra, Achilles' great speech to the embassy marks the moment when the hero falls into sin, and the definitive commentary on the speech is Phoenix' reply to it.

> Achilles has now become the victim of *atē*, the infatuation that leads to disaster. . . . It is all the worse because the divine ordinance which Achilles now violates is one of the most sacred, the law that mercy must be shown to suppliants. . . . In this scene Achilles definitely moves a step in the wrong direction. The recovery and repentance of Agamemnon remove what excuse he had before, and now he alone is to blame for the dire position of the Achaeans.[2]

Bowra's reading of the embassy scene is the key to his interpretation of the entire poem:

> As Phoenix has shown, [Achilles] has set himself up against the divine law, and he must expect the consequences. . . . Patroclus . . . is killed. . . .
> By the death of Patroclus Achilles is punished. . . . But his tragedy does not end here. The saddest chapter is yet to come. . . . Achilles has anger in his soul, and, though the death of Patroclus gives him a deep sense of guilt, it does not cure him of his anger. . . . Now his main idea is revenge. Revenge was quite legitimate in heroic morality. When Odysseus kills the suitors he would be thought entirely justified by the poet and his hearers. But when Achilles seeks revenge on Hector, his mood is different and its results less laudable. . . . His fury extends to others who are quite innocent. He slays Lycaon and refuses him the rites of burial. . . . He is not content with killing Hector. He has to maltreat his body after death. . . . But Homer is not content to leave Achilles and his story thus. His hero has sunk to degradation through a fault in his own character, and he can only be restored to honour and sympathy when this fault is healed.
> The healing comes in the last book, with the visit of Priam to ransom the body of Hector. . . . Achilles cannot withstand the request which comes from the gods that he should release the body of Hector. In this act he recovers his true nature. His anger has passed away, and he is himself again.[3]

Other critics take a very different view of the speech to the embassy —and of the story of the *Iliad*. Adam Parry comments on the great speech:

> Achilles . . . presents his own vision with a dreadful candour. And what this candour is concerned with is, precisely, the awful distance between appearance and reality; between what Achilles expected and what he got; between the truth that society imposes on men and what Achilles has seen to be true for himself. . . . The disillusionment consequent on Achilles' awareness of this cleavage, the questions his awareness of it gives rise to, and the results of all this in the events of the war, are possibly the real plot of the second half of the *Iliad*.[4]

This suggestion has been, in effect, taken up and developed by Cedric Whitman. Whitman sees Achilles in his great speech "passionately, and as yet dimly groping for something loftier than a system by which men pay when they must and steal when they can."[5] At this point, says Whitman, "Agamemnon ceases to be of any relevance to Achilles' concerns":

> The whole quarrel with Agamemnon was merely the match that lit a fire, the impetus which drove Achilles from the simple assumptions of the other princely heroes onto a path where heroism means the search for the dignity and meaning of the self.[6]

For Whitman, also, the interpretation of the great speech is the key to the interpretation of Achilles' story. Of Achilles before Patroclus' death Whitman writes:

> The wrath of the hero is a search for himself which is complete only when the poem is complete. . . . The wish for life, which he revealed in the *Embassy*, is still within him, and the conflict within him is intense. For mortal man, the will to be absolute entails, however unrecognized, the will to die, and a life-wish obscures it.[7]

Of Achilles after Patroclus' death he writes:

> Human ties have vanished utterly, and what remains, the inner divine force, no longer needs to feel after its appropriate terms, but reveals itself coldly in an agonized, overwhelming will to death. Achilles had given himself with his armor to Patroclus, and now he has no self.[8]

Of the ransoming he writes:

Since he has renounced his own life, Achilles can look, as it were, from a distance upon the living and their emotions, including his own. And the very detachment of his vision brings him closer than he has ever been to a real communion with his human fellows. . . . He is still the man of indomitable intensity and fierceness. He threatens Priam with death if he should anger him; for this yielding to ransom is not to be considered a correction, but a completion of his quest for honor. . . . There is no repentance here, nor rejection of the divine self-assumption in favor of humanity. It is an expansion of the assumption to include humanity. . . . Achilles has fulfilled himself: his divinity and humanity are one.[9]

And, in summary:

The highest heroes are not men of delusion. They are men of clarity and purity, who will a good impossible in the world and eventually achieve it, through suffering, in their own spiritual terms. It is the will to the impossible which resembles delusion until the terms are found in which it is possible.[10]

And:

The absolute is the ability and right of the heroic individual to perceive—or better, to conceive—law for himself, and then prove his case by action.[11]

Parry and Whitman begin from a fact Bowra disregards: the peculiar power of Achilles' rhetoric. Whatever else can be said for or against Achilles, it is hard to think of him as a hero merely self-indulgent or deluded; he seems to differ from his fellows in that he sees the world, not less well than they do, but more deeply. Whitman, on the other hand, seems to ignore the negative moral judgments passed on the hero by the other characters, human and divine, and apparently endorsed by the poet; in so doing, Whitman seems to me to miss the moral problematic of the poem. I wish to suggest another approach.

I begin by observing that these two interpretations have some points in common. It is perhaps worth stating these points, simple as they are, since they must, in my view, be accepted by any honest interpreter of the poem. They are, first, that Achilles is the central figure of the poem; second, that the poem moves through a long process of mounting tension and then to some sort of healing at the end; third, that Achilles' story is the story of a man who (at some point) disregards the norms of his society. For Bowra this departure from the norms is a deviance properly punished and repented; Achilles is at the end restored to his society, and the validity of the norms is reasserted. For

Whitman, Achilles is a kind of existential hero who leaves the safe
bounds of social convention and sets off on a quest for his true self—
and who thus comes to confront the Absolute and the Absurd. Whitman's Achilles both rejects and transcends the norms. We in our time
are familiar with this sort of hero—so familiar, in fact, that we should
be cautious about finding him in a poem as distant from us as the
Iliad. We should, perhaps, take another look at the wrath of Achilles.

THE WRATH OF ACHILLES

Achilles' wrath is in the first place grounded in his character. The most
reliable witness to Achilles' character is presumably his father, Peleus;
at least Achilles himself expresses unqualified devotion to his father
(XVI.15–16, XIX.321–22), and it seems that he himself would accept his
father's judgment. Odysseus quotes Peleus to Achilles:

> Sweet fool, surely your father Peleus told you,
> That day he sent you from Phthia to Agamemnon:
> "Son of mine, power Athena and Hera
> Will give, if they like, but you your great-spirited heart
> Restrain in your chest. For a friendly spirit is better.
> Hold back from strife, that inventor of trouble, so then
> The Argives will honor you, young men and elders."
> So the old man told you; you forget.
>
> (IX.252–59)

The same scene is described in more detail in Nestor's long speech to
Patroclus:

> Sweet fool, surely Menoetius told you this,
> That day he sent you from Phthia to Agamemnon;
> We were both there, I and bright Odysseus;
> We heard it all in the palace, just as he told it.
> We came to Peleus' house, those well-built halls,
> Collecting folk all across ox-rich Achaea;
> We found the hero Menoetius there at home
> And you, with Achilles. The old horseman Peleus
> Was burning fat ox thighs to Zeus of the thunder
> In his sheltered court. He held the golden cup,
> Pouring sparkling wine on the sacred fire.
> You two were serving the ox meat; we two came
> And stood in the porch. Achilles jumped up amazed;
> He led us by the hand and made us sit down,
> Put the guest fare before us, the right of guests.
> When we'd had joy of eating and of drink,
> I opened my speech and called you both to come.

You were both most ready, and those two told you much.
Old man Peleus told his child Achilles
To ever excel and to surpass all others;
To you Menoetius told it, Actor's son:
"Son of mine, Achilles outranks you in breeding,
But you are older; he is greater in force.
Speak to him thoughtful words and make suggestions,
Instruct him; he will obey you—to his good."
So the old man told you; you forget.

(XI.765–90)

Achilles is young. He is a great warrior, but less perfect in the arts of peace. He needs guidance and instruction (cf. IX.438–43); he has difficulty restraining his temper. All those who are close to him know this; he knows it about himself. He says:

There is no one like me among the bronze-clad Achaeans
In war. In assemblies other men are my betters.

(XVIII.105–6)

Achilles' wrath begins in an assembly, which he calls on the instructions of Hera (I.55). Achilles handles the occasion badly; he is not good at this sort of thing. Still, he is hardly at fault; he is doing what the goddess told him to do, and doing the best he can. Obviously the plague has brought a crisis. Obviously the plague has been sent by Apollo, and obviously the army needs to know the source of Apollo's anger and what can be done about it. Achilles goes straight to these points; he begins:

Son of Atreus, now I think, missing our goal,
We'll turn back home—if we don't die instead—
Since war and plague together destroy the Achaeans.
Come, let us ask some seer, or else a priest,
Or a dealer in dreams—for a dream, too, is from Zeus—
Who could tell us why Phoebus Apollo is angry . . .

(I.59–64)

Calchas offers to speak—providing Achilles will protect him; Achilles so swears, "even if you mean Agamemnon." Obviously the assembly needs Calchas' information, and Calchas deserves protection. The seer then informs the assembly that Agamemnon is indeed at fault. Agamemnon rises, in some ill temper, and says he will restore Apollo's priest his daughter; however, some recompense should be provided, lest the king be without a prize, "which is not fitting." Achilles asks where this recompense is supposed to come from. There are no undistributed prizes; the Achaeans will recompense Agamemnon from the spoils of Troy "three and fourfold"—if Troy ever falls. Agamemnon turns his ill temper on Achilles, and the quarrel between them begins.

In this brief scene some key facts of Achilles' character are set before us. Achilles is a man of great intelligence, but insensitive. He sees the situation clearly, but he does not see it as it appears to others. In particular, Achilles reveals no awareness of Agamemnon's probable reactions.

We can imagine how Nestor would have handled this situation. Nestor would have approached it obliquely, would perhaps have told an anecdote or two, would have soothed his audience with an assurance that the situation was not, after all, so desperate or insoluble, and, praising Agamemnon for his statesmanship, would at the same time have shown him, tactfully, what was expected of him. We know all this about Nestor because we see him at work at the beginning of Book Nine. Nestor knows that a king who is being asked to retract a previous action requires encouragement and support. Agamemnon's demand for recompense was a vague demand and could easily have been satisfied with vague reassurances that the Achaeans would certainly provide some substitute prize as soon as they had worked out some satisfactory way of doing so. When Nestor speaks, issues become blurred; that is part of the wisdom of elders.

Achilles is difficult to live with partly because he sees situations so clearly. This clarity of vision is the source of his powerful rhetoric and of his greatness as a warrior. Achilles gives himself over to the situation as he perceives it; he acts and speaks without shading or half-measures. A man of this kind is badly placed in a deliberative assembly. He sees the situation so clearly because he sees only a part of it. Achilles, with his instinctive rhetorical resources, dramatizes this partial vision to himself until it fills his view and leaves no place for qualifications. He says to Agamemnon:

> My prize is never equal to yours, whenever Achaeans
> Sack some Trojan castle, well provided—
> And yet the greater part of grievous battle
> Is work of my hands. But when there comes a sharing,
> Your prize is much greater; some small thing of my own
> I take to my ships, whenever I'm worn with battle.
>
> (I.163–68)

The formulaic phrase "a small thing of my own"—*oligon te philon te*—appears in the *Odyssey* in a context of begging (vi.208=xiv.58). That is probably the connotation here; Achilles pictures himself as a helpless creature fed on scraps. This is hardly fair. The two girls who are the focus of the quarrel—Chryseis and Briseis—were taken in the raid on Thebe (I.366–69; II.688–93). This raid was itself a theme of epic song;[12] references to it are scattered through the *Iliad*, and Homer seems to assume that his audience knows the story. In Book Six we learn that the most valuable prize of this raid, the king's wife, had been awarded to Achilles, who sold her back to her father, "taking measureless ransoms" (VI.425–27). Achilles was not so unrewarded after all.

In taking Briseis from Achilles, Agamemnon is of course acting outrageously. To Achilles this unfairness is especially bitter because so unexpected. Achilles is trying to rescue Agamemnon's army. If he speaks somewhat harshly to Agamemnon—well, that is the right of the assembly.[13] When Agamemnon insults him, Achilles naturally returns his insults. By the time Nestor gets the floor, it is too late. The best commentary on the whole scene is perhaps Aeneas' remark to Achilles late in the poem:

> We both of us have insulting remarks for the speaking
> In plenty; a hundred-burdened ship wouldn't hold them.
> Flexible is a mortal's tongue; its speeches are many,
> All sorts; the great field of words extends hither and yon.
> Whatever words you speak, such words you will hear.
> But why of strife and quarrels have we two need,
> To quarrel with one another, as if we were women?
> They fall to raging in heart-consuming strife
> And quarrel with one another out in the street
> With much that is true—and is not. For rage compels them.
>
> (XX.246–55)

The word I have translated above as "rage" is *cholos*; Agamemnon and Achilles fall to ranting like fishwives because *cholos* has come upon them both. *Cholos* has a somewhat wider range than "rage"; Achilles feels *cholos* when he looks for the first time upon the arms made by Hephaestus—and delight as well. His eyes "glitter beneath his brows as if flashing" (XIX.16–18). Odysseus fears that Nausicaa might feel *cholos* if a naked salt-covered stranger fell at her feet (vi.147). *Cholos* is a whole-body reaction, the adrenal surge which drives men to violent speech and action. *Cholos*, says Achilles later,

> drives even a sensible man to harshness;
> It is far sweeter than honey pouring within one,
> And in the breasts of men it rises like smoke.
>
> (XVIII.107–10)

14

There are two ways of dealing with *cholos*. It can be poured into violent action and in that way "healed" (IV.36). Or it can be "digested" (I.81; cf. IX.565); in the course of time the body will consume the *cholos* and the man will be calm again. Achilles' natural reaction is to take the first course; he decides to kill Agamemnon. But Athena intervenes and promises the "threefold gifts." Achilles replies:

> Your word, of course, goddess, must be respected,
> However great the *cholos*. For thus it is better.
> Who trusts himself to the gods will gain their hearing.
>
> (I.216–18)

Achilles withdraws to his ships, there to "digest his *cholos*" (IV.513) and await events.

We next see Achilles when the embassy comes to him "with glorious gifts and soothing words" (IX.113). The whole rhythm of events up to this point would lead us to expect that Achilles will take the gifts and that his wrath will be over. I believe that Achilles himself thinks he will take the gifts—until he has heard them. Here, I think, is the dramatic force of the long catalogue of gifts repeated almost verbatim by Odysseus from Agamemnon. The first time we hear this catalogue, we respond warmly to Agamemnon's reformation; each additional item is further proof of his new good will. When the same list is recited to Achilles, it falls flat, each item flatter than the last; ideally the audience and Achilles realize at the same moment that the gifts will not work, that the embassy must be a failure.

The phrase of Odysseus', mentioned earlier—"if you hate Atreus' son from the heart, himself and his gifts" (IX.300–301)—comes just at the end of the repeated catalogue. Odysseus himself is aware that his presentation is not going well. He inserts this phrase at the moment when he is leaving out the last four lines of Agamemnon's message, which had been:

> Let him be ruled; Hades, unsoothed, unruled,
> Is therefore hated most of mortals' gods.
> And let him accept that I am more of a king
> And that I can claim to be elder in my birth.
>
> (IX.158–61)

Odysseus, however, gains no advantage by suppressing a conclusion implicit in the body of the message. By his very act of recompense, Agamemnon asserts his superiority over Achilles. By offering gifts, he shows that he has them, and to spare. By offering Achilles seven towns and his daughter, Agamemnon is not offering to make himself any poorer; he is offering to include Achilles within his own sphere as his son-in-law and subordinate. Achilles twice says that Agamemnon had treated him "like a wanderer without honor" (IX.648=XVI.59). Such inclusion in the sphere of others is precisely the fate of wanderers, like Phoenix (IX.478–84) and Patroclus (XXIII.83–92), who had been taken in by Peleus. By the offered terms of settlement Agamemnon would convert Achilles into his dependent. That is why Achilles, while still making the somewhat contradictory claim that he has been unrewarded for his efforts, at the same time lays such stress in his reply on his own property and on the fact that he has a father of his own in his own country. Achilles knows that he is being asked to submit.

What does Achilles want from the embassy at this moment? Quite possibly he does not know. Achilles had wanted to kill Agamemnon and would now probably be content with nothing less than Agamemnon's humiliation. Perhaps an embassy that had come, not on Agamemnon's behalf, but, over the king's protests, on behalf of the rest of the Greeks would have been successful. In Book One Achilles says that, were the Greeks not worthless, Agamemnon would have lost the power to commit outrage (I.231–32). Here he says that the other Greeks will no longer trust Agamemnon; Achilles' case should teach them that their king is shameless and deceitful (IX.369–72). Agamemnon, Achilles says, must give back "the whole outrage" (IX.387). Achilles suffers, and his suffering can be soothed only by the suffering of the man who caused it. If Agamemnon lost his authority, he would surely suffer.

Achilles is offered the gifts on condition that he give up his *cholos* (IX.157, 260–61, 299). But he cannot do it; *cholos* is a *pathos*, not subject to rational control. At the end of the embassy Achilles tells Ajax that he is helpless:

> Telamonian Zeus-born Ajax, commander of men,
> In a way your speech is exactly to my mind.
> But still my heart swells with *cholos* at what
> I remember; he made me degraded among the Argives,
> Atreus' son, like a wanderer without honor.

> (IX.644–48)

Achilles feels that he has been evicted from his proper place in the world. Until he has recovered from this experience, he cannot return to his friends, however much they need him. In fact he would like to give them all up and go home. His troops have been telling him that, if they're not to fight, they might as well depart (XVI.203–6). The embassy seems to clarify this point in his mind also. There is nothing to wait for; he can leave in the morning.

But he does not go. He longs for home because home means for him his father—but his father sent him out to be a warrior; Achilles' mother may value his life before honor, but Achilles cannot disappoint his father's expectations of him. This idea of going home was always the weak point in his position; on this point, and this point alone, Phoenix and Ajax shift him.[14] He replaces his threat of departure by a vow: he will not fight until Hector comes to the camp of the Myrmidons and the fire reaches his own ships (IX.650–53). He thus commits himself to remain near the battle but not in it. Achilles is caught between a father who has sent him away and a king who wants to take him over and use him. He can think of nothing better to do, for the moment, than to take his stand on the margin of events.[15]

Achilles' great speech, by this reading, is an explosion of rage at the impossible position in which he finds himself. Achilles is an outsize figure. He is stronger, swifter, braver, than the other heroes, and his anger also is larger than any they could feel. And Achilles is a hero with exceptional powers of intellect and speech; he has a unique capacity to generalize his immediate experience and state it in universal terms. If he is deprived of Briseis, well, then, he has been stripped of everything and was given nothing in the first place. If Agamemnon behaves badly to him, well, then, Agamemnon is a fool, a glutton, a cheat, and a coward. Similarly, if he cannot find grounds for a return to battle, then no such grounds exist; nothing can recompense a man for risking his life. The speech is not a step toward a new synthesis but an overpoweringly vivid statement of a partial truth.

I cannot agree with Whitman that Achilles is here "groping for something loftier." He is groping, surely, but nothing comes to his hand. He tries to turn away from war, but war is his life and he cannot leave it. His speech is falsified by his act.

Nor can I agree with Bowra that Achilles here sins and opens himself to proper punishment. As the man he is, in the place he is, I do not see that Achilles could have acted otherwise. In the embassy, as throughout the poem, Achilles is less the creator of situations than their agent and victim; he does in each case what it seems to him must be done.

By Book Sixteen—the following day in the narrative but a long time later in the life of the poem—Achilles' *cholos* is gone; it has been "digested." Patroclus, instructed by Nestor, appeals to him to return to the battle or else send him, Patroclus, in his place; Achilles reviews his grievance once more and then says:

17

> Let us be done with all that. There was no way
> To keep the *cholos* unceasing at heart. Yet I said
> I would not stop my enmity until
> The war and the battle came to my own ships.
> But you, put my famous armor on your shoulders;
> Lead the warlike Myrmidons to battle. . . .
>
> (XVI.60–65)

The embassy had come a day too soon; now it might have had better success.[16] But it is too late; Achilles is bound by the vow he made on the previous day. He sends Patroclus instead.

The idea of sending Patroclus was suggested by Nestor. Achilles' vow was suggested by Phoenix' story of Meleager.[17] It is a tragic irony that the intractable Achilles falls into misfortune precisely because he is open to suggestion. It is another irony that the vow which traps him was drawn from him by his wish to respond somehow to the persuasions of his friends.

Achilles tells Patroclus not to pursue the Trojans but merely to push them back from the ships (XVI.80–96). Patroclus, caught up in the joy of battle, forgets these instructions and dies. Here Achilles' story turns and defines its ending.

With Patroclus' death a new clarity comes to Achilles. Life, which before had been so puzzling, becomes lucidly meaningless. Thetis tells him that if he kills Hector his own fate comes close behind. He answers:

> Let me die soon, since I was not there for my friend,
> To keep off his death. And he so far from his homeland
> Perished; he lacked me his guard in war.
> I'll never go back now to the land of my fathers;
> Not to Patroclus was I a light, nor to the rest,
> Our comrades—so many fell before bright Hector.
> I sit by the ships, an idle weight on the ground.
> . . . .
> Agamemnon king of men brought the *cholos* on me—
> But let us be done with that, although it grieve us—
> The heart in our chest by necessity held down—
> Now I will go, till I meet that dear head's slayer,
> Hector. My own death I accept whenever
> Zeus inclines to bring it, and the deathless gods.
>
> (XVIII.98–116)

What comes to Achilles at this point is not *cholos* but something much deeper. His spirit is constrained "by necessity" (cf. XIX.66). He has an absolute obligation to revenge his friend, and this obligation takes from him all further necessity for choice. Achilles launches his great *aristeia*, which fills Books Twenty, Twenty-one, and Twenty-two. This is a scene of overpowering action. Achilles fights with the river, and the gods fight with one another; at one moment the King of the Dead fears that the world will split and reveal the hateful realms below (XX.61–65). Through all this Achilles acts and kills with cold certainty and even a kind of joy. When he sees Lycaon, whom he had taken prisoner in an earlier battle and who, after being sold and ransomed, had returned to Troy only to come before Achilles a second time, Achilles says:

> Poor fool, a great wonder I see with my eyes.
> Surely the great-hearted Trojans whom I slew
> Will stand themselves up again from the misty West
> As this one came, escaping the pitiless day,
> Sold into sacred Lemnos. It didn't hold him,
> The gray salt sea, which holds so many unwilling.
> Come, then, let's try the point of this spear of mine,
> The taste of it, so that I may see and know
> If he can return from there, too, when it keeps him,
> The life-giving earth, which keeps down even the mighty.
>
> (XXI.54–63)

There is a kind of horrific playfulness in this. Lycaon appeals to him to be taken prisoner again; Achilles answers:

> Fool, don't tell me of ransoms or make speeches;
> Before Patroclus met his fated day,
> Then it was more to my mind to be somewhat sparing
> Of Trojans; I took many alive and sold them.
> Now not one escapes death, whomsoever the god
> Should place in my hands here before Ilium,
> Of all the Trojans, especially the sons of Priam.
> But, friend, you die too. Why do you cry so?
> Patroclus also died, much better than you are.
> Don't you see how I am, so fine and large?
> My father was brave, and a lady goddess bore me.
> But death is ready for me, and fate that rules us.
> It will come, a dawn or afternoon or midday
> When someone will take my life from me in war
> With a stroke of spear or with the bow-sent arrow.
>
> (XXI.99–113)

Since Patroclus has died, so must Hector; since Hector must die, so must Achilles; since Achilles must die, so all must die who stand before Achilles. With this logic Achilles is for a while content.

19

CHARACTER AND PLOT

Later in this book I shall return to the story of Achilles and, at the end, speak of its ending. The account so far has been (in a sense) intentionally superficial. I have said nothing of the fatality of the story, of the historic and cosmic reverberations which give Achilles' story depth and resonance,[18] nor have I explored the content of Achilles' private vision of man and world. More will have to be said; what is said here is that Achilles' separation from society is imposed on him by society; it is a piece of bad fortune.

Throughout the poem Achilles responds to other men and to events; throughout, his actions are dictated by his situation—given that his own temperament is a part of his situation. Achilles' wrath was provoked by an Agamemnon who left him no alternative to wrath; Achilles refused Agamemnon's gifts because he found himself unable to accept them. Achilles sent Patroclus into battle because he saw no other honorable course, and Patroclus' death forced Achilles to return to battle. This chain of necessary and conditioned acts extends, as we shall later see, through the death and despoilment of Hector and through the ransoming of Hector.

All this is to read the Homeric story from the surface down: from social relations to the individual acts they condition, from social situations to the individual consciousness they inform and provoke. That, I would contend, is the right way to read a Homeric story. In the *Iliad*, as I understand the poem, individuals are not seen as free, self-defining creatures confronting a society whose structure and values they are free to accept or reject. Rather, the Homeric actors are seen as embedded in a social fabric; they are persons whose acts and consciousness are the enactment of the social forces which play upon them. Thus the present reading of the Homeric stories implies an understanding of Homeric social psychology.

This understanding is not original with the present author. One critic who has written eloquently to the question is Herman Fränkel, who offers a sketch of the Homeric personality, a sketch I here summarize.[19] Fränkel offers an account of a kind of man who is not restrained by social norms but is rather constructed by them, and who therefore cannot separate himself from his society.[20] Homeric man, according to Fränkel, has no point of reference other than the society by which he might define himself.

For Fränkel Homeric man is characterized by "elementary vitality." He gives no thought to another life but fulfills himself in vivid experience of this life—experience joyful and sorrowful. However great his sufferings when confronted by harsh necessity, Homeric man still accepts whatever life brings him, including death.

Homeric man, by this reading, is both passionate and intelligent, both impulsive and lucidly reflective. This paradox is possible because his passions are "objective"—turned not inward but outward toward clearly perceived objects. Thus Homeric man does not become confused or depressed; he becomes angry with someone or grief-stricken by something, and in the most difficult situation he always retains the power to express himself in words.

Homeric man, being objective, has no innerness. He expresses himself completely in words and acts, and is thus completely known to his fellows. He has no hidden depths or secret motives; he says and does what he is.[21] Such a man is not an enclosed identity; he is rather a kind of open field of forces. He is open to others—to the words of other men and to the interventions of the gods. There is no clear line for him between *ego* and *alter*; he can recognize his own thoughts and wishes as having been implanted in him by another. Similarly, when he is in doubt, parts of himself become alien to himself; he argues with himself until he takes charge of himself and sees his way to action.[22]

Homeric man is "incapable of development"; this incapacity is a consequence of his responsiveness to new experience. He responds fully and uncritically to each situation, "and the mood which it induced in him passes with the situation without leaving a trace." The man *is* this sequence of states; his character is unified only in the sense that he responds in some characteristic way.[23] Thus for Fränkel the man is, not a synthesis of his history, but his history itself. Fränkel might have added that such a man is capable of surprising himself when a new situation evokes from him a previously unexperienced response.

Surely Fränkel, as he himself says, "sharpens and simplifies." Fränkel's description is intended to apply only to the *Iliad*, not the *Odyssey*, and even within the *Iliad* we can find exceptions. Odysseus, for example, is able to conceal his thought—for instance, when he leaves out the last four lines of Agamemnon's message. Agamemnon looks back on his past acts with regret, and in Hector's story (as we shall see) the recognition of error and the sense of responsibility play a crucial role. Helen is capable of self-contempt. And so forth. Nevertheless, Fränkel's analysis seems to me an essential starting point for moderns who would read the *Iliad*, for he reminds us to be careful in applying our own conception of character to these figures. Furthermore, his description of Homeric man applies, I think, better to Achilles than to any other

21

figure. This is perhaps as we should expect; as the greatest of the heroes, Achilles is also the perfection of the character type.

Achilles does not look back. He refers to earlier experience only occasionally, to report (without explanation) that he feels differently now. Achilles does not speak about his responsibility for his own acts. When Patroclus dies, his grief is total; he wishes he had never been born and accepts his own death. But there are no words of regret for having sent Patroclus into battle; he says only *ton apōlesa*, "I have lost him" (XVIII.82). In his brief speech of reconciliation with Agamemnon, Achilles says it would have been better if Briseis had died before they'd quarreled about her (XIX.59), but he does not blame himself—or Agamemnon either. While his quarrel with Agamemnon was in the forefront of his consciousness, he could think of nothing else; when this is no longer so, he has no interest in how it came about. Probably (he vaguely says) Zeus wished it (XIX.273–74). Achilles is a character strikingly lacking in both forethought and afterthoughts, and his judgments of others are as transitory as they are absolute.

This account of Achilles may seem to a modern reader to diminish him and to deprive him of his significance as the central figure of the *Iliad*. But perhaps the problem is with us, with our conception of heroic grandeur. In the *Iliad* (I contend) the greatness of a man lies not in his capacity to construct an inner synthesis of his experience but in his effect on others, whether that effect is voluntary or involuntary, whether for good or for evil. Character, in other words, acquires significance as it gives rise to plot.

Here a clarification is in order, and a qualification. Fränkel writes within the German tradition of *Geistesgeschichte*; for him "humanness has a history," and in describing the Homeric personality he is trying to reconstruct an early stage of that history. Achilles, for him, lacks "innerness" because the men of Homer's time lacked it; only as the culture developed new psychological states could the Greeks develop a new personal art, foreshadowed in the *Odyssey* and perfected in archaic lyric.

Possibly this view is correct, but we cannot be sure, and we should be cautious about moving so quickly from poetry to culture. It may be that the Homeric view of man has shaped the Homeric narrative, but it may be that the process has worked the other way. It may be that the men of Homer's day had more "innerness" than Homer allows his characters, just as it may be that we are more like Homer's Achilles than we like to think. Our lives also could be described as consisting of transparently socially conditioned speech and action; in fact the sociologist does this when he describes a man as a system of positions and roles.[24] If we have lost the knack of writing profound fiction from this point of view, then we have lost one valid way of seeing our own lives. That (I would suggest) is one reason the *Iliad* is interesting to us. But in any case we should remember that the *Iliad* presents us not with life but with an artist's view of life, a view probably characteristic of a whole poetic tradition and in that sense characteristic of its culture but still separable from its culture.[25]

The characters in a poem are as the poet made them, and he made them as he would have them for the needs of his work. When we think of the poem as a made thing, a construct, we abandon the point of view of the characters and take our stand with the poet. We ask what sort of meaning the poet is conveying and how he seeks to convey it; we shall find this meaning conveyed, not in the represented experience of any single character, but in the poem as a whole. We thus shift our interest from character to plot, taking "plot" in a very broad sense as that implicit conceptual unity which has given the work its actual form. We investigate the meaning of the work by asking how it hangs together, and thus we investigate what the poet is driving at.

In asking these questions we are, in effect, asking about the poet's own (implicit) poetics—not the external poetics of constricting rules but the internal poetics of the poet's aspiration. We ask what, for him, constituted a meaningful narrative. And we answer our question by finding out how—read in what way—his narrative is in fact meaningful.

THE POET AND HIS CULTURE

Since narrative is about men, the meaning of the narrative is a statement about men—men seen in a certain way. As we move from plot to character, we move also from the poet's poetics to the poet's psychology. In telling a story the poet employs and persuades us to certain assumptions about the sources and conditions of action. He thus (in effect) takes a view of culture. And further: since he is telling his story to an audience, the meaning he conveys must be a meaning *to them*. So we can go on to ask: What sort of audience would have found this story meaningful? Here (and only here) we reach culture itself.

Thus in order to justify one negative point—that the *Iliad* does not center on Achilles' inner experience—we have set ourselves a complex task. We shall have to detach ourselves from a set of ingrained attitudes—attitudes which constitute the implicit psychology and poetics of our own day. Implicit attitudes are difficult to refute because they are not quite stated anywhere. We can only try the experiment of looking at the poem in some other way. If our experiment is successful, we shall experience a certain disorientation, and at the same time we shall find in the work a new unity and a new meaning. This disorientation and discovery is the familiar (and invigorating) experience of cross-cultural studies. We shall attempt here to read the *Iliad* in its own terms.

For Bowra the *Iliad* centers on Achilles' sin; for Whitman, on his learning. Whitman says of Achilles that he "is actually not complete until the poem is complete. He is learning all the time."[26] For Fränkel, on the other hand, Achilles is incapable of either sin or learning; he is not that kind of character.[27] Here we accept this point and make another: Achilles is not that kind of character because the *Iliad* is not that kind of story. Certainly Achilles becomes isolated from his society; but since social isolation is a reciprocal process, that may tell us as much about the society as about Achilles. To the degree that we can see Achilles' situation as a special application of general themes within the poem, we can see the *Iliad*—the story of Achilles and the story of the war—as a unity. And in the process, as we reconstruct an appropriate context for the text, we shall learn (indirectly) something about the Greeks to whom Homer told his story.

The present inquiry is somewhat parallel to that conducted by John Jones in his book *Aristotle and Greek Tragedy*. Jones writes, not about Homer, but about Aeschylus and Sophocles, but his quarrel with the critics is much the same. Jones finds a pervasive assumption that the classic narrative must center on the inner experience of a single hero; this, for him, is a systematic misreading. For Jones (and this might almost be a translation from Fränkel) a character in tragedy is "significantly himself only in what he says and does."[28] The themes of tragedy are therefore man in his social relations; the tragic action is external rather than internal, "situational" rather than personal. Jones asks of us an act of the historical imagination; he asks us to break with the conception of narrative which has been ours since at least the late eighteenth century:

> The hero is a narrowing and distorting influence [on criticism] and nearly always baneful, and getting rid of him calls for bold action against a number of deep-rooted assumptions. We must open our minds to the possibility of an ancient—but Western—dramatic literature which cannot profitably be compared with Goethe's or Coleridge's Shakespeare.[29]

In comparing Aeschylus' Orestes with Shakespeare's Hamlet, Jones says:

> The one is isolated by his status-determined circumstances, the other by his *psyche*-determined incapacity to act. There is no

saying which of these dramatic solitudes is the more extreme, or the more eloquent.[30]

Here I am suggesting that the solitude of Achilles is similarly "status-determined."

My approach is like Jones's in another sense also, in that he pins his interpretation of tragedy to an interpretation of Aristotle's *Poetics*. Aristotle, he asserts, understood tragedy well, understood it as Jones understands it; that is, Jones finds in Aristotle an explicit statement of the principles of poetic form and purpose which he himself finds implicit in the plays. Naturally this brings Jones into conflict with the critics of Aristotle, who, according to Jones (and I agree), have subjected the *Poetics* to the same systematic misreading as the plays it describes. Taking as his fundamental text this statement from *Poetics* 1450a16—"Tragedy is the imitation, not of human beings, but of action and life"—Jones explains:

> The gulf between our preconceptions and the express doctrine of the *Poetics* can only be bridged through the recovery of some of the lost human relevancies of action. Aristotle is assaulting the now settled habit in which we see action issuing from a solitary focus of consciousness—secret, inward, interesting—and in which the status of action must always be adjectival: action qualifies; it tells us things we want to know about the individual promoting it; the life of action is the ceaseless, animating consideration of the state of affairs "inside" him who acts, without which action is empty and trivial, an effluvium. This movement from adjectival action to the substantive self would seem, were it conscious, not merely natural but inevitable. Were it conscious, however, we should have to admit that we are first rejecting Aristotle's injunction to make character serve action, and then replacing it with its opposite. Revealing a moral choice means, for Aristotle, declaring the moral character of an act in a situation where the act itself does not make this clear. Reader and spectator are apprised of the ethical colour of the action at this point of the play. To our sense of characteristic conduct Aristotle opposes that of characterful action: the essence of conduct being that it is mine or yours; of action, that it is out there—an object for men to contemplate.[31]

We also shall be seeking "lost relevancies of action" in a poetic image of "characterful action."

The modern focus on the inner experience of the individual, it must be added, is not so modern after all. Jones (like Nietzsche) traces the modern temper all the way back to Euripides and Socrates. From this point of view Aristotle's *Poetics* is retrospective and conservative; Jones says that Aristotle "expounds and defends a refined traditionalism."[32] In the field of systematic poetics Jones suggests that the line between the old way and the new can be drawn between Aristotle and Theophrastus[33]—so that Aristotle, while in one sense the founder of systematic poetics, is in another sense the last voice of the archaic and classic tradition in poetry:

> Aristotle has founded his book on the distinction between false imitation of human beings and true imitation of actions because he reckons it his first responsibility, as early as the fourth century, to oppose . . . inward-turning of attention and interest.[34]

Homer and Aristotle, from this point of view, mark the extreme chronological limits of a common conception of action and of narrative.

Fränkel also might have made this point had he noticed how Aristotelian is the Homeric psychology he describes. Fränkel notes that the Homeric view of man is at one with the Homeric narrative technique: as Homeric man is "objective," so Homeric narrative is "objective":

> A man is identical with his act, and can from his act be understood with complete validity; he has no hidden depths. This state of affairs gives the epic in its traditional form the right to exist. The objective report which the old epic gives us of act and speech expresses all that men are, since after all they are only what they say and do and suffer.[35]

So Aristotle says:

> Homer in general deserves our praise in that he alone of the poets knows what he is supposed to do. The poet should have as little as possible to say himself; that is not what makes him an imitator. The others are constantly involving themselves in the business, and imitate but little and infrequently. He, however, after a brief prelude brings on a man or a woman or some other character—not at all characterless, but having character.
>
> (*Poetics* 1460a5–11)

Homeric poetry is a poetry of surfaces, that is to say, of social phenomena. For Aristotle (and, I think, for Homer) such poetry is precisely a poetry of character, for character is transparently visible in speech and action. Aristotle also says that the later tragic poets (including Euripides) lacked character, although in the modern sense they provided far more refined individual characterizations of their figures.

26

But their characterizations did not give "an ethical colour to the action"; they were represented as more passive than active, more determined than free. For Aristotle action has meaning only when it is responsible, that is, only when it is grounded on deliberate choice. We understand the choice when we see the act and when we hear the grounds of choice stated; action, in other words, is to be understood through its justifications and its results. From this way of seeing it, men are fully fit to judge one another, and we in the audience are fully fit to judge the figures who enact the imitated event. We see that these figures are not fully free; they must respond to the situation in which they find themselves. But we also hear them reasoning about their situation, and we see their reasoned acts transform the situation. We judge the character by his reasons and by the effect of his acts.

Achilles and Hector

In my introductory sketch I spoke of Achilles' story primarily in terms of its causes. For the author of the *Iliad*, however, Achilles is a focal figure primarily because of his effect on events. The theme of the story is not Achilles but Achilles' wrath (*mēnis*) and its results:

> That cursed wrath, which caused numberless pains to Achaeans;
> Many mighty spirits it sent to Hades
> Of heroes, and turned them into prey to dogs
> And feast to birds.

(I.2–5)[36]

Once we begin to think of the effects of Achilles' wrath, we turn naturally to the story of Hector, for Hector is the focus of those effects. Achilles' story has two parts: Achilles' withdrawal from action and Achilles' return to action. In the first part, Hector is (unknowingly) Achilles' agent: Hector brings down upon the Greeks the defeat Achilles had prayed for and Achilles' mother had secured from Zeus. But Hector's strength goes beyond Achilles' wish; Hector kills Patroclus and brings Achilles back to the battle. In the second part, Hector becomes Achilles' victim: Hector suffers terror, death, and mutilation. The healing at the end comes only with the release of Hector from Achilles' hands. In some sense the story of the *Iliad* is the story of the relation between these two heroes.[37]

Achilles' greatness is a greatness of force and of negation. He is different from other men by his greater capacity to deny, to refuse, to kill, and to face death. He is a heroic rather than demonic figure because his negations are founded not on perversity of will but on clarity of intellect. Achilles' wrath originates and continues because he can see exactly what Agamemnon is and exactly what his proffered gifts really mean. Achilles pursues his revenge so grandly and so far—even beyond Hector's death—because he knows exactly how inadequate revenge must be to the suffering which provokes it. Throughout the poem Achilles fully enacts his condition as he, with peculiar clarity, conceives it. We shall find this same clarity, and this same absorption in immediacy, in the reconciliation which ends the poem. Achilles' absolute incapacity for illusion makes him throughout the poem an insoluble problem to others and to himself. At the end, as I read him, the poet presents this insolubility to us.

Hector, by contrast, is a hero of illusions; he is finally trapped between a failed illusion and his own incapacity for disillusionment. Hector is surely a figure less grand than Achilles, but it is Hector's story that gives Achilles' story meaning; Hector affirms all that Achilles denies. Treated in isolation, Achilles would be a mere existential cipher or borderline psychotic. Achilles achieves greatness only when we set him against the rich, functioning society of the Homeric world and see his tormented negations as, after all, a correct analysis of the contradictory internal logic of that world. Achilles brings destruction, first on Greeks and then on Trojans, because they have left him no choice. The source of his action is in their world; through the other characters, and particularly through Hector, we inhabit that world, and we see what problem it is that Achilles cannot solve.

It is also true that the poem would not move us if Achilles destroyed nothing of value to ourselves. Through Hector's story we come to see the wrath of Achilles as an event which has consequences for people like ourselves. Achilles is a strange, magical figure, with his immortal armor, his talking horses, and his sea-nymph mother, through whom his will has power even among the gods; Hector is a human creature, with wife and child, parents and brothers, friends and fellow citizens. Achilles' acts are always true to his shifting visions of himself; Hector has placed his life at the service of others. Between Hector and Achilles the outcome is never in doubt, for Achilles is superhuman, while Hector is only the sort of hero that we ourselves, at our moments of greatest aspiration, might hope to be. Through Hector's story, thus, Achilles is given a location in the human world. In the story of Hector Achilles appears as an emblem of those terrible facts men like ourselves can actually encounter. In Hector's story we see that, at the moment of such an encounter, wisdom and courage are not enough, that human strength and even human virtue can reach the limits of their efficacy.

The stories of Hector and Achilles are curiously discontinuous. They do not know each other. Achilles kills Hector, despoils and then later releases his body, not because Achilles hates Hector or forgives him but because in this way Achilles works out an action internal to himself. Hector's death is a debt owed by Achilles to Patroclus; Achilles releases Hector's body because at a certain moment Achilles is brought to see that Hector's death is not different from his own.

For Hector, on the other hand, Achilles is an unassimilable figure. He cannot be ignored, cannot be avoided, cannot be defeated, cannot even, at the end, be confronted with dignity. Throughout the story Achilles remains to Hector a riddle, an uncomprehended force. Between these two heroes there is a kind of vacant space at the center of the *Iliad*. This vacancy, at the end, the poet reveals to us.

Achilles is the great hero of the *Iliad*, and the *Iliad* is the story of the death of a hero; but Achilles does not die in the *Iliad*. The death of Achilles—or rather, his mortality—is a ruling fatality of the *Iliad*, but the pathos of the poem is concentrated in the death of Hector. The first line of the poem, as everyone remembers, is:

> The wrath, sing, goddess, of Peleus' son Achilles . . .
>
> (I.1)

We should also remember the last line:

> . . . so they completed the burial of horse-taming Hector.
>
> (XXIV.804)

In the account which follows we shall consider the story of the *Iliad* first as a kind of story, then as the story of what happens to Hector— in life, in death, and in the healing of death by the funeral.

1

IMITATION

THE NEXT TWO CHAPTERS constitute a largely self-contained essay in which we turn aside from the narrative of the *Iliad* and discuss some theoretical problems posed by the *Iliad* and by narrative in general. Here will be made explicit some critical assumptions left implicit in the later chapters. So far as possible those assumptions have been drawn from the Greeks themselves—although I have often tried the experiment of translating them into more modern language. The method employed in these chapters will therefore be historical, tracing certain aspects of the problematic of narrative art from Homer down to Aristotle.

THE FAMES OF MEN

People in Homer sing while they work; women sing at the loom (v.61, x.221), and a boy sings for the workers at the vintage (XVIII.570–72). For solemn occasions there are hymns, especially the *paiēōn* to Apollo (I.473, XXII.391). A man may sing for his own amusement, especially if he's had a bit to drink (xiv.464). Song is thus the common possession of the folk. But song is also the work of cultural specialists, the *aoidoi*, or "bards." As specialists, the bards are the vehicles and custodians of high culture. These men are *dēmioergoi*, "workers for the folk," who travel from place to place (xvii.382–85). They may be blind (viii.43–45, 62–64; *Hymn to Apollo* 172) and thus unfit for work; in compensation they are gifted by the Muse and honored by the folk. The bard is privileged at the feast, and his person is to some extent sacrosanct.[1]

Song in Homer is of two types, which we may call song-for-something and song-for-itself. In the first type, song accompanies dancing or ceremony; if a bard takes part, he acts as the leader of a group, which responds to him.[2] He sings a song they know, and they respond with countersong and rhythmic motion. Song for dancing is called *molpē*;[3] a song for mourning is called a *thrēnos* (XXIV.720–22); specific types of hymns have specific names. The folk, in other words, possess a stock of folk songs, organized by genre; such folk songs, throughout the history of Greek song, remained an important background and resource. The bard, in relation to such songs, is merely an exceptionally skilled performer.

Song-for-itself, by contrast, is sung by the bard alone and received by the audience in silence.[4] He does not sing a song they know; the theme of the song, the *oimē* or story, may be familiar, but the song itself is newly created in performance. Such songs are not strophic but were in a running meter, the hexameter; they are of no fixed length and derive their form, not from the music, but from the plot.[5] Only a trained bard, skilled in the formulaic language of the epics and the narrative possibilities of its themes, could create, apparently *ex nihilo*, in the face of his audience, a poem correct in meter and satisfying in content.[6] The bards employed and transmitted through painstaking application an art developed over many generations. From the beginning, Greek high culture devoted itself, before anything else, to the art of narrative.

The early bards told two kinds of stories: stories of the heroes (which involved relations between gods and men) and stories of the gods themselves (*Theogony* 99–101). Stories of the latter type are told, for example, in the *Theogony* of Hesiod and in the Homeric Hymns. Within the *Iliad* and the *Odyssey* there are two such stories: the Deception of Zeus in Book Fourteen of the *Iliad* and the story of Ares and Aphrodite in Book Eight of the *Odyssey*.[7] Such stories of the gods among themselves are generally lighthearted in tone and are often stories of playful tricks played by one god upon another. The gods live an easy life apart from us, and they live forever; they are in continual conflict but experience no real sorrow or permanent disasters,[8] and out of their conflicts they create the human world. The stories of the gods often tell the origins of things: How the Lyre Was Invented, or How Sacrifice was Divided between Gods and Men, or How Error Came among Men.

The stories of the heroes, by contrast, are stories of disasters and suffering, sometimes surmounted, more often simply endured. They tell of quarrels, stratagems, labors, and especially battles. These stories are historical, in the sense that they are set in the past, but they are not stories of historical origins. They tell, not of the founding of cities, but of their destruction. Man's life is set in contrast to the gods' life. At the banquet of the gods the Muses (like bards)

> taking turns, with their fair voice
> Sing the immortal gifts of the gods, and, of men,
> The sorrows—so much kept down by immortal gods,
> They live without sense or resource, nor are they able
> To find a cure for death or defense against age.
> (*Hymn to Apollo* 189–93)

The epic phrase for heroic story is *klea andrōn*, "fames of men."[9] *Kleos*, "fame," is an important term within the heroic world as repre-

31

sented by the epic; *kleos* is something the heroes prize and strive for. There is thus a curious reciprocity between the bard and his heroes. The bard sings of events which have a *kleos*; without the heroes he would have nothing to sing about. At the same time, the bard confers on his heroes a *kleos*, without which they would have no existence in the later world of the bardic audience. This reciprocity gives the epic a certain vivid intimacy, marked perhaps by the poet's occasional use of direct address to his own characters: "And then, Patroclus, you. . . ."[10] The bard is a kind of mediator between the heroes and the audience, a transmitter of *kleos* on behalf of both; thus the epic is given a grounding in the heroic ethic itself.

Kleos means, among other things, "news," as when Telemachus asks Eumaeus, "What's the news from town?" (xvi.461). One can hear the *kleos* of a particular event (XI.21, xxiii.137). *Kleos* is "what men say," and a thing has a *kleos* if it is talked about. Thus, an expedition or a war has a *kleos* (XI.227, XIII.364); a *teras*, "prodigy," has a *kleos* (II.325), and an object may have *kleos*, especially if it is in some way remarkable. Poseidon complains that the *kleos* of the Greek wall in the plain of Troy will extend "as far as the dawn is scattered" (VII. 451). The *kleos* of Nestor's shield "reaches heaven" (VIII.192). Armor is characteristically *kluta*, "famous." Armor has a history; a man is known by it, and a warrior acquires *kleos* when he wins on the battlefield especially famous armor (XVII.131). Also *kluta* or *perikluta*, "famous" or "very famous," are the craft works of women (VI.324, xx.72) and the gifts given in entertainment or ransom (VII.299, IX.121, XVIII.449, XXIV.458). These things are spoken about; men remember the gifts exchanged between heroes (cf. VII.300–302).

Like human things, human places also have a *kleos*. *Dōmata*, "houses," are characteristically *kluta*, and an *astu*, "city," is *periklutos* (iv.9, xvi.170, xxiv.154). Also *kluta* are the races of men (XIV.361) and the tribes of the dead (x.526). Things, places, and persons acquire *kleos* as they acquire an identity in the human world, as stories are told about them.

A man has a *kleos* which is his "reputation," either in general (iii.380, xviii.126–27) or for some particular quality. Thus a man may have the *kleos* of a warrior (XVII.143), a bowman (V.172), a spearman and counselor (xvi.241–42); one may have *kleos* for good sense (XXIV. 201–202) or for "craft and advantage-taking" (xiii.299). *Kleos* can be earned on the battlefield (V.3, XVIII.121), especially by some great act, such as seizing famous horses (V.273) or recovering the body of someone important (XVII.16). The commander gets the *kleos* for the sack of a city (ix.264). *Kleos* can also be earned in the games (viii.147–

48). *Kleos* is a reward granted by the folk in exchange for some difficult and important exploit and is thus parallel to the material reward given in the form of a prize or a share of booty (X.212–13, XVII.231–32). Nor can the two kinds of reward be set in the simple contrast of the social versus the material; the prize itself may have a *kleos* and confer a *kleos*, and a man is famous both for what he is and for what he has.

As a quality or possession *kleos* stands in relation and contrast to two other terms: *kudos* and *timē*. All three words may, in certain contexts, be translated "fame," but they mean quite different things. *Kudos* is a kind of luster or *mana* which belongs to the successful. *Kudos* is specifically personal; a man may be a *kudos* to others—a successful hero ornaments his city (XXII.435), just as fine harness ornaments a horse and is *kudos* to the horseman (IV.145)—but a man does not win *kudos* for another. *Kleos*, by contrast, is won by the warrior both for himself and for his father (VI.446, VIII.285). *Kudos* belongs only to the living; *kleos* belongs also to the dead.[11] *Kudos* is frequently a gift from a god; *kleos* is won by the man himself or granted by the folk.[12] *Kudos* belongs only to men, *kleos* also to women. *Kudos* is always positive; success brings *kudos*, failure merely *penthos*, "sorrow" (IV.416–17). (*Penthos* is an inward-turning, self-regarding feeling; the man who experiences failure feels himself diminished and draws into himself. *Kudos*, on the other hand, is a kind of star quality or charisma, an enlargement of the person.) The successful man feels that he matters more to others, and this feeling, his *kudos*, is his personal possession. *Kleos*, however, is in the keeping of others; a man's *kleos* consists of what others say about him. Since they may speak of his failures as well as of his success, failure also has a *kleos*—negative *kleos*, *duskleia* (II.115 = IX.22).

Timē also is bestowed on a man by others, but a man's *timē* is a valuation of him, while his *kleos* is a description of him. *Timē* means "honor" and also "status," especially the status of the king (VI.193, IX.616, XX.181); it also means "price" or "penalty" (III.286). In Homeric society, where every man was liable to be taken prisoner and held for ransom, there existed a kind of market in people; the value of a man (and therefore his honor and status) could be determined by finding out what his relatives would pay to have him back. Obviously men's *timē* fluctuated, and a man who had *kudos* would also have a greater *timē* (XVI.84). But *kudos* is an absolute quality, like health or strength, while *timē* is always relative: it is a measure of men's standing in relation to one another (I.278, XXIV.57). A man's *timē* is thus the index of his place in a zero-sum system; *timē* awarded to one must in effect be withdrawn from others. *Kudos* and *kleos*, by

33

contrast, are more nearly free goods, and the total amount of each within the social system will vary from time to time.[13] Where great events take place, men acquire *kudos* and society confers on men and their acts a *kleos*. When the men die, their *kudos* dies with them, but their *kleos* survives in the memory of men.

Kleos is thus a specific type of social identity. A man has a history, and for better or worse he must live with it. His story is in a certain sense himself—or one version of himself—and, since his story can survive his personal existence and survive his enactment of a social role, his story is from one point of view the most real version of himself. To think of life as a story is different from thinking of it in terms of praise and blame. A story is more than that; it has a shape—a beginning, middle, and end; in Homer a man may be conceived as a narrative, may conceive himself as a narrative. In the *Odyssey* the disguised Odysseus congratulates Penelope on her *kleos*, "which reaches heaven" (xix.108). Penelope responds that if only Odysseus came home, her *kleos* would be "greater and finer" (xix.128). Her struggle against the suitors is in any case admirable; but if her husband were at the end restored to her, then her story would have a fitting conclusion and dramatic meaning.

Kleos is specially associated with the gravestone.[14] Society secures its memories of the dead man by creating for him a memorial to perpetuate his name and remind men to tell his story (VII.86–91). He will not be utterly annihilated. Thus the *kleos* of the hero is to some extent a compensation to him for his own destruction. Achilles has a choice between long life and "imperishable *kleos*"; he cannot have both (IX.412–16). At the very end Hector recognizes his fate and knows that nothing is left to him except the hope of *kleos*:

> Now evil death is close, there is no more waiting
> Or turning away. Long ago this must have been chosen
> By Zeus and his son the Archer—and yet, before,
> They looked after me. But now my portion is here.
> Let me not perish, then, without effort or fameless,
> But in some great act, that men to come may know it.
>
> (XXII.300–305)

The last phrase, *essomenoisi puthesthai* (more literally: "for men-to-come to inquire about"), is a phrase used also of the gravestone.[15] By the greatness of his act the hero can create his own memorial; he impresses his existence upon the consciousness of men.

At such moments heroes become *aoidimoi*, "subjects for song." These famous acts are the *klea andrōn*, the themes of song; the singer tells the story his audience wants to hear. But it is also true that song creates or confers a *kleos*. In song events acquire a kind of permanence which confers on them something approaching immortality. A place in the tradition of song is the greatest prize the society can award its heroes, as Telemachus says of Orestes: "The Achaeans will carry his *kleos* afar and, for men to come, his song" (iii.203–4). Evil acts also can survive in this way; through song the society can award the negative prize of eternal infamy. Thus Agamemnon compares his wife with Odysseus':

> Blessed son of Laertes, resourceful Odysseus,
> Surely you took great excellence with your wife,
> So good is the mind of blameless Penelope,
> Icarius' girl. How well she remembered Odysseus,
> Her wedded man. The *kleos* will never perish
> Of her excellence. The immortals will make a song
> Delightful to mortals of Prudent Penelope.
> Not like Tyndarus' girl did she plan evil acts,
> Killing her wedded husband; a hateful song
> *She'll* be among men, and an evil name she'll give
> To women in general, even to a good housekeeper.
>
> (xxiv.192–202)

Thus, as the vehicle of the *klea andrōn*, heroic song is a kind of history; through epic the past is preserved from obliteration. The greatest praise one can grant a singer is that his account is true to the fact, as Odysseus praises Demodocus:

> Demodocus, I'd guess you're the best of any.
> You've learned from the Muse—Zeus's child—or Apollo—
> So well in order you sing the woes of Achaeans—
> All that was done and endured and labored by them—
> As if you had been there yourself or learned from another.
>
> (viii.487–91)

If song transmits the past to the future, the primary duty of the singer is to tell the past just as it was.

THE EPIC DISTANCE

But (for here we must catch ourselves up) we would be quite wrong to take Odysseus' praise of Demodocus as Homer's straightforward praise of his own art. There is nothing straightforward about it; the whole passage is shot with complex ironies. It is already an irony that Odysseus should hear the song of the bard. Epic song does not belong within the heroic world; it is excluded from the *Iliad*, where the bards appear in the narrative only to lead the mourning at a funeral (XXIV. 720–22). Achilles, it is true, sings *klea andrōn* and Patroclus listens (IX.186–91); but this is a special poetic effect. It is a mark of Achilles' unique self-reflective consciousness that he has become his own poet, or at least a poet of his own world. Similarly, Helen, who shares with Achilles the gift of self-reflection and the need for self-definition, works a great web,

> Double-folded and dyed, and worked with the many labors
> Of horse-training Trojans, Achaeans shirted with bronze,
> All they'd endured for herself in the wrestlings of Ares.
>
> (III.126–28)

Helen also says that Zeus has cast an evil fate on Paris and herself "so that later we could be a theme for song for men to come" (VI.358). Epic can only be hinted at and anticipated in the *Iliad*; epic describes the heroic world to an audience which itself inhabits another, ordinary, world.

Homer's heroes are larger-than-life figures, men who can throw such a stone as

> not two best men of the folk
> Could easily shift from the ground to a wagon with bars—
> Such as mortals are now. But he threw it with ease by himself.
>
> (XII.447–49)

These heroes inhabit a world different from that of Homer's audience. They use bronze weapons, not iron; they ride into battle on chariots from which they dismount to do their actual fighting; they do not eat fish; they are illiterate. No doubt Homer thought—as we think—that the stories he told had a historical basis, and no doubt he intended much of this to reflect the actualities of the past. Often he was wrong about that.[16] It does not much matter; what does matter is that the heroic world should be set apart. In another kind of literary tradition it might have been placed in the future or in the East. The technical features of the Homeric world have the same function as other features we might call poetic or conventional. Thus the heroes talk freely with the gods; they encounter monsters, speaking rivers, and giants; their corpses can be magically transported and protected from decay. A hero, further, never dies of wounds. He may be wounded and recover; but if he is to die, it will be immediately, on the battlefield. Heroes do not make casual remarks; they speak in speeches, each consisting of one or more complete hexameter lines. And so forth. All these features combine to establish an epic distance, to remind the audience that the story is not about their world.

In the *Odyssey*, however, the two worlds are to some extent collapsed. A naturalistic background is made to accommodate figures from epic and fantasy. Thus it happens that Odysseus can listen to the bard tell his own story; it is as if Octavius, in *Antony and Cleopatra*, should attend a performance of *Julius Caesar*. There is much that is playful in the ironies of the *Odyssey* and much that is serious; the poet inquires into the meaning of the heroic by testing it against the world familiar to his audience.

That is, the poet, by collapsing the epic distance, allows the two worlds to comment on each other. He often appears, further, to be making a comment on his own work as an epic poet. There is, for example, the question of truth in poetry.

In this poem, where the bard is praised for his truth, he is also uncomfortably associated with the liar. Odysseus himself is a kind of poet—he narrates four books of his own epic—and Alcinous says he is a bard, not a liar (xi.363–69). But Odysseus is of course a famous liar (xiii.291–95). He tells Eumaeus almost nothing but lies, and Eumaeus says that to listen to him is like being enchanted by a bard whose skill is from god (xvii.518–21). The only part Eumaeus disbelieves is the part that is true (xiv.363–65); presumably, being true, it is less carefully told and thus less convincing. It is said of Odysseus that "he always knew how to tell many lies like to truth" (xix.203). Almost the same phrase is used by Hesiod's muses:

> We know how to tell many lies that are like to the truth;
> And we know, if we like, how to utter the truth as well.
>
> *(Theogony* 27–28)

There is no reason to believe that the audience will be able to tell the two apart.

But we may suspect that the poet of the *Odyssey* is teasing his audience—as Hesiod's Muses are teasing Hesiod—with a false problem. Odysseus can comment on the truth of the bard's account: he was himself a witness of the event. The audience of epic, by contrast, has no access to the world of epic except epic. The poet invents or preserves the epic world in his own way, and we are entirely in his hands. What is transmitted, in fact, is not the story of the past but stories that have come from the past. And as we saw that a man's story is in a certain sense his most authentic identity, so also, in the case of events, the story of them has some claims to be called more real—because more enduring and more meaningful—than the literal truth of the event.

The matter of epic, as we saw, is *kleos*, but the themes of epic song themselves had a *kleos* (i.351, viii.74). The bard's stories, in other words, were not simply about events but *were* also events or objects in their own right—famous things in the world of things that are talked about, like Nestor's shield. The *kleos* of the song is the mark that, in it, history has been transformed into art. The audience does not ask for news of the fall of Troy but for one of the songs about it. The song acquires a value of its own, and men ask for it, not because they want to know something, but in order to enjoy the pleasure of song. A reversal then takes place. It seems that the event took place in order that a song could be made of it. The heroic world is a world of men and events that are talked about. In that way it is like our world; but, unlike our world, it seems to exist in order to be talked about. It has become the property of the poets and is turned to their purposes. It thus ceases in any ordinary sense to be a real world at all. Whereas the liar tells us falsehoods about the real world, the bard tells us the truth (a kind of truth) about a world become unreal. The epic immortalizes a *kleos*, but it is a news from nowhere.

The epic bard handles this point by referring to the inspiration of the Muse. The bard, that is, does not convey information acquired in the ordinary way; his knowledge comes from elsewhere, from outside the human world altogether. The Muse enables the bard to tell a story quite different from an ordinary human story. Homer puts the point this way in his prelude to the Catalogue of Ships:

> Tell me now, Muses who hold Olympus' halls—
> For you are divine, you were there, you know it all—
> We hear only the *kleos*, we know nothing—
> Who the leaders were, commanders of the Danaoi.
> The number of them I could not tell or name
> Not if I had ten tongues, and ten my mouths,
> My voice uncracked, and the spirit in me of bronze,
> Except you Olympian Muses, daughters of Zeus
> Of the aegis, remind me of all who went before Troy.
> Now I will name their captains and all their ships.

$$(\text{II}.484\text{--}93)$$

It is the Muses (or Muse—singular alternates with plural) who remember what we would otherwise forget. Thus it is explained that the stories they tell us, while somehow close to us and full of meaning, hold a meaning far from our ordinary experience. They are complementary to ordinary experience. Epic is both a remembering and a forgetting. The Muses are the daughters of Memory—*Mnēmosunē*;[17] but at the very moment Hesiod gives them this parentage, he calls them "forgetfulness of trouble and a rest from anxiety" (*Theog.* 55). When we hear heroic song, we remember that world and forget this one. We are transported. The bard sings

> With god-given knowledge his words, charming to men,
> And they, motionless, eagerly listen whenever he sings.
>
> (xvii.518–20)

The epic distance—the conquest of history by art—gives rise to a contrast between the themes of song and their effect. Epic song tells stories of violent action; but when the stories are told, a tranquillity descends upon the folk. The bard sings of sorrow and death, but his songs give pleasure. The themes of heroic songs are themes of ruin and disorder, but the song itself is an ordered thing, and heard as such.

THE MUSE

The poet of the *Odyssey* is, among other things, the first great critic of the *Iliad*.[18] By his collapse of the epic distance he is able to dramatize the problematic of his narrative art. He points to narratives suspended between reality and unreality, between history and fantasy, claiming the merits of both. The poet is free to tell us whatever he likes without losing his claim to actuality; he is in a sense inventing the world he describes.

The archaic Greeks resolved this problematic mythologically, by reference to the Muse. A sacred authority was conferred on the poet, and it was thereby declared that everything in his poem was just as it should be.[19] The poets were figures with a special status, parallel to that of the priests, whom, in this relatively unpriestly society, they to a large extent replaced. Poets were central, integrative figures within archaic culture; in fact they held this position among the Greeks until, toward the beginning of the fourth century B.C., they were forced to give way to the philosophers.

In Homer and Hesiod the work of the bard is said to be like the work of the orator. Public speech that is proper is *kata kosmon*, "ordered" (II.213–14); the bard also sings *kata kosmon* (viii.489). Both create order in others—the orator in public space, where he puts an end to strife, the bard in the private heart, where he heals distress so that "gladness fills the folk" (ix.6). Hesiod goes so far as to say that the two are inspired by the same Muse; in his praise of Calliope, leader of the Muses,[20] he says:

She also attends upon the respected kings.
Whomsoever they honor (the daughters of great Zeus)
And watch over his birth among the Zeus-bred kings,
Upon his tongue they shed the sweetest moisture,
And the words from his mouth fall soothing. Then the folk
All look upon him as he dispenses right
With straight justice. He makes his speech securely
And with swift skill stops even a great quarrel.
For that is the use of kings in their wisdom; the folk
They can in assembly bring round from harm to good
Easily, talking them over with gentle words.
Like a god they greet the king in the meeting place
With soothing respect; he excels where men are gathered.
Such is the holy gift of the Muses to men.
     And from the Muses and from Archer Apollo
Are men who are bards on the earth, and skilled with the lyre;
Kings are from Zeus. He is blessed whom the Muses
Love. Sweet from his mouth there flows the voice.
If one keeps sorrow in his new-grieved mind
And dreads the pain at his heart, yet still the bard
(The Muses' squire) sings *klea* of previous men
And of the blessed gods who keep Olympus.
Soon he forgets his grief, nor of his care
Remembers. Quickly the gifts of the goddesses persuade him.

(Theogony 80–103)

Both the king and the bard are praised, not because their words are true but because they are effective. Both have authority, and both draw their authority from Zeus, the divine source of authority. Both create a common world and thus make it possible for men to live in the world and with one another. The bard and the king are thus parallel figures, and poetry is firmly established as a public fact with public uses. The heroic world is kept alive by the bards as the common possession of the public; heroic epic secures the public by giving it a world alternate to its own, a world between unreality and reality which its members can contemplate in common. From this point of view the epic is a social institution, and the Muse is appealed to, as a god is so often appealed to in culture, to legitimate the institution. When the bard speaks of his inspiration by the Muse, he objectifies his own capacity—dependent as much on the responsiveness of his audience as on his own skill—to create among the folk a second reality, a poetic world which has a standing parallel to that of objective fact.

The heroic world was thus a "collective representation." The reality of the heroic events was a reality secured and validated by the recurrent collective experience of successful poetry. In this experience the audience felt the presence of the poet's god.

Mythological solutions do not answer questions; they merely set them aside by shifting them to a level at which they cannot be answered. For this reason mythological answers cannot survive criticism; they presume, rather, the absence of criticism. But the Greeks were nothing if not critical. The history of Greek culture after Homer can be seen as a progressive "demystification" of the world—of poetry with the rest. By "poetry" the Greeks meant always, before anything else, the *Iliad*, so the question can be put in this form: What is the standing of Homer once he has been deprived of the authority of his Muse? In tracing this question we shall come, by way of Socrates' quarrel with the sophists, to Aristotle's *Poetics*. We shall see that Aristotle answers, not a new question, but this old question—which he is for the first time in a position to make explicit. Since we also live in a demystified world, since for us also the Muse can be only a metaphor, Aristotle's question must be our question. It is the question of the human meaning of imaginative narrative art—in particular, as a leading example, the *Iliad*.

The Poet and the Teacher

The leading instruments (if not sources) of demystification among the Greeks were the sophists; their activity centered on a reevaluation of the power of the word. Sophistry developed contemporaneously with democratic institutions, and these implied a redefinition of oratory. The typical archaic orator had been the judge or king, the creator of community who arbitrates and finds middle ground between factions. The people (the new democratic arbiter) acted without speech, by voting for one speaker or the other. The typical orator became the litigant, the party to a dispute, and rhetoric came to be conceived primarily as a competitive activity. Mediating rhetoric, in which the speaker attempts to speak on behalf of the whole community, was restricted to a few ceremonial occasions, such as state funerals, and received little theoretical attention.

The new competitive rhetoric required no Muse to legitimate it. It was a technique; the means were justified by the attainment of the end. In Homer and Hesiod the power of the word had seen itself as a kind of virtue; for the sophists rhetoric became a martial art, in the service of either virtue or vice.[21] As it became technical, rhetoric also became demystified; the sophists began to write books and give lessons explaining the sources of rhetorical power.

All this had an effect upon attitudes toward poetry. It occurred to men trained in rhetoric that the poet also is a speaker with an audience; the poet was praised for his ability to make an effect on that audience, to provoke *pathē*, "emotions," as though emotional impact were the purpose of poetry. Thus Ion, the performer of Homer, says:

> I can see the audience down there crying, moved to outrage, swept away by wonder at the poem. . . . If I can set them to crying, I will laugh when I carry off the prize; but if they laugh, I will cry for having let the prize get away.
>
> (Plato *Ion* 535e)

Poetry in the fifth century became increasingly technical, with some loss to its dignity.[22] And poetry, like rhetoric, was drawn into the format of democratic procedures, with the poets competing before a panel of judges. But, with all this, poetry never became rhetoric. For one thing, poetry maintained some distance from everyday life—comedy through fantasy, tragedy through the heroic world inherited from Homer. The crucial warning was issued early, when Phrynichus, after *The Sack of Miletus*, was fined by the Athenians for "reminding them of their own troubles" (Herodotus 6.21). Poetry (in spite of a few experiments with contemporary themes) continued to concern itself with an alternative reality, and the poets preserved their special relation with the public. Poets were awarded prizes, but poetry never became merely a means for winning prizes. The poet continued to speak on behalf of the public, and poetry continued to be a source of community, especially in Athens.

The poet's authority, however, was secularized. He lost the standing of prophet and acquired the standing of teacher.[23] On this one point, both parties and umpire in the debate which fills the second half of Aristophanes' *Frogs* are agreed:

> AESCHYLUS: Why should one admire a poet?
> EURIPIDES: For cleverness and wit, that we make better Men in the cities.
> AESCHYLUS: And if you didn't do this But found them fine and noble, left them rascals, What's coming to you?
> DIONYSUS: Death, no need to ask.
>
> (*Frogs* 1008–12)

The classification of the poet as teacher made some sense for the didactic and sententious poets—Hesiod, for example, and Simonides—whose work, in any case, occupied a large part of the elementary school curriculum.[24] It was more difficult to classify the narrative or dramatic

42

poet this way. The narrative poet does not explain anything; he shows us something. We do not feel ourselves instructed but affected. Furthermore, the affect we feel, the *pathos*, is often negative: we feel terror or grief or outrage. And yet the experience is a sort of pleasure. Perhaps the poet teaches us, but it is hard to say how; it is hard to say anything about poetry except that it works.

The problem is stated—with a comic solution—in a fragment of Timocles, a comic poet contemporary with Aristotle:

> Friend, just listen, I'm going to tell you something.
> Man is an animal born to constant trouble,
> And many sorrows come packed up with life;
> Some breathing-spells from care he has invented,
> Like this: his mind forgets his own affairs;
> He gets entranced by other people's troubles;
> It's pleasant—and educational as well.
> Just take the tragic poets, for example;
> They help a lot. Suppose someone is poor;
> He'll find that Telephus is poorer yet—
> Then being poor is not so hard to take.
> He's crazy? He can look at Alcmaeon.
> His eyes are sore—but Phineas' sons are blind.
> His child has died? Niobe is his comfort.
> He's lame—but he can stare at Philoctetes.
> Some old man is in trouble—he learns of Oeneus.
> Everything greater than mankind ever suffered—
> Other people's bad luck—once he's got that,
> His own misfortunes aren't so hard to take.

> (*apud* Athenaeus 223b)

The comic effect of this passage lies in the discrepancy between the first half and the second. We can take it that the general description was well understood by Timocles' audience. Tragedy, which shows us heroes in trouble, releases us from trouble; it further grants us a pleasure mixed with education. But how does it have this effect? The poet contents us with his comic answer: tragedy shows us that "there's always somebody worse off than you are."

We can suppose that this answer amused Timocles' audience because it answered a familiar question to which they themselves had no ready answer. There was a mystery about poetry. The power of poetry was undeniable, but the meaning of that power remained to be explained.

Into this gap between power and meaning slipped, with characteristic agility, Socrates—who turned the mystery of poetry against the poets. Socrates (or Plato's version of him) revived the doctrine of inspiration,

43

but to opposite effect. The archaic Muse had conferred authority on the poet; Socrates introduces the Muse to deprive the poet of authority:[25]

> I went to the poets—those of tragedy and dithyramb and the rest—because I thought that there I could catch myself in the act of knowing less than they did. I took in hand their poems—the ones they seemed to me to have worked on the hardest—and asked them what they meant (I thought that way I might learn something from them too). I am ashamed, gentlemen, to tell you the truth; however, it must be told. I could almost say that just about any bystander could have spoken better about the things these men themselves had made. So it did not take me long to realize this about the poets: not by wisdom do they make what they make, but by some kind of nature and inspiration, like the seers and the prophets. These too say many and beautiful things, but they know nothing of what they say. And I came to see that that was roughly the condition of the poets.
>
> *(Apology* 22a–c)

In other words: poems happen—like thunderstorms; since neither comes "accompanied by an explanation," you cannot learn anything from either. About poems Socrates says:

> We cannot ask them questions about what they say; and when the many bring them into conversations, some say the poem means this, some say it means that; they are conversing about a thing which they cannot put to the test.
>
> *(Protagoras* 347e)

For Socrates there is a mystery about both the source and the meaning of poetry; and, being mysterious (this is the peculiar Socratic step), poetry is fundamentally uninteresting.

Socrates' position, like most morally urgent positions, is founded on a circularity. What is worth knowing is established by reference to a concept of what is worth knowing. Having established the one necessary task of man—the understanding of the ground of his own actions—Socrates can set aside everything else as irrelevant.[26]

This does not mean that poetry must be rejected; it means only that it must be reevaluated and the poets deprived of any independent authority vis-à-vis the philosopher. For Socrates (as Plato represents him) all valid activities are one with dialectical philosophy and therefore can be included within it. Thus in the *Phaedrus* rhetoric is redefined as an art of speechmaking which properly belongs only to philosophers. In the *Republic* politics is redefined as an art of ruling which properly belongs only to philosophers. Similarly, poetry could be redefined as an art of imaginative composition which properly belongs only to philosophers. Plato nowhere makes this point,[27] perhaps because he spoke to an audience, not of poets, but of politicians and speechmakers, or perhaps because he thought that the Dialogues themselves made the point plainly enough.[28]

In any case, Socrates' position is clear: if the poet is to have the status of teacher, he must be judged as a teacher; we should not praise him for being moving, or charming, or full of pictures of life. Furthermore, the status of teacher is really the only status worth having. This leaves the poet no special place to stand; he is (like the rest of us) a philosopher or nothing.

IMITATION AS EXPERIENCE

Poetry, once set aside in this way, comes back into the Socratic discourse at another level. As Plato's Socrates describes his own enterprise, he must also describe the world in which that enterprise takes place. Poetry is a part of that world and must find a place in that description. Thus Socrates finds himself talking about narrative and dramatic poetry —and specifically about Homer—especially in the *Republic*, Book Ten.[29] Socrates asks in effect: What kind of thing is a dramatic narrative, and how are we to consider it among the things we know? We should be clear that the question is not, at least initially, a question in aesthetics or literary criticism but a question in metaphysics and epistemology. Yet it was in this Socratic discussion that Plato made his contribution to literary criticism and firmly established at the center of it the term "imitation."[30]

Socrates' world picture, his metaphysics and epistemology, were created in conflict with the sophists, and the Socratic position can often best be understood as a response to a sophistic challenge. Let us therefore go back to one of the few surviving texts of the sophistic, Gorgias' *Praise of Helen*.

The *Praise of Helen* is a playful rhetorical display piece, written in a highly artificial style, in defense of Helen of Troy. Gorgias' case is that Helen went with Paris for one of three reasons: she was coerced, she was persuaded, or she was in love. The device of the speech is to collapse the second and third into the first: persuasion and love, says Gorgias, are both forms of coercion. Therefore Helen was at no point responsible for her acts.

Gorgias twice refers to imitative art, first in the section on persuasion, where poetry is introduced to demonstrate the power of the word:

If speech was her persuader and her soul's dissuader, against this not hard is the defense and the release from the offense, as follows: Speech is a great potentate, which, though insignificant in body and invisible, yet has godlike powers. For it is able to halt fear and take away sorrow and create in us joy and increase in us pity. . . . Poetry altogether I deem and name speech having meter. To those that hear, it enters shivering, full of fears and pity, filled with tears and longing turned to sorrow; alien are the acts and bodies, yet by their good fortune and ill fortune an inner experience through the words comes upon the soul.

(Gorgias *Helen* 8–9 [Diels-Kranz⁸])

The point here is that the power of words is unconnected with their reality; we know that the events of the play are unreal—or in any case have nothing to do with us (they are *allotria*, "alien")—but they move us anyway.

In the section on love, Gorgias refers to painting; here his object is to demonstrate the power of things, of experience, and to show that this power is similarly unconnected with reality:

Through vision also the soul is shaped in its tendencies. For straightway when warlike bodies, to be warlike, put on warlike dress of bronze and iron, some for defense, some for attack, if the vision beholds them, it is startled and startles the soul, so that many times men flee in their confusion from impending danger as if it were actual. Habitual character, though strongly implanted by the law, is evicted by fear, which arises from the vision; this latter, when it comes, makes us careless of that judged noble by law and of that made good by victory. Already some, seeing fearful things, lost their present thought for present time; so much did fear quench and distract the mind. Many fell into vain travail and dread disease and incurable madness; such images of things seen did vision inscribe in the thought. . . .

And then the painters, when from many colors and bodies they compose one perfected body and figure, delight the vision. The making of statues and the working of ornaments provide pleasant sights to the eye. Thus is engendered a vision, with sorrow for some things, desire for others. Many causes, in many people, for many things have provoked love and desire, for both objects and bodies. If, then, Helen's eye, pleased by Alexander's body, induced desire and contention of love, what wonder?

(Gorgias *Helen* 15–19)

Gorgias' point here is that we are frightened, not by the enemy, but by the look of the enemy; the appearances of things work on us because we take the appearance for the thing. The proof is that the plastic arts, which exist purely in order to appear in a certain way, work on us and please us.

Gorgias' argument thus moves twice: from experience in general to art and back to experience. Experience is first explained by reference to poetry, then by reference to painting. The experience of imitative art is taken as typical of experience in general. We are affected by art, which we know to be unreal; we should know that all experience is similarly affecting and similarly unreal. All experience, thus, is a kind of passivity, and the meaning of the experience is simply its power over us. Gorgias rests his case on the absolute power of appearances; if Helen found Paris' words persuasive or his person pleasing, she was helpless to resist her own state of mind.

Gorgias does not draw attention to the unreality of art in order to dispraise the artist; on the contrary. His argument is parallel to that in the *Dissoi Logoi*, where the fact that lying is permitted in art—"In tragedy-writing and painting the man who cheats us most thoroughly by making things like truth is best" (*Dissoi Logoi* 3.10 [Diels-Kranz[8]]) —is taken as evidence that lying ought to be permitted everywhere. Similarly the artist, in creating a quasi reality of appearance and imposing it on the world, is doing nothing different from what everyone and everything does, since everything that is, appears, and is known to us as appearance. So, Gorgias does not have to deny the poet the standing of teacher; rather he assimilates all teaching to poetry and makes of all learning a *pathos* or passivity. Thus he can set science, rhetoric, and (sophistic) philosophy together:

> That persuasion entering through speech shapes the soul as it wishes, one must learn first from speech about the things above the earth, which exchanges opinion for opinion, extracting one, inserting another, and makes things unbelieved and unclear obvious to the eyes of opinion. Second come the contests we are compelled to carry on through speech, in which one speech delights a great crowd and persuades when written with art, not spoken with truth. Third come the contentions of philosophical speech, in which is displayed the rapidity of insight, how variable it makes the belief of opinion. One can speak of the power of speech toward the mobilization of soul as one speaks of the mobilization of drugs toward the nature of body. Just as various drugs draw various humors from the body and put an end, sometimes to disease, sometimes to life, so also, of speeches, some please, some terrify, some put confidence in the unwilling, some by a sort of evil persuasion drug and charm the soul.
>
> (Gorgias *Helen* 13–14)

The doctrine of the absolute power of appearances is a core doctrine of the sophistic, related to the doctrines that right and wrong are whatever men take them to be, that justice is whatever those in authority declare it to be, that whatever a man thinks to be true is for him true as long as he thinks it. All these doctrines rest on a basic assertion that we are in no position to criticize our experience, to declare some of it valid and some of it invalid.

Behind this doctrine—which we may call exoteric—lay another esoteric (though hardly hidden) doctrine: that if the power of appearances is absolute, it is a power which can be exercised by anyone able to control appearances. This power the sophists offered their initiates, those who would be, not the patients on whom the drugs acted, but the doctors who administered them, not the audience of the social drama, but its poets. Sophistry, by teaching the power of appearance, would make tyranny possible—a tyranny all the more absolute for being unperceived.

This second doctrine made the sophists popular and dangerous—and vulnerable to Socrates' dialectical questions: What does your doctrine say about yourself? Where do you place yourself in the world you describe? Is there not a contradiction between the explicit doctrine you teach and the implicit doctrine that governs your behavior—and that of your pupils? The assimilation of teaching to *pathos* could not apply to the sophists' own teaching, at least when it went beyond a mere display of their power and came to imparting that power to another. At that point there must be some criticism of experience, if only the sort which distinguishes effective technique from ineffective.

Socrates took his stand vis-à-vis the sophists on the absolute necessity of criticizing experience. He also renewed the notion that the experience of imitative art is typical of experience in general, but renewed it to opposite effect. After all, the sophists had made a fundamental mistake. It is not true that the poet lies to us and convinces us that we are hearing truth; rather, we enjoy his story in the way we do precisely because we take it as a story. We do not admire the statue because we think it is a man; we admire it as a statue of a man. The experience of imitative art is therefore typical, not of uncritical, but of critical experience.

Imitation is a pervasive term in the Socratic discourse[31] because the imitative object is the typical less-real thing, the thing which demands to be taken as what it is not and therefore demands of us, on the most primary level of recognition, some mental activity. When we see a picture of grapes, we know we are not seeing grapes; that is the basis of our praise of the imitation. There would be no point in praising

48

an actual bunch of grapes for looking just like grapes. Furthermore, since we praise the imitation by reference to the original, it follows that we appreciate the imitation by reference to something which we do not, directly and at the moment, experience. When we point at the picture and say, "Those are grapes," we are stating our recognition, not of the picture which is before us, but of the grapes which are not before us; the object of our knowledge is not the object which we see but another object which we do not see but of which we are reminded.

Socrates (or Plato's version of him) generalizes this point and makes of it the Theory of Ideas. When, he says, we point at a bunch of actual grapes and say, "Those are grapes," we are referring, not to the particular bunch, but to the general idea of "grapes" which we have in our mind and of which we are reminded by seeing the particular bunch. Socrates calls the particular bunch an imitation of the form of grapes. He relies on the term "imitation" to encourage us to take all immediate experience as the less-real—as experience which demands of us the mental activity of abstract interpretation.

Socrates' introduction to the discussion of imitation in Book Ten of the *Republic* is thus somewhat disingenuous. We "are accustomed to make the hypothesis," he says, that there is a form of each thing and that there are objects which are imitations of the form. Thus we can describe imitative art, which imitates objects, as an imitation of the imitation and twice-removed from reality (*Republic* 596a–597b). It is characteristic of the *Republic* that (unlike most of the dialogues) it argues downward from principles to application. We should not forget that the dialectical process had worked the other way and that the notion that things were imitations of forms was originally derived from the notion that pictures were imitations of things.

Thus we can understand the place of the argument on imitation in the whole pattern of the *Republic*. It is introduced as an epilogue, along with the argument demonstrating the immortality of the soul, the two arguments being followed by the myth of judgment. These two arguments belong together; together they form the basis of the Socratic moral urgency. The argument on imitation reminds us that experience must be criticized; the argument on the soul reminds us that we have in ourselves the power to criticize experience and rise from a position of mere passivity. Placed in this world, the soul is like a creature who has lain long in the sea, "worn and corrupted by the waves"; we can guess at its real nature only when we consider

its philosophy and when we notice the things it catches onto and the conversations it desires, because it is akin to the divine and immortal and ever-existing; we must think what it would be like if it gave itself over to such pursuits and by this impulse rose from the sea in which it now is, crusted over with rock and shells as we now are, because of our present entertainment here on earth, overgrown with things earthy and rocky and with wildness as a result of this so-called prosperous entertainment.

(*Republic* 611e–612a)

Socrates' rejection of poetry in the *Republic*, Book Ten, is a part of Socrates' definition of philosophy. The poet—to pursue the metaphor—swims in the element in which we find ourselves immersed and sings of man's actual condition; the philosopher seeks to rise into some purer atmosphere and speaks of man, not as he is, but as he could be. Socrates' rejection of poetry is, furthermore, hypothetical; poetry is harmful to those "who lack the antidote [*pharmakon*] of knowing how things actually are" (595b). Socrates speaks of the effect of poetry on those who take it as a substitute for truth. He here contrasts the philosopher with the completely unphilosophical poet, just as he contrasts the philosopher in the *Gorgias* with the completely unphilosophical rhetorician and in the *Theaetetus* with the completely unphilosophical practical man. In each case the aim is to show us something about the philosopher; there is no intention to deny the possibility of a philosophical rhetoric, a philosophical practical life, or a philosophical poetry.

Socrates begins with painting, because figurative art is the clearest example of what we mean by imitation. His real topic throughout the passage, however, is the poets (cf. 603b, 605a–b)[32]—and especially Homer. His basic quarrel is with those who claim that since all aspects of life are represented in Homer, Homer understood all aspects of life. This would be like saying that a man who has made sketches of all kinds of craftsmen understands every craft (598b–d). The imitation of a thing is not a knowledge of it but only "some sort of play" (602b).

Socrates goes on to explain what he means by "knowledge." Knowledge is founded on science, which numbers, weighs, and measures and in this way constructs a stable world. The world of appearances is in itself unstable, since things constantly appear different; the painter exploits this very instability. Thus he teaches us to pay attention to the flux of immediate experience and distracts us from our task of testing and stabilizing experience (602c–603b). Similarly, the poet exploits the phenomenal instability of the ethical world, in which good and evil constantly appear different (603d). Here again the imitator, by drawing our attention to the surface of experience, distracts us from our task. Socrates does not assert that there is a science of ethics, but he does find an equivalent to science in the ethical sphere: reason and the law, which demand that we stabilize ourselves. When we suffer some ill fortune, "the loss of a son or something else of great importance to us," then

> that which commands us to stand firm is reason and the law, while that which draws us into grief is the suffering [*to pathos*] itself. . . . The law says that it is noblest to stay calm as far as possible in misfortune and not to complain, on the premise that the good and evil of these things is unclear and that taking them hard does nothing to improve matters; no human thing is worth great seriousness, and the position which we should adopt as quickly as possible is cut off from us by grief. . . . I mean that we should take counsel about what has happened, and, as in the game of pebbles, play our pieces according to the fall of the dice . . . ; we should not, like children who have been struck, hold tight to the place and pass our time in howling.
>
> (*Republic* 604a–c)

Here Socrates' argument turns back from the question of knowledge to his original ethical concerns. Throughout, his objection to imitative art has been that it is too intelligible. Because the artist is content with the play of appearances, he can show us the world as we often see it, and his pictures will be immediately recognizable to us—unlike the pictures created by science, which often look completely absurd until we have heard the theory explained and the evidence laid out. Socrates is perhaps the first of those thinkers to whom this dialectic between appearance and reality is also enacted on the ethical level. Here the distinction is between the way we feel about our experience and our rational capacity to choose and to act. Fiction, which is "an imitation of the experience [*pathos*] of others" (604e),[33] encourages us to respond and to feel. It thus encourages in us a responsive attitude to our own experience and cultivates in us an emotional attitude toward our own situation. Thus the poetry of *pathos* appeals to the less-rational part of ourselves[34] and tends to create in us a condition in which we are incapable of rational action (606a–b). Therefore, on the hypothesis of the *Republic* (that an education could be created completely in the service of philosophy), Homer and the poets must be excluded from the state:

> If you admit this pleasure-giving Muse either in song or in speech, then pleasure and pain will rule in your city, instead of the law and the reasoning which seems best at any given time to the community.
>
> (*Republic* 607a)

Chapter 1

At the end of Plato's section on imitation, Socrates makes a promise and issues a challenge:

> All the same, let it be stated that if pleasure-giving poetry and imitation have anything to say for themselves, we for our part would be glad to hear it, because we know how much we have been enchanted by them. . . . So we would grant to their patrons, those who are not poets but lovers of poetry, to say something on their behalf in prose: that they are not only pleasant but also useful to civic life and to the life of man. And we will give them good hearing. It would surely be a gain if they should turn out to be not only pleasant but also useful.
>
> *(Republic* 607d)

This is the challenge to which Aristotle (consciously or unconsciously) responds in the *Poetics.*

IMITATION AS A MODE OF LEARNING

Aristotle's treatment of poetry is characteristically eclectic and to some degree synthetic of previous thought. Aristotle extends or renews the Homeric tradition by identifying the central organizing principle of the poem as the story—no longer called *kleos,* but *muthos,* "plot." Aristotle follows the sophistic in treating poetry as a *technē,* "craft," and by finding the special power of that *technē* exhibited in the *pathos* felt by the audience. Aristotle has his own characteristic interest in the kinds and history of human things; he is interested in the development of poetry and wants to define clear genres. All these elements are in the definition of tragedy:

> Tragedy is, then, an imitation of an action serious and complete, which has magnitude, in pleasure-giving language, different kinds in the different parts, done by actors and not reported, through pity and fear achieving the purification of these emotions.
>
> *(Poetics* 1449b24–28)

A tragedy, that is, tells a story having a certain kind of content and with certain formal characteristics; it uses certain means, which are prescribed by the tradition of the genre; and it produces a specifiable effect on its audience. Of "purification"—*katharsis*—we shall say more later. Here I note that Aristotle shows himself the heir of Plato by calling the play an "imitation" *(mimēsis).* He is concerned to rescue this term from the pejorative connotations inflicted on it by Socrates:

> It would seem that, in general, two causes produced poetry, and these by nature. In the first place, imitation is bred into man

52

from childhood (this is the very point in which he differs from the other animals—in that he is most imitative—and he makes his first learnings through imitation), as is the pleasure everyone takes in imitation. And a sign of this is what happens in fact; for things which give us pain when we see them give us pleasure when we look upon the most accurate images of them, for example, shapes of the most despised animals and of corpses. And the cause of this is as follows: learning is delightful not only to the philosophers but to men in general, although they have some smaller share of it. That is why they take pleasure in seeing the images; for it happens that, when they look upon them, they learn and reason out what each thing is, for example that this is that. (But if one has not actually seen the thing before, then it is not *qua* imitation that it produces the pleasure but through workmanship or color or some other cause.)

Imitation being natural to us, as are also harmony and rhythm (for the meters are obviously parts of rhythm), from the beginning those most naturally so inclined, proceeding by small steps, produced poetry out of improvisations.

(Poetics 1448b4–24)[35]

Aristotle goes down to the ground of nature because, for him, nature does nothing in vain; an activity specific to man and usual among men in general must be an activity whereby men are human. Obviously, not all men are poets, but Aristotle finds the roots of poetry in universal tendencies—tendencies seen even in those still-to-be-developed human beings we call children. Children from infancy dance, chant, and sing; we have some innate tendency to use our bodies and voices to structure space and time. Thus the music of poetry has primitive roots. So also does the imitative content; man is the most imitative of the animals. No doubt this has to do with his power to manipulate symbols. A man can make of himself a symbol, as when the child says, "I'm a vampire, and I'm going to eat you," and thus becomes a performer. And the child, like all of us, takes pleasure in recognizing imitations; thus he becomes an audience. Aristotle grounds imitative poetry on the most primitive sort of recognition: the child who looks at a picture book and says "cow." Aristotle says that the child thereby has some share of the philosophical pleasure of learning.

But here we have a problem. What does the child learn? That a thing can be an imitation? But the child does not point and say "picture of cow"; he says "cow." He recognizes, not the imitation, but the original. And the original—cow—he already knew; otherwise he would not have recognized it in the imitation. So in what sense can he be said to learn anything?

The key word in Aristotle's passage is *sullogizesthai*; Aristotle says that "we reason out" what each thing is. The learning occurs in this process of reasoning out, which itself occurs because the imitation presents us with a problem. A picture of a cow is really very little like a cow. In fact, an imitation must be unlike the original to be an imitation; an imitation cow which was just like a cow would be a cow. Imitation implies certain likenesses in a context of unlikeness. A picture of a cow shares with a cow certain common features; by these features we recognize the model. We identify horns, udder, tail—and we say "cow." That is the syllogism: we say, "Everything with these features is in some sense a cow. This thing has those features. Therefore this thing is in some sense a cow." The content of our learning is not "cow" but "features-of-cow." A mere sketch of these features properly arranged on the page is enough to prompt our recognition; we thus learn something about what we mean by a cow. For purposes of recognition, at least, these few features define a cow. The picture is thus a kind of concept; it presents us, not with a whole cow, but with some basic or underlying cow.

The essence of imitation (to borrow a term from Claude Lévi-Strauss) is reduction;[36] or, as Socrates says, the imitator "makes everything because he only lays hands on some small part of each thing" (*Republic* 598b). Socrates should have added, however, that the corollary of reduction is form. The imitation is qualitatively simpler than the original; thereby it can be more coherent; being less complex, it can be more intelligible. So in a certain sense the imitation is more of a cow—that is, more obviously a cow—than a cow is. That is why the imitation is pleasant—more pleasant than the original. Being made for us, it speaks to us far more directly than anything can in nature. In a certain sense the picture shows us a cow so that we can really see it.

From this point of view, imitation is the discovery of form in things. But we must remember that the form thus revealed to us, while it is really (because recognizably) a form of the object, is in no sense a definitive or absolute form. There is no question of the painter presenting us with some Platonic cow-in-itself. Just as there is no upper limit to the description of an actual cow—there is always more detail to be supplied, more relevant relations to be stated—so there is a potentially infinite number of different valid imitations of a cow. It was a principle of the Picturesque that "a cow is never out of place in a landscape"; the cows imitated by the painters of this genre were ornaments within a humanized natural world and were quite different objects from those presented under C in the child's alphabet. No imitation replaces any other imitation; and while each in its own way reveals some formal knowledge of the original, the aggregate of all imitations does not constitute any systematic knowledge of the cow; each in its own way remains a certain picture of the whole cow, monadic and independently valid.[37] Thus, while the pleasure of imitative art (from this point of view) lies in learning, the artist does not thereby become a teacher. He does not explain anything to us. Rather he sets us a soluble problem, a problem which always remains to be solved over again in some new way the next time it is set.

The artist thus (and Lévi-Strauss saw this point also)[38] is opposite to the scientist. Science explains the whole in terms of its parts and explains typical effects in terms of typical causes. Imitative art, which is in a certain sense more superficial than science (since it deals in appearances), is in another sense more profound; whereas science deals with abstracted elements, categories, and processes, an imitation states (in some specific way) the whole being of the thing. Each imitation rises from some inclusive, if schematic, intuition of the patterns found in experience. By the vision of the imitator, the parts are reduced to a whole, and their wholeness is revealed, perhaps for the first time. As Aristotle puts it:

> This is why poetry is more philosophical and more serious than history; poetry speaks rather of the universal, history of the particular. Now it is a universal that a certain kind of person turns out to do or say a certain kind of thing in accordance with probability or necessity; this is what poetry aims at, although it gives the persons proper names. But the particular is what Alcibiades did or suffered.
>
> *(Poetics* 1451b5–11)

The Probable as the Universal

But (and here we must catch ourselves up again) the distinction between poetry and history is not really relevant to what we have said so far. Of particulars too there is a universal[39] which makes them recognizable and imitable; from such imitations something can be learned. A portrait of Alcibiades might well reveal to us some essential or underlying Alcibiades. The story of Alcibiades could be told with fidelity to literal fact and yet in such a way that the rhythm and form of the events stood revealed. The responsible narrative historian tries, in fact, to do just that. In terms of what we have said so far, history is simply a narrative imitation written under a special discipline: that it must be literally true. But everything recognizable is an equally valid imitation.

Thus the position, as interpreted so far, does not really meet the Socratic indictment. It is not enough that we learn something; we must also learn something important—something more important than Alcibiades or cow. Aristotle is ready to make this claim as well, and, interestingly enough, he is more ready to make it for fiction than for history.

Fiction is a new term—or rather it is not yet a term; there is no word in Aristotle which can be translated just this way.[40] Fiction was in Aristotle's day a new genre, just emerging. The Homeric epics, as we saw, stood between history and fiction; there was no other place for them to stand, for the two had not yet been distinguished. History and fiction evolved in relation to each other and at the same time. History comes to full self-consciousness in Thucydides' Introduction (I.20–22), where he firmly turns his back on the storytellers and the legends which have "won their way into the world of myth." Self-conscious fiction begins with Agathon's *Anthos*, in which "the events and the proper names are made up, and nonetheless it pleases" (*Poetics* 1451b22–23). The problematic of narrative fiction can for the first time be explicitly stated by Aristotle because in Aristotle's time it had for the first time become clear that the meaning of a story need not have anything to do with the actuality of the events narrated.[41]

For Aristotle—and we shall see that this point is crucial—the heroic stories derived from epic are located firmly in the category of fiction. If the audience believes that they actually happened, this belief is merely (so to speak) one of the poet's rhetorical resources:

> In the tragedies they cling to actual [*or* preexisting] names. The reason is that what is possible is believed. When things have not yet happened, we do not yet believe that they are possible; while it is obvious that what has happened is possible. For it would not have happened if it had been impossible.
>
> (*Poetics* 1451b15–19)

> Even if he turns out to make a poem of what happened, he is · nonetheless a poet. Nothing prevents some of the things that happened from being such things as probably happen and possibly happen; according to *that*, he is their poet.
>
> (*Poetics* 1451b29–33)

> It is obvious . . . that it is not the task of the poet to tell us what happened but the sort of thing that would happen and is possible according to probability or necessity.
>
> (*Poetics* 1451a36–38)

In these three passages (which I have quoted out of order to clarify my point) Aristotle names the kind of universal imitated in fiction. Fiction shows us what sort of thing is possible, probable, or necessary.

The key term here, "probable" (*eikos*), is borrowed by Aristotle from fifth-century rhetorical theory. In a pleading, the litigant told the story of the case—of course in the form most favorable to himself. He might call witnesses to the truth of his narration or cite evidence which supported him. The rhetoricians taught him to take a further step: he could argue that his version of the story was the sort of thing one can expect to happen, while his opponent's version was inherently improbable.[42] Rhetorical instruction thus led to inquiry into the kind of story that men find probable and are generally prepared to believe, and this inquiry laid the ground for the emerging craft of fiction. For Aristotle, the poet of fiction collapses the argument from probability into the narrative itself; instead of telling a story and then defending its truth on the grounds of its probability, he tells us a story which we do not have to believe to be true but which we do believe to be the sort of thing that "is likely to happen in accordance with probability or necessity."

Probability and necessity have to do with the relations between cause and effect and between events and the conditions of events. Whereas the rhetorician takes the conditions and consequences and uses them to reconstruct the event,[43] the poet of fiction begins from the event and constructs around it appropriate conditions and consequences. The rhetorician says: "The accused had motive, means, and opportunity; we conclude that he (probably) committed the crime." The poet starts out to tell the story of a crime and says to himself: "I must provide my criminal with (probable) motive, means, and opportunity." The rhetorician says: "You know that this sort of man does such things; you should believe that this man did them." The poet asks himself: "What sort of man shall I make my criminal? What sort of man is likely to do such things?" The rhetorician says: "You know that criminals generally run away; the accused demonstrates his guilt by the fact that he left the city." The poet says: "After he has committed his crime, what will my criminal do? I suppose he will run away."

The poet, for Aristotle, has made a single *muthos*, a plot, when he has made a chain of events with this sort of internal logic. The perceived relations of cause, condition, and event, as we say, "hold the plot together." Probability and necessity are the sources of unity.

> Tragedy is the imitation of a complete and whole action having some magnitude. . . .
>
> To give a simple definition: it is of such magnitude that when things happen in sequence according to probability or necessity

it turns out that there is a change from good fortune to ill fortune or from ill fortune to good fortune.

(Poetics 1450b24–25 and 1451a11–15)

The change in fortune requires magnitude; it takes a certain scale to accommodate change. But the plot will not be "whole and complete" unless the change is probable or necessary. Aristotle goes on:

> Plot is not, as some suppose, a unity because it is about one person. There are many and unlimited things which happen to a single person; there is, of some of them, no unity. Thus there are many actions of a single person from which no unity of action arises. So all those poets seem to have been wrong who have composed Epics of Heracles and of Theseus and such poems. For they think that, since Heracles was one, there is a single plot about him. But Homer, just as he excels in other respects, also seems to have seen this clearly, whether by art or nature. When he composed his *Odyssey*, he did not include everything that happen to [Odysseus], such as being wounded on Parnassus or pretending to be insane at the gathering of the host—there being no probability or necessity that, when one of these things happened, the other would happen; rather, he constructed his *Odyssey* around a single action of the kind we mention, as also his *Iliad*.

(Poetics 1451a16–29)

Homer found stories about Odysseus in his tradition; he told, however, not those stories, but the story of a plot he had himself invented. Stories can be borrowed, plots cannot; the invention of a plot is the essence of the invention of a (narrative) poem *(Poetics* 1451b27–29). The plot is the story conceived in a certain way, in terms of relations between conditions and events, causes and consequences. One story can give rise to many plots as the story is reconceived. The poet can borrow his stories from anywhere—from other poets, from history, from his own memories and dreams. He can make his stories up. His power as a narrative poet is his power to conceive the story as unified by an internal logic of probability and necessity and to convey this conception to us. That, for Aristotle, is the characteristic wisdom of the narrative poet.[44]

The poet, in making his plot, discovers a form in the story, an internal logic. He then tells us the story in such a way that we also see the inner logic of it. When we "get" the plot—when we recognize its unity—we do so because we recognize the probability or necessity of the sequence. We "believe" the poet, we call a story "true to life," when we are led to say that, yes, such a man would indeed say or do such things under such conditions and with such consequences. On the premises the poet has set before us, his story does indeed follow.

The premises can be absolutely outlandish; the characters can be placed anywhere—in Hell, in outer space, in fairyland. Fiction is a thought-experiment and is hypothetical. We are quite ready to suspend our disbelief, in the sense that we are ready to grant the poet the premises he needs for his plot. Frequently a premise involves the introduction of an impossibility into the familiar world. What if the actual god Dionysus should appear in a rather ordinary Greek town? What if a rather ordinary Athenian citizen succeeded in making a private peace with Sparta? From these hypotheses develop consequences; the poet displays these consequences in such a way that we recognize their causes.

But there is then a paradox about the poet's display of causes. Insofar as he traces the event back to its first cause—to his own premise—he has shown us nothing, for the first cause is by fiat. If Iago is absolutely evil, he is not interesting as a character, for there is nothing to be explained about him. So we do not ask: Why does Iago do such evil acts? He does them by definition. Iago's significance within the story lies rather in the impact of this unconditioned evil on a world recognizably like our own. From the premises, that is, develop intermediate causes; the poet inquires into these intermediate causes and resolves his inquiry when he shows us that the consequences of his premises develop according to probability or necessity.

The first causes are for the sake of the intermediate causes; the poet sets the stage in order to tell us a story. The story develops by an interplay among thought, character, and action. As the characters confront the events, they change, and the changes that occur within them give rise to further events. These changes are like changes we know. The poet creates his world, but he does not create it just as he wishes. The beginnings are invented, but the consequences follow as they really would. In this sense, fiction presents an unreal world which is about the real world. In this sense also, the principle of all fiction, however fanciful, is realism. The poet is an imitator, not of actual events, but of events which have real (that is, recognizable) causes; the story is probable, not because it tells of the kind of events we would expect to see, but because it shows us the kind of action which, once the poet has explained it to us, we would expect to happen under the conditions he has set.[45]

We can thus define fiction as the outcome of a hypothetical inquiry into the intermediate causes of action, an inquiry which has led the poet to the discovery and communication in a story of some universal pattern of human probability and necessity. The characteristic learn-ing, the "this is that," is the recognition of this universal. The poet does not teach us this universal; in order to recognize it, we must already know it. We are all familiar with the shock of recognition narrative art can bring us, the sense of having brought to the surface some intimately held and perhaps unwelcome truth, as when we say: "Yes, given Othello, Iago, and Desdemona, it could not be otherwise." The poet thus shows us something more about something we already knew; he picks out of the pattern of probability certain characteristic features which, in his presentation, enable us to recognize it as a pattern.

PLOT AS KNOWLEDGE

Aristotle's treatment of fiction, with its emphasis on the inner logic of plot, may seem curiously one-dimensional. Obviously there are other sources of form and unity in narrative art. There is, for example, what we might call rhetorical form, the unity imposed by a poet who is careful to command and control his audience's attention, to excite in them just those expectations he intends to fulfill, and to provoke them to ask just those questions he intends to answer.[46] There is what we might call musical form, form produced by the interplay of sym-metry and asymmetry, dissonance and harmony. There is what we might call thematic form, in which incident is connected to incident through the common content of the notions and meditations they pro-voke in us. All these kinds of form can be characteristic of what Aristotle calls the "episodic plot, where the episodes follow one another without probability or necessity" (*Poetics* 1451b34–35). This sort of plot Aristotle says is the "worst," yet Odysseus' narration, *Odyssey* ix–xii, is of this kind, and we do not think of it as an inferior fictional narrative. The incidents of Odysseus' narration are not connected to one another by probability or necessity—there is no inner logic which determines that they should occur in just this order—but the narrative is formed and unified in other ways.[47]

I do not think that plot is central in all fiction. A work of fiction is often as much about its author ("implied" or actual) as its char-acters; it may show us how one man sees the world or be a unified reflection upon the process of fictional creation itself. What would Aristotle have made of *Tristram Shandy?*

I suspect that Aristotle's argument is sharpened and limited by his desire to respond to the arguments of the *Republic*, Book Ten, and that he pins his case to the inner logic of plot because in this way he can argue that fiction is a source of knowledge, knowledge which we absolutely require and which we have no other way of acquiring. In other words, that fiction enables us to recognize patterns of probability and necessity gives fiction an ethical standing. In order to make this point, it will be necessary to turn from the *Poetics* to the *Ethics*, and specifically to Aristotle's account of happiness:

> But perhaps that happiness is best is a formulation which obviously commands agreement; one would be glad, however, to be told more clearly what it is. Perhaps we could get at it this way, by stating the function [*ergon*] of a human being. Just as in the case of a flute-player, sculptor, or any craftsman, or of anything that has a function or action [*praxis*], the good of it and the doing-it-well [*to eu*] are thought to be in its function, so one might have the same thought about a human being—if indeed he *has* any function. Are we to say that of a shoemaker or a carpenter there is a function and action, while of a human being not, but he is by nature functionless [*argon*]? Or just as there is an obvious function of the eye and the hand and the foot and in general of each part, so should one propose some function of the human being also, beyond all these? But then, what in the world can it be? Life is something obviously shared, even by plants, but we are looking for something particular. So one must set aside the capacity for nurture and growth. Next comes the capacity for perception, but this is obviously shared even by a horse or an ox or any animal. There remains some kind of capacity for action which belongs to a creature capable of speech [*or* reason: *logos*].
>
> But this latter can be meant in one of two ways; we must state that we mean the capacity in its actual functioning [*energeia*]— for this seems to put it more adequately. If the function of a human being is an actual functioning of the soul according to reason, or not without reason, then exactly this is man's specific function, and it also is the function of a serious [*or* excellent: *spoudaios*] man, just as the lyre-player and the excellent [*spoudaios*] lyre-player have [the same function], and, in a word, it is generally so; the superlative achievement with relation to the [relevant] virtue [*aretē*] has to do with the function. Of a lyre-player, this is to play the lyre; of an excellent [*spoudaios*] lyre-player, to play it well [*to eu*]. If so, then the human good is an actual functioning of the soul in accordance with virtue.
>
> (*Ethics* 1097b22–98a16)

The most important terms common to the *Ethics* and the *Poetics* are *praxis*, "action," and *ēthos*, "character." In both books, character is for the sake of action—but differently. In fiction, character is explanatory of action; we believe the poet because we believe that such a man would do such things. In ethics, character is praised or dispraised by reference to action; we want our sons to be such men because of the actions such men do. In neither sphere does character have any standing by itself. The poet shows us nothing of importance when he draws a character sketch without reference to an action, for the same reason that there is no merit in possessing a good character which is not enacted. Character is the potentiality which comes to actuality in action.

The poet, when he imitates an action, shows us a picture of the actual functioning of human souls. When the imitation has a unified plot, we see that the action follows by probability or necessity from the premised characters and conditions. The poet thus shows us a reduced and clarified (although not at all definitive) picture of the causes and conditions of human happiness and unhappiness; as we recognize the probability of his plot, we come to know certain features of those causes and conditions. There could be no knowledge more important to a "creature capable of speech."

We should not, however, confuse the kind of knowledge gained from fiction with the kind of knowledge gained from ethics. On the contrary: the two complement each other. Ethics investigates the causes of happiness in us; the subject matter of ethics is the virtues. Ethics, however, is an incomplete science because virtue, though it is a necessary condition of happiness, is not a sufficient condition. Virtue is only a potentiality for happiness:

> It is possible for the developed capacity to be present without producing any good effects at all, for example in sleep or when for some other reason there is loss of actual functioning. . . .
> Just as at the Olympics it is not the finest and strongest who are crowned but rather the competitors (for some of them are victorious), so also in life the actors [*prattontes*] of fine and good deeds achieve it.
>
> (*Ethics* 1098b33–99a7)

Yet ethics, as a science, extends no further than a description of the capacities. Fiction, on the other hand, imitates the actual functioning of the virtues in action:

> Tragedy [and fiction in general] is an imitation, not of human beings, but of action and life—and happiness and unhappiness are in action, and the end [*telos*] is a certain action, not a kind-of-thing [*poiotēs*]. They are certain kinds of persons according to their characters, but they are happy or the reverse according to their actions.
>
> (*Poetics* 1450a16–20)

Ethics discusses kinds-of-thing: the general kinds of activities rightly called happiness, the general kinds of capacities required for such activities, the general kinds of process, deliberative and otherwise, which will enable men with such capacities to choose well and thus function well in actual situations. All these kinds-of-thing appear in fiction under the headings of action, character, and thought; but they appear in fiction as specific instances, not general types, not as possibilities or potentialities, but as actualities.

Because happiness does not consist in the possession of the virtues but in their exercise, virtue is not the sole cause of happiness. Circumstances must also be propitious:

> Obviously there is also some need of exterior goods, as was said. For it is impossible, or not easy, to do what is fine without resources. Many things are done, as with instruments, so with friends and wealth and political power. When people are lacking in certain things, they decry their own prosperity—lacking such [other] things as good birth, fine children, good looks. For a man cannot be completely happy if he is extremely ugly to look at or ill-born or lonely and childless; he is even less so if his children are worthless, or his friends, or if they are good and die. So just as we were saying, there is apparently some need also of such comforts.
>
> (*Ethics* 1099a31–99b7)

Our lives are not entirely our own; life is shaped by the interplay between ourselves and our circumstances. Happiness is always at risk. This risk and interplay are the study of the poet, who is thus a student of the relation between the virtues of man and the conditions of their exercise. Compare Aristotle's use of a poetic example:

> Many are the changes and various the chances of life, and it is possible for the most straight-coursed man to fall into the wreckage of great mischance in old age, as is told in the Trojan story about Priam. But a man so used by ill luck and dying miserably is called happy by no one.
>
> (*Ethics* 1100a5–9)

Ethics and fiction have a common subject matter—*praxis*; but they approach it from opposite directions. Ethics, which is a science, "replaces . . . an effect by its cause," while fiction, which is an art, produces an image "homologous with the object."[48] Ethics is about the conditions of happiness; it treats happiness only potentially. Fiction is about unreal happiness and unhappiness, but it treats these in their actuality. We should not conclude that fiction is unconcerned with the causes of happiness. Ethics works from actor to action and prescribes; it says that such a man will live in such a way and that that is good. Fiction works from action to actor and describes; it shows us that such an action could have been done by such a man, that it is probable. Fiction shows us particular instances of happiness and unhappiness in such a way that we can see the causal relations between the actor, his situation, and the event.

Ethics is about *praxis*, but ethics never achieves an understanding of *praxis*; or, to put the point another way, because happiness is in the fortunate interplay between virtue and circumstance, happiness is finally unintelligible. The success or failure of an action is known only by its results, and since every result leads to a further result, the final result is never before us. Hence the dilemma: Shall we call no man happy until he is dead? But if happiness is an actual functioning and the dead are not actual at all, how can they be happy? Besides, it is possible for a man to live happily and yet become unhappy after death through "dishonors and the misfortunes of his children and descendants in general" *(Ethics* 1100a20–21). The actor commits himself to the future and thus never knows his own act; since the future is without limit, there is no moment when the returns are in.

Similarly action, since it is with others, is never self-contained. Having said that happiness is a certain kind of self-sufficiency, Aristotle goes on:

> The self-sufficiency we mean does not belong to man by himself, to a man living his life in solitude, but with parents and children and a wife and in general friends and fellow citizens. . . . But of these things one must set a certain limit. As one reaches out to one's parents and their ancestors and to one's friends' friends, it goes off into infinity.
>
> *(Ethics* 1097b8–13)

No man is an island, but to treat his fate as inextricably entangled with the present condition and future adventures of the entire continent is to rob him of personal identity altogether. Some limit must be set, even though the limit be to a degree arbitrary. Action, to be intelligible, must be perceived to occur within a definite social field and to have definite consequences. Such limitation of our perception in life is analogous to the discovery of narrative form in fiction. By the imposition of limits we discern, in both cases, the pattern of a *praxis*.

Praxis I have here translated (as is customary) "action." The word might equally be translated "accomplishment" or "event." *Praxis* means, among other things, a transaction in commerce or an action at law. The word has implications of completeness, of activity rounded to a definite outcome.[49]

Litigation and commerce, like games, impose limits on our interactions; within these limits we know how we are obligated and to whom, and we can measure acts against their consequences. The situation so delimited defines which actors are more or less successful than others. Such limits give our choices meaning. Where the limits are not set by rules, however, we must discover them for ourselves. We thus impose a form upon our understanding of human things. We do not hold that men are responsible for or involved with the fortunes of all those with whom they might have come in contact. We speak of happiness as bounded by birth and death, or even in smaller units; we say that such a one had a successful college career, a good war, a rewarding working life. Thus we construct around the central actor or actors an intelligible pattern of events, with a beginning, middle, and end, and a listable cast of characters. We make a life, or some part of a life, into a story. Only in this way can we form any judgment of it. Similarly we must think of ourselves as actors in a story. We must perceive our relations as finite and our acts as testable against some definitive outcome; otherwise our ethical situation "goes off into infinity" and the will is puzzled.[50]

Storytelling thus rises directly from the need for ethical intelligibility, as we saw in our examination of Homeric *kleos*. A life conceived as a *kleos* becomes a kind of work of art. The hero by his acts is constructing the matter of a patterned story "for men-to-come to inquire about." For those others the hero's life has meaning insofar as it has become a story.

Yet the hero's actions cannot in themselves be a story; a story requires storytellers. Facts do not bear their meaning on their faces; they acquire meaning when they are well told. In the telling, an action becomes a plot. But this gives rise to the problematic of narrative, for the well-told story becomes an object of interest in itself. In the terms we are using here, it has crossed the line from history to fiction.

Narrative history rises from a reflection on the experience we already have—a reflection not analytic but synthetic. In telling our own story we gain control of our experience; we give it form and share its meaning with our audience. Thus Odysseus and Penelope tell each other the whole story of their twenty-year separation (xxiii.300–343); this is a necessary completing step in the reconstruction of their marriage. Storytelling is a way of knowing and sharing knowledge of the matter of life.

When the story is told for its own sake, however, as fiction, there must be a further forming of experience. History forms events into a plot; fiction starts with an idea for a plot and generates events. The form of the action, which was in history the conclusion of the thought process, is in fiction the beginning. History is a response to experience; fiction is a response to some idea of experience. That is what Aristotle means when he says that poetry is "more philosophical" than history. He does not mean that the poet is a philosopher. Narrative remains on the level of the particular: it tells of these men in this place. In this sense, fiction, like all imitative art, remains "mid-way between schema and anecdote."[51] The poet is more philosophical only in that he founds his claim to our attention, not on the literal matter of his story, but on the human universal there revealed. The sequence is clearest in the case of historical fiction, when the poet, captivated by the story of Alcibiades, retells that story as the Tragedy of Alcibiades. He will then tell us what "a certain kind of person turns out to do or say . . . in accordance with probability or necessity." The facts about Alcibiades are then no longer important (although the poet may choose to adhere to them either as a special discipline on his art or to help enlist our belief in his narrative); frequently the poet will be ruthless with the facts. He has in effect constructed a new Alcibiades, who is what he is in relation to the poet's plot. For Aristotle, and for us, the *Iliad* is historic fiction of exactly this kind.

In this way Aristotle resolves the problematic of narrative, between truth and falsehood: it can be false in its particulars, he says, yet true to life universally. By taking this step Aristotle also—almost incidentally—resolves the problem of epic distance. The heroic world for him consists of a set of premises on which fictions can be founded; these premises, being the collective possession of the literary tradition, have the special merit of being familiar Troy fell, the heroes spoke with the gods, Achilles was brave—all these things are known to the audience. The poet, when he creates a plot, shows us an action which follows—given these premises—in accordance with probability or necessity. Thus the *Iliad* appears to be about things very far away and long ago, but what we learn from it is a universal which applies also to ourselves.

Aristotle is able to call the poet both philosophical and instructive without making him into either a philosopher or a teacher. The poet does not teach because he does not, primarily, concern himself with his effect on his audience. As a maker of plot, he must seek out the intermediate causes within the world and for a while consider his characters more real than his audience. No wonder he appears to his audience inspired or possessed.

The poet, further, does not ask general questions; he does not ask: What is justice? loyalty? forgiveness? He asks instead: How was it that Achilles refused the gifts? What would he say in refusing them? He answers these questions concretely; he is not making an essay but a story. Once he has conceived situation and character so clearly that he can speak for Achilles, he is done. He has said what he had to say in telling his story. No wonder any passerby can say more about his poem than he can.

THE EFFECT ON THE AUDIENCE

Aristotle's focus on the inner logic of plot sets a program for criticism. We—the passersby—can ask: How is it that this story is probable and necessary? What universal patterns can be discerned in it? How does the action follow from the premises? To a large extent these questions have set the program for the present essay on the *Iliad*. It is only fair to say, however, that this is not Aristotle's own program. In the *Poetics* he does not explore the meaning of texts; he examines only the general kinds of things which in a dramatic text engross and move us. The emphasis remains (and in this Aristotle shows himself the heir of the sophistic) on the *pathē*, the emotions produced in us by fiction—and especially the tragic emotions, pity and fear. Of these I shall have more to say in the next chapter.

Yet it remains true that for Aristotle a dramatic text moves and engrosses us when we recognize in it some comprehensible pattern of causes—and that it moves us most when this pattern comes to us unexpectedly and thus extends our understanding. Aristotle says:

> The imitation is not only of a complete action but of things pitiable and fearful; such things most happen when they happen contrary to expectations because of one another [*di' allēla*].
>
> (*Poetics* 1452a1–4)

Casual events, however horrific, do not move us to pity and fear; those emotions are excited by a narrative with meaning.[52] The best kind of meaning is that of the inner logic of the events, the *di' allēla*. When these events are "contrary to expectation," when they reveal to us a pattern of causal relations which we had not seen before, then we are most shaken and enthralled. So the characteristic *pathē* of the plot cannot be separated from its characteristic learning; *pathē* and learning together constitute the characteristic value to us of a well-made narrative.

I suspect that Aristotle meant by *katharsis* exactly this combination of emotion and learning. Aristotle himself has nothing to say about

katharsis in the *Poetics*; the word occurs once only, in the definition
of tragedy. On this one word an enormous body of commentaries has
arisen.[53] Since Aristotle gives us no other guide (with the exception
of an obscurely related passage in the *Politics*), we can interpret *katharsis* only by interpreting the *Poetics*.[54] Here I notice only that the
objects of imitation mentioned in *Poetics* 4, "the most despised animals
and corpses," are the typically impure or unclean things; Aristotle
there says that we take pleasure in imitations of them because from
the imitation we learn something. So perhaps learning itself purifies.

Tragedy, says Aristotle's definition, purifies pity and fear through
pity and fear. This appears to be a paradox until we remember that
the play is something we both experience and know. The *pragmata*,
the events of the story, work on us in certain ways. But as we come to
perceive the unity of the plot, its inner logic, we reconceive our own
emotions as the necessary conditions of our comprehension of a formally coherent order. We set our own emotions at a certain distance
from ourselves; like the story itself, they stand between reality and
unreality and are purified as we come to conceive them within the
formal order which the work provides.

This interpretation of *katharsis* cannot be convincingly defended
from Aristotle's text. It will be defended in this book only by its
application. In chapter 5 I shall explore, in connection with the *Iliad*,
the notion that, in art, purification takes place through the comprehension of a unified structure and is equivalent to the discovery that
the work is in fact perfectly founded on its own premises.

2

TRAGEDY

Socrates in the *Republic* had already given a general statement of the content of fiction:

> "We say that imitation imitates men in action; their actions
> are either constrained or free; as a consequence of their actions
> they think they have acted [*or* fared: *pepragenai*] well or badly,
> and in all this they feel pain or pleasure. Is there anything be-
> yond this?"
> "Nothing."
>
> *(Republic* 603c)

Men in action, in other words, freely determine their own fate, yet they make these determinations under constraints. In action they pursue happiness; sometimes they succeed, sometimes they fail. Their success or failure appears to them in two ways: objectively, as a matter about which they have an opinion, and subjectively, as experienced gratification or suffering. The imitation of an action, insofar as it sets before us a recognizable universal, must then enable us to perceive relations between these things: between freedom and the constraints on freedom, between acts and their consequences, between opinion and the *pathē*. That is the general content of fiction.

Aristotle refines this analysis by adding to it an account of the causes of action:

> Since the imitation is of an action, it must be acted by certain
> actors, who must be of some certain kinds according to their
> character or thought (since it is through these latter, we say, that
> actions get to be of a certain kind, and there are by nature two
> causes of action, character and thought, and according to these
> all men succeed or fail)—while the imitation of the action is the
> plot. I mean by this word "plot" the sequence of the actings
> (*pragmatōn*); while character is that according to which we say
> the actors are of a certain kind, and thought is in their explain-
> ing something in speech or making plain their opinion.
>
> *(Poetics* 1449b36–50a7)

By locating the source of action in the character and thought of the actors, Aristotle reminds us that the sphere of action per se is the sphere of freedom. While action is limited by constraints, a "con-

69

strained action"—a *biaios praxis*, as Socrates calls it—is a contradiction in terms. What a man is forced to do he does not do; he endures it.

The actor's free choices are conditioned by his virtues and resources. His act will be characteristic of himself, and it cannot (except by happy accident) be better than his understanding of the situation. In showing us character and thought, the poet is showing us the probability or necessity of the action as done by that actor so situated. He is showing us a relation between action and the conditions of action in the actor.[1]

These conditions are not constraints on the actor. His character and thought are his own responsibility; both can be changed by his own act. Often a story is about such change—about learning or reformation or discovery.

Those things which can be made otherwise by choice, effort, and the application of knowledge constitute the sphere of culture. These things are the specifically human things. In imitating an action and showing us the sources of action in the actor, the poet is imitating the actuality of culture.

Culture is also the subject matter of fiction in another sense. Acts are done in a manner judged proper and for ends judged desirable. Action is thus in accordance with values and norms, and values and norms are prescribed by culture.

For us, as students of culture, values and norms are culturally and historically conditioned. Thus we *explain* a man's actions in terms of the values and norms of his culture. For the actor it cannot be so.[2] His values do not explain his actions to himself; they *justify* his actions. One end or procedure can be justified in terms of another, but action must finally be grounded in unconditioned values and norms.[3]

Values and norms are thus not constraints on action but (teleologically) the sources of action. Values appear as constraints only to the unsympathetic observer. When a man acts according to a code with which we have no sympathy, his action will always appear to be a form of madness, however well we understand the rules of the code, however well we can see that his acts correspond to the code. The sense of honor of the Samurai, the suspicious care of the Dobu magician, are states of mind we find it difficult to share. Insofar as we cannot share the state of mind, we can only *explain* the action arising from it, not see it as *justified*. Thus we lose the meaning which the act has to the actor; we see it not as free but as determined.

In imitating the actuality of culture, the poet of fiction looks at action from the point of view of the actor. He shows us men pursuing happiness as they understand it and succeeding or failing in their own terms. A condition of the poet's communication with us is our sympathetic understanding of the values and norms presumed by the work. The more distant the poet's culture from our own, the more difficult this is likely to be.

Values and norms, however, while culturally conditioned, are not arbitrary. They are not privately invented but arise out of and for the sake of the functioning of whole communities—communities which continue over time. Communities function under natural constraints and can continue to function only so long as they respect the ground of nature. Thus the values and norms of any enduring culture can gain our respect and even our sympathy as one of the ways in which men have found it possible to live in this world.

Once we have entered into the values and norms presumed by the work of fiction, we shall be able to see it as a dramatization of the relations between the *actuality* of culture—the actions by which men enact and create their own situations—and the *ground* of culture—the ideas and ideals (always only partially explicit, differently understood by different actors within the culture) in accordance with which and for the sake of which they enact and create as they do.

Action, we said, takes place within constraints. These constraints constitute the sphere of nature; they are things which cannot be made otherwise. The sphere of nature is a sphere of force, of things which may be exploited, enjoyed, or endured but which cannot be altered, which are both the precondition of culture and the problem of culture. Nature is the matter to which culture is the form, but we encounter nature *qua* nature at the (frequent) moments when the matter is not pliable to the forming hand of culture.

Nature surrounds man with an enduring order, a cosmos. Man himself also has a nature; he must respect his own capacities and his fixed limits. He has organic needs, passes his infancy in a state of dependency, comes in two sexes, and is mortal. Culture must respect these facts. Furthermore, man lives in history, which, as an irremediable constraint on his action, also (paradoxically) forms part of the sphere of nature. The ancient proverb says that one thing is beyond the power even of the gods: to make undone what has been done.

The frontier between nature and culture is flexible; what is uncontrollable for one culture is by another seen as an area of human responsibility. Our own age has seen an enormous expansion of the sphere of culture. Culture states its own limits, and in this sense nature is a cultural product.

Furthermore, cultural patterns themselves acquire the standing of nature insofar as they are unquestionable and fixed. Habit is a kind of second nature; social structure is perceived as natural so long as there is no thought of changing it. If it is true that "The poor we have always with us," then the poor are as natural as any other species.

Thus each culture has its own nature—its own way of having nature —and the relations between culture and nature will be particular to particular cultures.

Fiction, which is founded on premises, states the constraints which shape the action it imitates. Fiction thus invents a hypothetical nature. The scene of fiction is governed by rules which may or may not be the same as those of the ordinary world. In fiction men can exist without food; they can be born mature; they can pass freely from sex to sex or be without sex; they can live forever. Furthermore, the poet of fiction invents facts previous to the action he imitates; he thus founds his action on an irremediable previous history which constrains it.[4]

Fiction, however, is not about those constraints but about the action founded on them. It follows that fiction, while not bound by the laws of nature, is bound by the laws of culture; otherwise it is unintelligible. Thus in fiction a princess can promise her friendship to a frog in exchange for the return of a ring; the frog can return the ring and claim the promise. All that is possible. But the story will not be a story about a promise unless the princess is free either to keep her promise or break it. If it is a story about a promise, then it is impossible that the princess should have no obligation to keep her word or that the frog should not be disappointed when she breaks it. And if the princess breaks her promise, we must be entitled to conclude that she is less than perfectly virtuous; whatever else she says and does must somehow be in keeping with this conclusion. Whatever the premises, the inner logic of the action must follow some rules we understand; the alternative is not a new meaning for action but no meaning at all. It is in this sense, then, that all fiction is naturalistic. If, for example, magic powers are granted a character in a story—a ring of invisibility, for instance—the interesting question is always: Given that he is some sort of man we know, what is he going to do with it?[5]

The interpretation of a work of fiction thus has, in schema, two aspects. We must first identify the premises of the work, the hypothetical constraints on action. Then we can reconstruct the action and show its probability and necessity.

PREMISES AND PROBLEMS

Some premises of the work give little difficulty; these are premises stated in the work itself. The poet states previous events and sets a scene: "John and George, two telepaths, have quarreled over a woman." We call this statement of premises the "exposition."

More difficult are premises derived from the culture. A work of fiction presumes (unless it explicitly or implicitly notifies us otherwise) the laws of nature—not nature itself, however, but nature as it appears to the poet's culture. For his own audience this poses no difficulty; but if we come from far off, we shall have to do some reconstruction.

Most difficult are premises derived from the tradition of the art. For the *Iliad* we have given such premises the collective name "the heroic world." The tradition of the art is itself a cultural product; but as it comes to be generally understood within the culture, its rules become a kind of second nature, and each story founded on the tradition serves to reinforce the quasi reality of its rules.

(Parenthetically we may add that the story told by the poet—the story he converts into a plot by his perception of its probability and necessity—may be a traditional story, known already, in its broad outlines, to the audience. Their knowledge of the outcome of the story will shape their perception of the intermediate incidents. I shall return to this point in chapter 4, in the discussion of fatality.)

Aristotle's name for these difficulties is *problēmata*, and he devotes chapter 25 of the *Poetics* to them. For Aristotle a *problēma*, at least one that can be solved, is an apparent flaw in the poem which is really a flaw in our understanding of it. Sometimes (says Aristotle) our failure will be ignorance of the poet's language. More interesting to us in the present context are the *problēmata* which arise from the poet's work as an imitator:

> Since the poet is an imitator . . . he must always imitate some one of three things: either the sort of thing that was or is, or the sort of thing men say or think, or the sort of thing that ought to be. . . .
>
> Say he has imitated impossibilities. . . . This is a fault, but it is all right, if thereby he reaches his aim . . . that is, if in this way either this part or some other part is made more striking. An example is the pursuit of Hector. . . .
>
> Or else, [he has imitated] what men say, as in the case of the stories about the gods. Perhaps these are neither good nor true, and Xenophanes is right—but still, men did tell them.
>
> Or perhaps it is not good thus, but it was that way, as in the case of the line about the arms: "Their spears stood upright on their points"—for that was, at the time, the custom, as it is now among the Illyrians.
>
> (*Poetics* 1460b7–61a4)

In this section Aristotle lays out the task of the critic in a framework of comparative studies. Any poem which comes from a culture distant from our own—and the *Iliad* was already such a poem for Aristotle—will contain much that appears absurd. But most of these absurdities will disappear in the course of reconstruction. We must first consider the poet's use of his own poetic means. Acted on a stage, the pursuit of Hector would appear ridiculous, but the absurdity is not noticed in epic narration, and the scene excites a sense of wonder appropriate to the epic (*Poetics* 1460a14–17). Then we must ask what sort of stories were proper to the tradition of the art. We may not believe in the Homeric gods, but we should not therefore exclude them from the epic. Finally, we should allow for the differences between the poet's cultural experience and ours; we would not set up spears on their points, but we know people who do. This sort of behavior is within the known range of cultural variation, and we are entitled to assume that Homer's picture is based on observation.

Homer's epic (to run through the points in reverse order) implies an ordinary world which is not our ordinary world. Homer's audience understood the meaning of the terms *temenos* and *klēros* and understood the pattern of landholding those terms imply. They knew what a herald was, what his privileges were, and what he was supposed to do. For us those things remain to be reconstructed.

Then there is the category of "the sort of thing men say or think," that is, of points which are obscure to us because we do not think as Homer's audience thought. One is tempted to place in this category (for example) the *problēma* raised by the phrase "gets intelligence in his chest" (XIII.732), for this phrase is obscure to us until we understand that for Homer's audience the seat of all subjective life, including thought, was not the head but the thoracic cavity. From another point of view, however, it would be more correct to return this *problēma* to the first category; for to the degree that the Homeric audience simply believed that thought was in the chest, this location of thought was an aspect of their actual world. We might do better to say: "The Homeric Greeks did their thinking with their thoracic cavities," just as we might say: "The Homeric Greeks purified objects with sulfur, because sulfur is the stuff of which thunderbolts are made." It is not accurate to say that "they *believed* that objects could be purified in this way," for purity is a matter of belief, and if a people believes the object pure, it is pure. And a thunderbolt is really a matter of belief also—a special way of conceiving the lightning, and those who have thunderbolts are presumably entitled to tell us what they are made of. A culture, in other words, includes both a set of social institutions and a picture of nature, and both will have to be reconstructed if we are to understand the culture's poetry.

All this is the strictly historical aspect of the reconstruction of Homer's premises. One such reconstruction is presented, in some detail, in M. I. Finley's book *The World of Odysseus*.

Finley's book is a great achievement and is one of the foundations of the present essay. I would point out one difficulty in it, however: having completed his reconstruction, Finley cannot quite locate it historically. Shall we follow Schliemann and believe that, since evidently there once was a siege at Troy, the *Iliad* describes what took place there? But the *Iliad* must have been composed centuries after the fall of Troy, and many descriptions in the poem have the ring of the poet's own experience. Shall be suppose that the poem describes the poet's own world? But it is evident that the poet archaizes. Shall we then place the Homeric world not in Homer's time, not as far back as Mycenaean times, but in, say, the tenth and ninth centuries before Christ? That is Finley's own solution.[6] But many details belong earlier or later than that. Shall we then say that the world of the poem is an amalgam of many periods?[7] But we do not believe that there was ever a time when rivers rose from their beds and spoke or when the winds ate dinner in a great hall, and we find it nearly as hard to believe that there was ever a race of men by the Mediterranean who ate no fish or that chariots were ever used in war as the heroes used them. Eventually we are forced back on "the kind of thing men say or think"; we speak of the unfamiliar features of the Homeric world as a mixture of elements drawn from Homer's own culture, of historical memories, and of poetic conventions.[8]

Poetic conventions pose a special problem; they are between reality and unreality in just the same way as the particular fictional narrative founded on them. The acceptance of a convention involves a systematic suspension of disbelief; we accept the convention as a necessary condition of being told this sort of story. Yet the convention is valueless unless it has some relation to truth, that is, makes it possible to tell a certain kind of story in which we recognize a certain truth. The convention is for the sake of the story, and the story has a universal meaning.

THE PROBLEM OF THE GODS

Aristotle's example of "the sort of thing men say and think" is "the stories about the gods." Insofar as the gods of the *Iliad* are the same as the gods accepted by Homer's audience—insofar as the Zeus and Apollo of the story are representations of the Zeus and Apollo from whom the Greeks of Homer's day received omens and oracles, to whom they prayed and made sacrifice—to this degree the peculiarities of the Homeric gods fall in the same category as thought-within-the-chest and purifying sulfur. The Homeric gods are then features of an actual culture and are to be interpreted as such. If, however, we assume (as seems reasonable) that Hesiod's *Works and Days* represents actual religious belief at the time of Homer—or something very like it—then we must admit that the gods of the *Iliad* are very different creatures.

Hesiod's gods stand behind the forces of nature; they send the weather, disease, and the fertility of the land. They are guarantors of moral norms; they punish the guilty, although not as adequately as one might wish. They are accessible to prayer and sacrifice, although here, again, their responses are not entirely reliable. They are sacred beings, solemnly invoked.

The gods of the *Iliad*, on the other hand, are generally frivolous, unsteady creatures, whose friendship or enmity has little to do with human justice. They do not appear in the narrative as guarantors of human norms or as the sources of natural process. These Iliadic gods may use the means of nature—thunderbolt and earthquake—but they do not guarantee a cosmos; their interventions are erratic and personal. Most important, the gods of the *Iliad* are lacking in *numen*; they are in fact the chief source of comedy in the poem. We can, I think, explain this difference most easily by assuming that the gods of the *Iliad* belong to the conventional world of epic and were understood as such by the audience. Just as the epic tells, not of men, but of heroes, so also it tells stories, not of gods conceived as actual, but of literary gods.

The relation between the two sets of gods is made subtle and difficult by the fact that the members of the two sets have the same names. The line is not firmly drawn between them. The one genuinely numinous entrance of a god into the action is the very first (I.45–53); here it seems that, in drawing a picture of a plague brought down by impiety, the poet has evoked the Apollo of ordinary belief. In chapter 5 I shall assert that the similes, also, reflect ordinary religious belief; the result is a certain discontinuity with the poem. The Zeus of the simile, who sends a flood on the fields out of his anger with men "who by force determine crooked justice in the assembly" (XVI.387), is hard to reconcile with the Zeus we know so well from Homer's scenes on Olympus. Similarly, the characters in the poem sometimes speak of the gods rather as members of Homer's audience would have spoken of them. But when we say "the Homeric gods," we mostly mean the gods whose doings, loves, hates, and quarrels are known to the poet and are told by him as part of his story; and these gods, I would assert, belong to the conventional world of the epic.

The divine interventions, therefore, set us *problēmata* having to do with the correct interpretation of literary convention. Take, for example, the moment in Book One of the *Iliad* when Achilles decides to kill Agamemnon. Athena comes down from Olympus, invisible to all but Achilles, takes him by the hair from behind, and dissuades him. We could take Athena's intervention merely as a manner of speaking, as the way in which the poet expressed the idea that Achilles had changed his mind. In other words, the audience sees the scene as a representation of a familiar kind of event—a man, about to do one thing, pauses and then does another—but dressed up with a bit of epic apparatus.[9] But the gods of the *Iliad* cannot be reduced to bits of apparatus; they are definite characters with a story of their own, both among themselves and in their interactions with men. Athena comes because she has been sent by Hera, whose idea the assembly was in the first place. Hera suggested the assembly because she wanted to help the Greeks; the occasion turned out to be a disaster; she is now trying to minimize the damage. However erratic the gods may appear to the heroes, they are known to the audience to be intelligent, self-willed creatures, more or less consistent in their purposes, who intervene in the action when and as they do for discernible reasons. These gods are no epiphenomena; they are a part of the phenomenal world, which they help to shape and by which they are affected.

Here also we may imagine that the epic convention has been infiltrated by ordinary belief. When the poet says of Lycaon, "god cast him into Achilles' hands" (XXI.47), he is not thinking of any particular god. The word is simply used, like the neuters *to theion* or *to daimonion* of later Greek, as a residual cause for an event which seems both significant and accidental.[10] But most of the time the gods of the epic are personalities, not impersonal potencies; they are characters with their own thoughts and their own place in the action.

I suggest a different interpretation, according to which the arrival of Athena is a completely literal event *within the poem*—an event as literal as, for instance, a visit by Menelaus to Agamemnon. Such literalism, I suggest, is acceptable to the audience because they understand that they are being shown, not the Athena of cult, but the Athena of epic. Such divine visitations are the sort of thing that happens to heroes, and in poetry.

It would follow that the relation between the epic world and the ordinary world is not a relation to be stated part by part but as whole to whole. The two worlds correspond, not in detail, but through the universal revealed by the poet. The audience watches the scene and discerns in it a human situation which has been given concrete form by the poet in a way consistent with the premises by which he works.

It would further follow that the scene between Achilles and Athena may well be taken by the audience as having little to do with the relation between man and god as they would normally understand that relation. Rather, the scene shows them (to make an artificial abstraction from the particularity of the scene) something like this. A man becomes angry with the authority to whom he is subject and proposes to himself an act of absolute rebellion. By such an act he would resolve the situation: either he would perish himself or he would put an end to the authority he can no longer tolerate. But this same man then receives instructions from a higher authority, an authority he is absolutely obligated to obey. However, the higher authority which prevents his act is, at the same time, powerless to resolve his situation. The man therefore, baffled, withdraws from action and (so far as he can) withdraws from the situation. From this withdrawal further consequences follow. The essential scene, thus, is the man between two authorities; one of the authorities is divine, but "divine" is merely a specific version of "higher."

From this point of view the Homeric gods are justified by the view of man they make possible. Homeric man is placed between animal and gods; yet, as we shall see, he is in some crucial respects a higher being than either. This ordering of the cosmos places man in a position of great dignity and yet greater vulnerability; this is perhaps the cosmic order particularly appropriate to tragedy. It is then no accident that tragic poets, most particularly Shakespeare, have over and again revived or reinvented something like the Homeric gods as the theological premise of tragedy.

The Poet as Student of His Culture

The heroic world, we have said, is a less-real world which exists for the sake of song. In this sense it is unhistoric. Yet song is for an audience and in this sense is located in history. In reconstructing the heroic world, we implicitly reconstruct the audience which understood it, the audience for whom the *Iliad* was not (in this particular Aristotelian sense) problematic. In this broad sense any careful study of Homer is a contribution to the study of Homer's period. We may not be able to tell from the poems whether the men of Homer's day could read and write or whether they respected hereditary kings. But we can tell that they knew what a hero was and what was expected of him and that they were engrossed by stories on themes of loyalty and valor, rage and mourning. In this sense, and really only in this sense, the

Iliad is a direct source for its own period; and the best literary criticism, the criticism which best reconstructs the premises and meaning of the piece, is also the best history.

The poet may or may not imitate the details of his culture. But if his work, as a whole, is to be intelligible to his audience, he must have a profound understanding of his culture. Therefore, if we assume that the work is intelligible, we can deduce the culture from the work.

Earlier I said that fiction is the outcome of a kind of inquiry. This inquiry is conducted by the poet when, in the course of inventing a plot, he asks himself: How would this happen? Who would do this? What would he have in mind? Of course this inquiry is conducted on the level of the concrete. When the poet asks himself: What sort of mother would Coriolanus have? his response is not some general formulation, but Volumnia.

Inquiry, however, implies a question. We are interested in Coriolanus' mother because Coriolanus is extraordinary. Poetry is not about the typical but about the wonderful, because the wonderful gives rise to questions about probability and necessity.

Some actions bear their meaning on their faces, as when a man touches fire and flinches. This is not a story. There is also no story when the event occurs "of itself and by chance." The poet justifies his inquiry when he makes an interesting story, when he shows us the inner logic of events which at first appeared inexplicable. The events of such a story occur "contrary to expectation because of one another."

Because action is the actuality of culture, the conditions of action are the form of culture. As he invents a plot, as he relates action to its conditions, the poet inquires into character and thought. These are culturally determined. Men are as they have learned to be, and they think as they have learned to think. A wonderful (that is, puzzling) action is, as it were, the figure; culture is the ground. In showing us the probability and necessity of the action, the poet reduces the figure to the ground. Coriolanus is a kind of monster, but he is a characteristically Roman monster. The city created him and must live with him. So in watching Coriolanus' career, we come to understand something about the perils of a heroic ethic—perils to the hero himself and to the city which attempts to employ the hero as an instrument.[11]

Because he proceeds on the level of the concrete and imitates an (imagined) actuality, the poet is interested in the consequences of acts —not only for further acts but also for experience. *Pathos* is an essential part of fiction; the poet asks not only: How does this happen? but also: How does it feel? Through his imitation of *pathos* the poet enables us to experience the action, as it were, from the inside. We not only see the causes of events; we also experience the felt meaning of the event to the actors.

The source of *pathos* is not in the sufferer; *pathos* is inflicted on the sufferer by others, by chance, or even by his own act, in which case he will appear alien to himself. A central question in tragic drama is the question: How could I have done this to myself? *Pathos* is felt as such when it appears to some degree ungrounded and therefore not appropriate or fit. Therefore *pathos* always poses a question to the sufferer and (in an imitative work) to us. This question itself may be the source of the poet's inquiry and thus of his plot; perhaps the source of the *Iliad* was its ending and the question: Why should Priam suffer so? What does this suffering mean?

Of *pathos* also there is a probability and necessity; we can ask: What sort of man would feel this way? What would he come to think and say when confronted by his own suffering? The full plot constitutes a coherent order of *pathos* and *praxis* brought to unity by the poet's conception of the inner logic of the whole.

The poet's premises, then, are hypothetical, but the inner logic of the action—the intermediate causes which follow from the premises—is created by the poet in accordance with the rules of culture. Thus we can state the use of fiction to culture. The poet puts the rules of culture to use under intelligible constraints and asks how they would then function. He imaginatively tests the limits of his culture's capacity to function.

In fiction all the resources of culture are tested. We can have a story on a purely technical theme, a story of the cure of a disease or an escape from a prison. But the serious themes of fiction are themes of ethical values and norms. When values and norms are tested, the story is in a special sense dramatic.

It is a cliché that drama requires conflict. Mere conflict, however, does not generate drama; mere conflict belongs to the realm of nature and can be appropriately settled by force. Drama arises within the sphere of culture and out of the ambiguities of cultural values and norms.

Actors have a saying: "No villain is a villain to himself." The actor who is playing, say, Tartuffe should realize that, from Tartuffe's own point of view, all his actions are proper and justified—or at least quite forgivable. This is what makes Tartuffe an interesting character: we can see the action from his point of view. Otherwise (as I said earlier of one reading of Iago) the villain is a mere premise of the plot, a kind of force of nature with which the other actors must cope.

The pretended piety of Tartuffe, the sexual charisma of Anatol Kuragin, are, taken in themselves, admirable to us, since charisma and pretense are necessary to the functioning of culture. Furthermore, these villains are admirable to themselves; they are aware of their partial virtues and contemptuous of the virtues which they lack. This self-approval is a source in them of self-confidence and courage and licenses them in their own eyes to exercise their intelligence in a self-willed manner. Courage and intelligence are also virtues; these partial virtues make the villains dangerous and bring them into conflict with the partial virtues of others. The poet traces the interplay of these partial virtues as they develop into an action. The poet's own sympathies are clear; he is on the side of Orgon's family and on the side of Natasha. Yet it is also clear that these victims bring their disasters on themselves—in a sense; it is their weakness which makes them vulnerable to exactly those partial and distorted virtues in which the villains excel.

The ethical themes of these stories are thus not in their outcomes; that Tartuffe is punished while Anatol Kuragin is not is a relatively superficial fact. The ethical interest of the story lies in the power which the villain exercises in the first place. Through him we see that the culture cultivates kinds of excellence—social powers—which are destructive. These villains are characteristic products of their societies; that the society cannot control them to its own satisfaction marks a lack of ethical coherence in the society. A society can be injured through the distorted application of its own values and norms. An imitation of such an action calls upon us to reconsider the proper measure and balance in the application of our own values and norms.

The poet is thus a student of his culture, but in a specific sense: he is a student of the culture's characteristic abnormalities. The poet encounters his culture in two forms: in his subject matter and in his audience. The poet must know the norm, the presuppositions of his audience; initially he knows this norm only in order to vary from it, to present to his audience a story which is problematic, with a character who is a deviant. In his presentation of the story, however, the poet rediscovers the norm as the solution to the problem which he himself has created. He shows us that the deviant of his story is also characteristic of the audience's culture. In revealing that the causes of the action are according to probability or necessity, the poet reveals that the norm is also present in this abnormal version of it. He shows the audience something new about what they already knew and so interprets the culture to itself.

81

The poet of fiction thus stands in contrast to the ethnologist. The ethnologist describes an alien culture; he must state the norm of that culture to an audience which does not know it. He attempts a description of the culture as a whole, of its most pervasive patterns, and aims to reveal a functioning system. The poet of fiction, by contrast, speaks to his own culture, to an audience which knows the norm but has not considered its implications. The poet investigates the norm in situations and in relation to characters where the norm implies dysfunction —situations in which and characters to whom the norm fails to prescribe the proper end or to furnish the necessary means. These situations are the stuff of dramatic art.

In an important sense the ethnologist's picture is an ideal picture, while the poet's view of culture is more realistic. Culture functions smoothly only in general and in principle. The values and customs of a live culture do not constitute an inclusive set of rules for action and self-consistent beliefs; a culture is rather a tissue of ambiguities, of tensions and unresolved problems. Perhaps we understand a culture best when we know what conflicts are most likely to arise in it and what problems are most likely to prove insoluble. The poet pursues such an understanding; that is what makes him an imitator. Drama is possible in art only because it is the normal condition of life.

A Definition of Tragedy

Within the domain of fiction, tragedy has a special claim on our attention. We begin again from Aristotle:

> Since the imitators imitate actors, but these must be either excellent [*spoudaioi*] or worthless (for character is nearly always according to these two particular criteria, in that people in general differ in their character according to their virtue or vice), then [the actors] must be better than we are or worse or the same. . . .
>
> And this is exactly the difference which divides tragedy from comedy. The latter wants to imitate people who are worse, the former, better, than the men we know.
>
> (*Poetics* 1448a1–18)

In order to interpret this passage, I remind the reader of two previous points: first, that fiction presumes the cultural norm; second, that the imitation is a reduction of the original. These points will be taken in turn.

Previously we spoke of the cultural norm as it appears to the actor. We thus spoke of the norm as prescribing ends and identifying means: the actor has some idea of what is worth doing and some ideas of how to do it. Now we speak of the cultural norm as it appears to the spectator of action. For the spectator the norm establishes a set of expectations: he expects men to choose certain ends, and he expects them to use certain means in pursuit of those ends.

But there is an ambiguity in the term "expect," as we can see in the two sentences: "I did that because I thought it was expected of me" and "I really think I did as well as could have been expected." We expect of men—that is, we require of them—that they pursue happiness in accordance with virtue; since we have some experience of the world, however, we also expect that they will often fail to do so. Our joint expectations of one another constitute the cultural norm, which therefore exists on two levels: the ideal norm prescribes ends and identifies means; the descriptive norm estimates, under given conditions, how likely people are to respond to the prescription of the ideal norm. Cultural norms vary on both levels; different men at different times and places have different ideas of virtue and happiness, and they also have different expectations as to the likelihood of encountering, in actual experience, men who are virtuous and happy.

Comedy and tragedy, in Aristotle's definition of them, differ in their implied descriptive norms. They share a common ideal norm; comedy and tragedy imply the same ethical standards. But they differ in their expectations of achievement. The poet of comedy establishes a pervasive expectation that his characters will behave badly, the poet of tragedy that his characters will behave well. Each presumes the descriptive norm of his culture, but in a reduced form.

The difference between comedy and tragedy, by this definition, originates in the different perspectives adopted by poets as spectators of culture. Obviously there will be wide variation. Poets of comedy will range from the detached amusement of the comedian of manners to the *saeva indignatio* of the committed satirist; poets of tragedy will vary from the compassionate affection of the domestic naturalist to the full-fledged idealization of the heroic bard. In each case, however, the perspective adopted, like the conventions of the art and the hypothetical starting point of the action, is a premise of the work.

This does not imply that in a comedy all the characters are vicious or that in a tragedy all are virtuous. On the contrary. As we saw, a work of fiction becomes problematic in that it develops from, and varies from, its premises; but in comedy we are surprised by virtue and success, in tragedy by vice and failure. The typical comic hero, from this point of view, is the Dionysus of the *Frogs*—a fool and a coward who turns out, at the end of the first half of the play, to be unexpectedly brave and, at the end of the second half, to be unexpectedly wise. The typical tragic hero, as we shall see, is a good man who falls into vice and error.

The tragic poet's reduction of his culture's descriptive norm thus directs his hypothetical inquiry toward a specific set of problems. Assuming, he says, that men are generally virtuous and wise, under what circumstances will their wisdom and virtue fail them? The tragic content of *Othello,* from this point of view, is not in Iago's vice but in the failure of Othello and others to perceive it; the tragic content of *Hamlet* is not in Claudius' crime but in Hamlet's inability to devise a response. Tragedy is thus seen as a hypothetical testing of the limits of the virtues.

This definition of tragedy establishes tragedy as a subgenre of fiction and also grants tragedy a privileged status within the domain of fiction —for the following reason. It is the function of both the lyre-player and the excellent lyre-player to play the lyre; the excellent lyre-player performs the function well. The excellent performance defines the function; when we hear the lyre played well, we understand what all lyre-players are trying to do. Similarly, the virtuous man defines the function of a man; he is the man par excellence. The tragic poet, who imitates *spoudaioi,* excellent men, thus inquires, not merely into certain kinds of men, but into man per se. Assuming, he says, that men have the resources which culture sometimes provides, under what circumstances will those resources prove inadequate? The tragic poet thus tests the limits of culture. Whereas the poet of comedy shows us the unexpected functioning of something we had presumed to be dysfunctional, the poet of tragedy shows us the unexpected (and yet probable or necessary) dysfunctioning of the functional.

It follows that when we speak of fiction as an inquiry into culture, we speak, generally, of tragedy; for in tragedy culture itself becomes problematic. Thus (from this point of view) tragedy is, not merely a genre of fiction, but the ideal type of fiction; or we could say that all fiction, insofar as it becomes serious, insofar as it is founded on an inquiry into the functioning of culture, approaches the type of tragedy. I think here, for instance, of the difference between *Le Médecin malgré lui* and *L'Ecole des femmes.* In the former, ignorance masquerading as expertise conquers a situation and redeems it; the result is pure comedy. In the latter, a partial conception of virtue and honor is punished for its partiality and yet is seen to retain a certain validity; the result is high comedy tinged with reflective seriousness. Both works are equally perfect, but the second has a greater range and power. In the same way, the *Odyssey,* which, as Longinus said, "approaches a comedy of manners," is as perfect a work as the *Iliad* but less deep. The *Odyssey* sets aside the heroic ethic and proposes a functioning alternative; the *Iliad* accepts the heroic ethic and yet inquires into its limitations and self-contradictions. The *Iliad* is thus a more profound work, for it leads us to a recognition of the internal limitations of one of man's most perfected ideas of his own possible virtues.

PITY AND FEAR

Aristotle associates tragedy with certain specific *pathēmata*—experiences or emotions—evoked in the audience; these he calls pity and fear. Something more can be said about tragedy when we approach it from this side, from the feelings it evokes; we begin with Aristotle's account of these *pathēmata* in the *Rhetoric*, more exactly, from the chapter on pity (2.8):

> Pity we define as a kind of pain evoked by evident evil, painful or destructive, which befalls a man undeserving of it and which one might expect to suffer oneself or that one of those close to him might. . . .
>
> Those who are utterly destroyed do not feel pity (for they do not think they will suffer anything more; they have suffered already); neither do those who think themselves superbly fortunate [feel pity]; instead they are insolent. . . .
>
> Rather [those who feel pity] are the sort of persons who think they might suffer [such a thing themselves; these are] those who have suffered it already and escaped; older people because they are more sensible and experienced; the weak; the relatively cowardly; the educated—because they can see the problem [*eulogistoi gar*]. . . .
>
> But those who are much terrified do not feel pity in that they are concerned with their own suffering. [People feel pity] if they think that worthy men do exist, for a man who denies their existence will think everyone deserving of evil. . . .
>
> People pity those they know, unless the relationship is very close (in the case of close relatives they feel it is about to happen to themselves. That is why Amasis, as they say, did not weep when his son was led out to execution but when he saw his friend begging. That was pitiable, but the other [sight] was dreadful). . . .
>
> People pity those who are like themselves in age, in character, in capacities, in social status, in birth. For in virtue of all these [similarities] it is more obvious that the possibility exists [that it could happen] also to themselves. . . .
>
> (*Rhetoric* 1385b13–86a26)

There are a number of points to make about this passage. In the first place, we learn that, according to Aristotle, pity and fear are not coordinate emotions; rather, fear gives rise to pity under certain conditions. Pity is fear which has been mediated by a certain distance—and by a certain closeness. We do not feel pity for ourselves or for those so close to us as to be parts of ourselves; we feel pity only for others. On the other hand, we do not feel pity for misfortune pure and simple; we do not feel pity for men *qua* men. We feel pity for unfortunate men who are like ourselves, because then we imagine ourselves in the place of the other.

In the *Rhetoric* Aristotle speaks of the pity evoked by a description of actual events. But from his definition it is easy to see why pity is evoked by imaginative works. Since the event described in a work of fiction is imitated, and therefore unreal, it is set at a certain distance from us. Yet to the degree that fiction reveals a universal, it can be perceived as a statement as much about us as about the characters imitated. Fiction presents persons like ourselves and situations (potentially) like our own. Furthermore, the imitative work communicates the universal, not abstractly, but by presenting certain particulars; thus the universal is made vivid and moving to us. Similarly, Aristotle recommends a certain theatricality to the rhetorician:

> Necessarily, those who press into service gesture and vocal technique and costuming and acting will in general be more pitiable (for they make the evil appear close, putting it before our eyes as impending or just past . . .). For the same reason signs [are pitiable]—for example, the clothing of those who have suffered, and such stuff, the acts and speeches and so forth of those who have suffered.
>
> (*Rhetoric* 1386a31–b4)

Next, we observe that pity is felt specifically for the undeserving. Pity, it follows, will seldom be evoked by comedy, for the comic poet, as we saw, tends to deny "that worthy men exist." But the tragic perspective may be expected to discover the pitiable, for that perspective asserts both that virtue exists and that it is inadequate to happiness.

Pity, then, is evoked by a perceived lack of fit between the qualities of men and their circumstances, especially when that lack of fit is elaborated in the direction of the ironic or the fateful, that is, when adverse circumstances seem to give evidence of a hidden pattern hostile to man.

> [It is pitiable when] some evil results from a source where one had a firm expectation of good, and when this happens many

times, and when the good arrives when the suffering is past remedy, as when what came to Diopeithes from the King came when Diopeithes was already dead.

(*Rhetoric* 1386a11–14)

Thus we may expect the tragic poet also to discover ironic or fateful patterns; investigating the limits of man's cultural resources, he is likely to see man, not only as inadequate to, but also in contest with, the patterns of nature and cosmos.

Pity is evoked most surely by the misfortunes of *spoudaioi*, of excellent men (*Rhetoric* 1386b5). Pity is also felt most surely by *spoudaioi* —by men who believe in the excellence of others because they know of their own excellence. The audience which feels pity is described by Aristotle in some detail: they are older men, men who have known trouble and escaped it, men of some education, men who are somewhat cowardly, men with something to lose and some anxiety about losing it. Pity is, in fact, the *pathēma* specific to the *bon bourgeois*—middle-aged and middle-class, with some advantages and real insecurities. Such men, from the point of view of the *Politics*, are the pillars of the functioning political· community (see *Politics* 1295a25–b34). From the point of view of the *Poetics* such men are the ideal audience for tragedy. Aware of both the resources of the cultural order and its limitations, they are most responsive to the poet's inquiry into the functioning and dysfunctioning of culture.

Aristotle's treatment of pity, finally, allows us to understand the importance of the tragic *pathos*. Through the undeserved suffering of the characters of tragedy the problem of culture is brought home to us. Through culture man has transformed his world and made it habitable, but this transformation is only partial. Primal disorder continually reasserts itself around man and within him. Disorder limits the scope of culture and leads it into internal contradiction. Thus the enterprise of man is frustrated and his purposes confused. In their struggle with such disorder others have been defeated, and we, since we are like them, may be defeated also. When we feel pity for others, we become aware of our own limitations. Tragedy, which evokes pity, leads us to face the hard truths about ourselves. We might prefer to think that the world is on our side, that goodness will always be rewarded and vice punished, that virtue is a sufficient cause of happiness, that suffering is not real. As mature men, however, we should be strong enough to recognize that it is not so. A story which avoids this recognition may be a perfect work of art, but it falls short of the truth about the human world:

The second-best pattern is that called first by certain people,
I mean the story that has a double pattern, as in the case of the
Odyssey; it ends oppositely for the good people and the bad.
This has been thought first because of the weakness of the
audience; the poets cater to the audience and compose a kind
of wish-fulfillment. However, the pleasure of such stories is not
proper to tragedy but closer to that of comedy. For in comedy
even the greatest enemies (according to the story)—for example
Orestes and Aegistheus—go offstage at the end as friends, and
there is no slaying of anyone by anyone.

(*Poetics* 1453a30–39)

Tragedy is painful because life is difficult; the tragic poet looks
deeply into life and shows us the hard truth he sees. We must add,
however, that not all art which evokes pity and fear will qualify as
tragedy; the *pathēmata* are mere experience unless they are justified
by the learning they accompany. In a true tragedy the *pathos* is imitated, not for its own sake, but as an element of the *praxis*. The tragic
poet is not an imitator of misfortunes but of actions; it is not the
misfortune of a character but the failure of an action which, when
interpreted to us by the poet, evokes tragic learning.

TRAGIC ERROR

This point leads Aristotle to his taxonomy of plots:

Since the composition [*sunthesis*] of the finest tragedies must
be not simple but complex, and this in imitation of fearful and
pitiable [events] (for that is particular to this sort of imitation),
it is in the first place clear that one ought neither to show [1]
worthy men moving from good fortune to misfortune (for this
is neither fearful nor pitiable but impure [*miaron*]) nor [2] worthless people moving from ill fortune to good fortune (for this is
the least tragic of all; it is neither human-hearted [*philanthrōpon*]
nor pitiable nor fearful) nor again [3] the thoroughly bad man
cast from good fortune into ill fortune (for such a composition
would have the human-hearted quality [*to philanthrōpon*] but
neither pity nor fear; for the former is for a man in undeserved
misfortune, the latter for one like [ourselves]—pity, that is, for
the unworthy, fear for one like [ourselves]—so that the event
will be neither pitiable nor fearful).
The intermediate remains. This is when [4] a man who does
not excel in virtue and justice falls through no vice or crime into
misfortune but through some kind of error [*hamartia*]—one of
those who have great reputation and good fortune, as, for exam-

ple, Oedipus or Thyestes and the notable men of such families.
So a fine plot must . . . move not to good fortune from ill
fortune but from good fortune to ill fortune, not through crime
but through a great error, made by just such a man as [we have
described] or at any rate by a man better than that rather than
worse.

(Poetics 1452b30–1453a17)

The undeserved misfortune of a good man is in life most pitiable;
this is the kind of event on which the rhetorician, for instance, relies
in order to move his audience to pity and fear. Why does it not move
us in art? Because the story is imaginary and the poet has himself
invented the misfortunes. If a poet (one thinks of Thomas Hardy in
his blacker moods) simply torments his hero with unexplained catastrophe, the *pathos* seems merely arbitrary and distasteful. The *pathēmata* of tragedy, as much as the characteristic learning, are evoked
from us by the poem as an imitation; we are stirred when we recognize
certain essential features of a reality we already knew. But the poem
is imitative in its intermediate causes; the *pathos* is moving only if we
find its causes in the action, in character and thought developed according to probability and necessity.

In his taxonomy of plots Aristotle contrasts two terms: *philanthrōpos*
and *miaros*. These terms are parallel with pity and fear and, like those
two, name attitudes or feelings evoked in us by the work of fiction.
(Strictly speaking, *miaron*, which means "filthy" or "distasteful," is
parallel with *phoberon* and *eleeinon*, "fearful" and "pitiable," since it
names a quality which evokes an attitude. *To philanthrōpon*, on the
other hand, which I have here translated "human-hearted," is parallel
with *phobos* and *eleos*, fear and pity; it names the attitude itself.)

Philanthrōpon is a compound, parallel in formation with *philo-
mousos* or *philathēnaios*. Just as those terms name a man who has a
taste for music or a liking for Athenians, so the *philanthrōpos* is a
person with a taste for mankind—someone who "likes people," as we
say.[12] *Miaron*, with its connotation of uncleanness, should be the opposite of that which evokes the *katharsis*, and at a deep level *miaron*
does have this connotation in the *Poetics*. But at a more superficial
level, and in this context, it is more relevant that, in classic Greek,
miare, the vocative, is a familiar and harsh insult—as we might call
someone "disgusting" or a "filthy swine." If the *philanthrōpos* is someone who likes people, the *miaros* is someone or something nobody
likes; that is the parallelism between the two terms.

What is the relevance of these terms to tragedy? Let us remember
that tragedy is an inquiry into the strengths and weaknesses of culture.

It will then follow that a tragedy taken as a whole—what Aristotle here calls a *sunthesis* or composition—will evoke an attitude toward culture as a whole. If we see the culture functioning smoothly, so that virtue results in happiness and vice is appropriately punished, our attitude toward the culture will be positive. We will then feel *philanthrōpos*, glad to live with our fellow man, glad to rely on the cultural order. If, however, the culture is seen to be dysfunctional, our attitude toward it will be negative. We cannot, however, reject it (remembering that the poet describes the culture from the inside and interprets the culture to itself); the culture is our home, and we have nowhere else to go. We will feel confused and disaffected; mankind will become to us distasteful. *To miaron* provokes what later writers have called *anomie*.

Aristotle's first three plots cover these two possibilities in reverse order. The misfortune of a good man leaves us with a sense that the culture is ineffective. We feel no pity or fear, because we know that the misfortunes were simply invented; but we also find that the poet has shown us no actions which could overcome misfortune. He has shown us an image of man naked to circumstance; it is this diminished image of man which leaves us with a distaste for man.

The success of a bad man is also distasteful; if the cultural order is to reward and celebrate such as these, we want no part of it. Our *philanthrōpia* is diminished, and we turn away from the human world.

The third plot—in which a bad man ends badly—does show us the culture functioning well, and it is a satisfactory plot, up to a point. Half of the double ending of the plot of the *Odyssey* shows us an outcome of this kind; and if we read that poem as it was meant to be read, we feel nothing but temperate satisfaction in the slaughter of Penelope's loathesome suitors. The shortcoming of such a plot, from Aristotle's point of view, lies in its superficiality; it "caters to the audience" and, as it were, overpraises culture.

In the fourth kind of plot, as in the first, there is a *pathos*: there is undeserved misfortune; but the two are quite different. In the first, the *pathos* is simply inflicted by the poet; in the fourth, the cause of the *pathos* is in the *praxis*: the suffering is due to error (*hamartia*). Aristotle carefully distinguishes error from vice and crime (*kakia* and *mochthēria*); vice and crime, plain bad character, are by fiat and, like any other first cause, uninteresting. *Hamartia* is the act of a good man gone wrong under pressure; *hamartia* is an intermediate cause. The actor's error enacts a change which has come over him in the course of the action, a change which comes about according to probability or necessity.

A plot of this kind shows us culture both functioning and dysfunctioning. Error is imposed on the actor by the limitations or contradictions of his culture; he is more or less forced to go wrong. His cultural resources are seen to be inadequate to the demands of the action; he probably or necessarily does the wrong thing at the very moment he is trying hardest to do right. Such an error evokes pity and fear, not only because we see that if we made a similar error we would suffer similarly, but also because we see that under similar circumstances we would probably or necessarily make the same error.

Yet it is right that those who go wrong should suffer; we accept the outcome even as we pity the actor and fear the consequence of his act. Society, at least from the Greek point of view, is rightly impatient of sincere effort and well-meaning but misguided muddle; it rewards nothing but adequate performance.[13] The tragic error may be the error of a good man, but it is really an error; and if it brings catastrophe on the actor, he gets no more than he deserves. We, if we are *spoudaioi*, would accept such an outcome in our own case also. The tragic *pathos* is thus a reassertion of the values of the society. In this way the *pathēmata* are purified; the poet's inquiry into culture is both a criticism of culture—for it shows culture to be a source of error—and an affirmation of culture—for it shows error properly punished. Finally, we must note that the punishment of error, if it is to be proper, must be properly limited and that the fundamental goodness of the erring actor must be respected. After error and its *pathos* come healing and an ending (a topic to which I shall return in chapter 5).

Error, in any case, is from this point of view the pivotal tragic event, and the interpretation of error is the focus of the poet's inquiry. In his error the actor enacts the limitations and self-contradictions of his culture; through his imitation of error, the consequences of error, and the healing of error, the poet leads us, not to a rejection of culture, but to a reaffirmation of it it on a new level of troubled awareness.

THE WRATH OF ACHILLES AS TRAGIC ERROR

An interpretation of the tragic error embedded in the story of Achilles' wrath will serve both to exemplify the abstract principles here stated and to return us to the *Iliad*. Achilles' wrath is a collective error; it is not the unilateral act of one actor but the outcome of an interplay between actors within a defined social situation. The wrath, further, is the starting point of the poem—the rest of the action begins there—but it is not a premise of the poem; the poet shows us that the wrath is a probable outcome of a preexisting situation. The wrath is thus in itself an intermediate cause; in it a potential instability in the community is enacted as an actual (and insoluble) conflict. We therefore interpret the wrath by stating its sources and tracing its development from potentiality to actuality.

The wrath originates in a quarrel between Agamemnon and Achilles. Both of these figures are problematic. Agamemnon is king of kings, dominant by virtue of his inheritance of the scepter of Zeus and the greatness of his personal domain (II.100–108). A community has need of such a dominant figure; the existence of a single paramount authority limits conflict, guarantees solidarity, and enables the community to function. Odysseus states the principle:

> Many lords are not good. Let there be one lord,
> One king, to whom crafty Cronos' son gave
> The scepter and decrees, to be their king.

(II.204–6)

The king is the "agent of the community principle";[14] he is the arbiter of disputes,[15] commander-in-chief in war, and host at the dinners which are also meetings of the council, meetings at which collective policy is threshed out.

Yet the king does not have arbitrary authority. In a society more aristocratic than feudal he is *primus inter pares*—one among the leading heroes, yet apart from them and their leader. Nestor states his role:

> Son of Atreus, take charge; you are most the king.
> Share a feast with the elders; it's fit and seemly.
> Your huts are full of wine that Achaean ships
> Daily from Thrace fetch across broad ocean.
> All entertainment is yours; you are king over many.
> When many are gathered, you'll trust the one who best
> May give you counsel.

(IX.69–75)

And again:

> Noble Atreus' son, great king Agamemnon,
> In you I conclude, from you I begin, since of many
> Folk you are king, and Zeus has guaranteed you
> Your scepter and decrees, to give them counsel.
> There is great need that you speak a word, and hear one,
> And complete another's, when his heart may move him
> Toward good. It rests with you, however it starts.

(IX.96–102)

Throughout the poem Nestor and Odysseus struggle to maintain Agamemnon's authority, not out of personal loyalty to him but because they see him as the channel through which policy can be made coherent and effective. The role of the king requires him to be both responsive and authoritative; he should hear good counsel and convert it into public policy by sealing it with his personal approval. This is a difficult role, and Agamemnon was not chosen for it; he was placed there by an accident of birth.

Agamemnon is a weak character—vacillating, easily depressed, often anxious and unfair. He is not a bad man; he is devoted to his brother, has considerable personal courage, and achieves moments of brilliance as a warrior. But he occupies a social role which is (as it were) too big for him. He would surely be an adequate warrior of the second rank, but as king of kings he finds demands made on him which are beyond his powers.

Achilles is problematic in a different way. His very existence is the result of an anomaly: the marriage between Peleus and Thetis, the mortal man and the immortal goddess. Homer does not tell the story according to which Thetis was courted by both Zeus and Poseidon but was married to Peleus when the gods learned that Thetis' son would be greater than his father. He may well have known this story, however, and may have expected his audience to know it. Homer presents the gods' gift of Thetis to Peleus as rather in a class with Aphrodite's gift of Helen to Paris; in both cases an apparent benefit turns out to be a disaster. Achilles is the only child of this misalliance between nymph and mortal, and he will not live to inherit. In one sense, of course, this early death is his fate; in another sense it is the consequence of his character and role.

Achilles is a marginal figure, half god, half man, suspended between the worlds. To both his parents he is problematic. For his immortal mother he is a link with the mortal world of death and grief; his existence makes his mother subject to feelings which gods are supposed to be spared. Thetis herself is marginally placed among the gods; she has links to the Titans and a special claim on Zeus (I.393–406). Through her Achilles has a special link to divine power; at the same time, her grieving immortality confers on Achilles a bitter consciousness of his own mortality.

If Agamemnon has inherited a social role which is too big for him, Achilles has inherited a role which is too small for him. Not that Achilles has any claim on Agamemnon's role; he is even less fit to be king of kings than to be a warrior among warriors. Achilles, in fact, has no proper place in the human world; his very virtues, extravagant and incomplete, make it impossible for him to be at home there or anywhere else.

Thus we define the potentiality of the *mēnis*. Achilles and Agamemnon confront each other: two men out of place, disaffected with themselves and with the order of things around them. The poet brings this situation from potentiality to actuality by adding to it one chance event: the fact that Agamemnon possesses, as a prize of war, the daughter of a priest of Apollo.

The priest is himself a somewhat problematic figure; he is a cultural specialist who stands somewhat outside the status order. Or, to put that another way, he is a low-status person with special powers. The priest attempts to ransom his daughter, and Agamemnon refuses, remarking only that the priest should be glad his sacerdotal emblems save him from personal injury. Agamemnon sees no reason why he, a powerful man, should give way to someone insignificant and weak.

This is the first error in the series; the poet marks it as an error by telling us that the folk shouted on behalf of the priest. It is the folk who will suffer for Agamemnon's error, and they do their best to prevent him from making it. In ignoring their shout, Agamemnon is undercutting his own position; his kingship (while inherited) is an accountable position, an instrument of public and collective authority. When Agamemnon ignores the folk, he is cutting himself off from the source of his own power and abandoning his claim to moral authority.

This error, as the first step in the action, is uncaused—yet it is not improbable. In the first place, Agamemnon suffers from the paradox of authority: authority often seems to confer power to do everything except what the person possessing it wants for himself. As Agamemnon says later, with rather touching openness, he kept the girl because he liked her (I.112–15). But precisely because he is king, Agamemnon is not allowed to follow his own inclinations; he has more power than other men but less freedom. This paradox has puzzled wiser men than Agamemnon.

In the second place, the priest's demand confronts Agamemnon with an ambiguous situation. In keeping the girl, he undercuts his own power; but if he gave her up, he would also, in another sense, undercut his power. The girl was his share in a distribution; she is a *geras*, a mark of status, Agamemnon's proof that he is a warrior among warriors. In losing his share, Agamemnon loses status; he, who is supposed to be the highest figure, would become lower than those around him. As he says later:

> Let me not alone of the Argives
> Be without a *geras*, for that is not fitting.
>
> (I.118–19)

In Homeric society, authority is secured by the exercise of authority, and status by the display of status.[16] Agamemnon's status and authority, as we saw, are necessary to the functioning of the community. Agamemnon could thus fairly claim that in disregarding the folk he is acting on their behalf. He is showing himself in control of the situation and thus securing the office of king.

Of course Agamemnon is *not* in control of the situation; his refusal of the priest's ransom brings him into conflict with Apollo. Agamemnon's error is his failure to recognize the strength of the forces against him. He has failed to cope with one of the most difficult situations with which authority can be confronted: a situation which requires one to surrender immediately, before things get worse and surrender will be more expensive.

Agamemnon's error draws down the plague; the plague brings on the assembly that becomes the setting for the *mēnis*, the wrath. This assembly is instigated by Hera "in her care for the Danaoi, because she saw them dying" (I.56). Hera does not, however, put it in Agamemnon's mind to call an assembly and apologize; rather she stirs up Achilles. This is a procedural error; assemblies are supposed to be called by the king. Why does Hera make this error? The poet does not tell us. Two reasons come to mind: first, the assembly is called to deal with Agamemnon's error; thus Hera may have thought it inappropriate that he should call it. Second, Achilles is closer to the gods than the other heroes are, and Hera may simply have found it more natural to go to him. Both are bad reasons; they come from and serve to amplify the very anomalies which Hera should be concerned to soften. Agamemnon is threatened by his own error and by Achilles' rival status; if the community is to be secured, Agamemnon must be supported, not further attacked. Thus Hera (as so often happens) in her effort to heal a situation reenacts it and makes it worse.

The assembly is called to reverse Agamemnon's previous error. If this is to happen with minimal social cost, Agamemnon must find the strength to give way calmly and with dignity; Achilles must help him. Both men are superbly ill-equipped for the roles they must play. Furthermore, the situation cannot be resolved without the help of Calchas. Calchas, the seer, is another problematic figure; like the priest, he is low in status but has a special potency, not because of his influence with the gods but because of his knowledge of them. Calchas, in fact, is an expert, and experts have always posed a problem to authority; like a tyrant's surgeon, Calchas has, within his own sphere, the right to instruct his superiors. Calchas is aware of his own anomalous position; he knows that authorities are not pleased to be told inconvenient truths. Calchas therefore asks Achilles for protection, and this Achilles promises. Achilles thus, on Calchas' behalf at least, declares himself independent of Agamemnon. Achilles, in calling the assembly and in opening it as he does, presents himself as a threat to Agamemnon's position.

Thus, by the time Agamemnon gets the floor, he is already embattled. He finds himself trying to do several things at once: to excuse himself, to reverse himself, and to reassert his authority. Given the confusion in which he finds himself, he does not do badly. He gives instructions for the return of the priest's daughter and for sacrifice to Apollo; he thus takes command of the reversal of his own error and exercises authority in admitting his previous misuse of it. He also, however, asks for recompense. This is a fatal error, not because the request is unreasonable, but because Agamemnon is not the proper person to make it. Nestor or Odysseus should rise and suggest that, given the king's magnanimity, the princes and folk will surely be unwilling to see him without a prize. In making the demand on his own behalf, Agamemnon makes it seem personal rather than official, a matter of private greed rather than the maintenance of propriety and status. He lays himself open to a charge of avarice, and Achilles promptly puts this name upon him (I.122).

This is the beginning of the harsh language which from here on echoes through the debate as the two parties amplify each other's rage. Agamemnon does not initially say that he is going to take Achilles' prize; he says he might take someone's—Achilles' or another's. Achilles, taking this threat as directed against himself alone, threatens to go home. Agamemnon, more or less forced to call Achilles on this threat, tells Achilles to go if he likes, and promises to take Briseis from him; seeing himself threatened with mutiny and desertion, he finds no other way to regain control of the situation. Achilles, in turn, makes up his mind to kill Agamemnon.

Both men have behaved badly but differently. Achilles has spoken and acted thoughtlessly; as always, he sees a point and goes straight to it, feels an emotion and gives way to it immediately. Agamemnon behaves badly in a more culpable way, in that his wrongdoing is more than a response to the situation; he does wrong in an attempt to deal with the situation. Achilles' anger is more spontaneous, Agamemnon's more systematic; Agamemnon acts out his anger in a definite injustice: the taking of Briseis from Achilles.

Later Agamemnon ascribes his wrongdoing to *atē* (IX.115–20). *Atē* is a kind of moral blindness or damaged deliberative capacity; it is a name for a state that comes over men in certain situations. In his speech of apology in the assembly of reconciliation Agamemnon says:

> I am not the cause
> But Zeus and fate and the fury that walks in mist
> Who in the assembly sent on me savage *atē*
> On that day when I took from Achilles his prize.
> But what could I do? A god brings all this on,
> The eldest daughter of Zeus, Ate, who blinds us,
> Cursed. Her feet are soft—for not on the ground
> Treads she, but walks right on the heads of men
> Harming mankind.

(XIX.86–94)

Agamemnon then tells a long anecdote of how Zeus himself was once subject to Ate and in his rage threw her out of heaven, so that she now frequents the works of men.

It should be observed that Agamemnon is not disclaiming responsibility; on the contrary, both times he refers to *atē* he is taking full responsibility and offering restitution. He is not trying to deny his wrongdoing but rather to describe its quality. It should be further observed that Zeus, in his anecdote, is tricked by Hera into saying something which he does not mean. Zeus, in our terms, does not do wrong at all; he makes a mistake because he is not clever enough to see what is happening to him.

And, says Agamemnon, this is just what occurred in his own case. His act was really wrong but in a certain sense was imposed upon him by the situation. In the assembly, events occurred with such speed and in such confusion that he, as we say, "got it wrong"; he was (as it were) deceived by the event. His act, in Aristotelian language, was a *hamartia*,[17] an act originating not in *mochthēria*, some baseness of character, but rather the error of a moderately good man, the sort of error such a man would make in such circumstances according to probability or necessity. And in his careful development of the scene, the poet presents to us an analysis of the conditions of *atē*; he shows us the probabilities and necessities which give rise to error. Agamemnon, in trying to act nobly and well, has acted basely and unjustly—yet we see exactly how he came to that point. Agamemnon's error is thus the enactment of ambiguities and contradictions within the culture—contradictions which come to the surface in a situation of stress. Hard cases make bad law, and bad kings.[18]

When Achilles is ready to kill Agamemnon, Athena intervenes. The rest of the story springs from this divine inhibition of Achilles' act. Achilles' wrath is not acted out directly but with massive indirection; Achilles' appeal to Thetis sets in motion the plan of Zeus. Thus the initial error spreads until it encompasses in its destructive consequences Troy and the leader of the Trojans, Hector. The tragedy is in motion.

3

THE HERO

The epic picture of the world was formed and transformed during the Greek dark ages, during the gap or vacant space in Greek history between the fall of citadels—Mycenae, Tiryns, Pylos, Troy—and the revival of towns in the eighth century B.C. Whatever details of Minoan or Mycenaean culture may persist in the poems, the Homeric picture of society in general belongs to the dark age and the early age of recovery. Homer shows us people living in small groups, dependent on one another for their mutual security against a hostile world.[1]

When the background condition of life is a condition of war—when men feel themselves free to steal from anyone with whom they are not acquainted and to plunder and exterminate any town against which they have a grievance—men must place great trust in those close to them. Thus combat generates a tight-knit community. A Homeric community consists, in effect, of those who are ready to die for one another; the perimeter of each community is a potential battlefield. Under these social conditions, war is perceived as the most important human activity because the community's ability to wage defensive war is perceived as the precondition of all other communal values.[2] Within the community there can be families, productive labor, property, religious and social ceremonies, but all these depend for their existence on the valor of the warrior.

The burden of a Homeric battle falls on a few leading men. The anonymous mass may appear on the battlefield, but they are insignificant in the course of the war; battles are won and lost by those who step forward from the mass, the *promachoi*, those who "fight among the foremost." These are the *aristoi* or princes, men who own armor and chariots, who are trained to the art and labor of war. To these leading warriors the Homeric language gives the name of *hērōes*, heroes.[3]

Thus heroism is for Homer a definite social task, and the heroes are a definite social stratum. The name is given to those who are, have been, or will be warriors. This is the Homeric governing class, the propertied class, and also the class on which the burden falls of maintaining the community. The most lucid statement of the hero's role and task is Sarpedon's speech to Glaucus, spoken in the depths of the battle by the ships:

Glaucus, why is it we two are most in honor
In our place at the feast, with meats and many cupfuls,
In Lycia? Like gods all men behold us.
Why hold we a great grant-farm by the banks of Xanthus,
Fair with orchard and corn-rich plow-land?
For this: that we now with the foremost Lycians
Must stand and exchange the blows of searing battle
So that one may say, some Lycian with his armor:
"They are not so fameless, that rule in Lycia,
These kings of ours, that eat the fattened flocks
With the honey-sweet choice wine. It seems their force
Is good, since they fight with the foremost Lycians."
Sweet fool, if only escaping this one war
We two would be able, ageless, immortal,
To live, then I'd neither fight with the foremost
Nor would I send you to battle that wins renown.
As it is, since the winged death-bringers stand beside us,
Countless, which mortals cannot escape or shun,
Let us go, to work our boast or submit to another's.

(XII.310–28)

Sarpedon sees that the privileges of the warrior serve both to mark
the warrior's special status and role and to hold him to the execution
of his task. The warrior's privileges are a kind of reward granted in
advance; the community accumulates a debt which it collects from the
warrior on the battlefield (IV.338–48). The warrior's advantages and
prestige thus serve to maintain in time of peace a social class which
properly functions only in time of war, on the battlefield.

But as the community's need of warriors generates a social organization, it generates also a paradox. War is initially an unhappy necessity,
the precondition of protected community. But as the warriors become
a class or caste, the advantages—and more important, the prestige—of
the warrior become in themselves desirable. War thus acquires for the
warrior a certain positive value. Heroism is initially a social task; it
then becomes a definite set of virtues associated with the performance
of this task. The warrior's virtues, further, entitle him to claim a social
status. But he can claim that status only if he can show that he has the
virtues, and he can demonstrate the warrior's virtues only on the battlefield. If his own community is not at war, the warrior will seek out combat elsewhere. Glaucus and Sarpedon are not fighting in defense of the
Lycians; they are far from home, fighting, not on behalf of their community but on behalf of their own status within it. Thus the young

Nestor also traveled far to prove himself a hero among heroes (I.260 ff.). And so it happens that the community's need for security and for defensive warfare generates a warrior ethic, which then gives rise to aggressive warfare—which is a threat to security. This double meaning of combat—defensive and aggressive, altruistic and egoistic—is fundamental to the *Iliad*.

All this is commentary on the first half of Sarpedon's speech; the tragic power of the speech is in the ending. In the first half Sarpedon praises the warrior's role; in it, he says, a man becomes godlike. In the second half Sarpedon (as it were) steps back from his own picture and says: all this is only a social illusion. The hero may appear godlike, but he is only mortal.

But this shift of perspective enables Sarpedon to justify heroism in another way. Man dies in any case, but he can choose to die well. He becomes a hero because he cannot be a god. In his nature the hero remains like other men, but culture bestows on him a value; he does not survive, but he is remembered. The hero knows this, and his knowledge enables him to go forward. It is a curious kind of knowledge, however; for if the hero knows what he is receiving, he cannot forget that the price he pays is his own existence.

All men are born to die, but the warrior alone must confront this fact in his social life, since he fulfills his obligations only by meeting those who intend his death. The community is secured by combat, which is the negation of community; this generates a contradiction in the warrior's role. His community sustains him and sends him to his destruction. On behalf of community he must leave community and enter a realm of force. The warrior can protect the human world against force only because he himself is willing to use and suffer force, "to work his own boast or submit to another's." The warrior stands on the frontier between culture and nature.

The power of Sarpedon's speech lies in its implicit recognition of the contradiction. To die for something, he says, is better than to die for nothing—and that is, after all, the alternative. In accepting death he shows himself searingly aware of it. The hero is in a sense rescued from mortality; he becomes godlike in status and immortal in the memory. At the same time he is uniquely conscious of his own mortality.

The greatness of Homer's heroes is a greatness not of act but of consciousness. There is not much nobility in the act of war, which is in itself a negation of human things, barbaric and impure. But there is a nobility in men's capacity to act and at the same time comprehend themselves and their situation. Homer's heroes have the power to step back and conceive themselves, suspended between culture and nature, as godlike and mortal.

Sarpedon and Glaucus, in particular, form a kind of chorus on the Trojan side. To Sarpedon's speech in Book Twelve corresponds Glaucus' speech in Book Six:

> Tydeus' son, great-hearted, why do you ask my breeding?
> Like to the breed of leaves is that of men—
> Leaves that the wind pours earthward, and others the tree
> In its strength puts forth, as the season of spring goes forward—
> Thus the breed of men puts forth and withers.
> If you wish even so to learn, then you may know
> My breeding; there are many men that know it.

(VI.145–51)[4]

For a moment Glaucus moves back and sees men as the gods see them (cf. XXI.464)—creatures as ephemeral and insignificant as all the other creatures of nature. Yet Glaucus goes on to recite his genealogy, and concludes:

> Hippolochus bred me, and I say I am from him.
> He sent me to Troy, and gave me much instruction:
> Always to excel and be held beyond others,
> Nor to shame the race of my fathers, who were much the best
> That grew in Ephyre and in broad-plained Lycia.
> Of this breeding and blood I claim to be.

(VI.206–11)

As the theme of Sarpedon's speech is community, the theme of Glaucus' speech is kinship. Kinship and community generate the institutions of *oikos* and *polis*, household and city, and thus the whole fabric of the human world. Within this fabric, men have identities and roles, relations and obligations, and thus are capable of the virtues.

Glaucus' speech is implicitly a praise of kinship; he displays his pride in his lineage, his breeding. Yet Glaucus also reminds us that kinship, which appears to be founded on nature, is really a fact of culture and another social illusion. Only within the order of culture do men have proper names and individual identities; as creatures of nature they are perfectly ephemeral. Nature cares nothing for the life of the individual and everything for the life of the species. To speak of the generations of men as like the growing of leaves is to see oneself as, after all, insignificant.

Thus the warrior, placed on the edge of culture, is in a position to form a view of culture as a whole. Culture has created a human world within which men can live. The warrior knows that world to be in-

102

substantial. Culture, which appears to us in our social lives so solid and enduring, reveals itself on the battlefield for what it is. The values conferred on life by culture are the only values we have, but they are a secondary product, sustained only by men's common assertion of them. For the warrior, culture appears as a translucent screen against the terror of nature. The heroic vision is of meaning uncertainly rescued from meaninglessness.

HEROIC WRATH

This discussion brings us back to the wrath of Achilles, which we are now able to see as a specific version or transformation of the heroic consciousness. Heroism presumes a reciprocity between hero and community. By Agamemnon's act in Book One this reciprocity is broken. Achilles' spontaneous response is the wish to kill Agamemnon; this would be a social act and would file a de facto claim with the community of his own righteousness against Agamemnon. "He would break up the assembly and kill Agamemnon" (I.191)—that is, Agamemnon would die and the rest would go home, giving silent consent to an act of excusable violence.

Athena prevents Achilles' spontaneous response; Hera has sent her "in care and concern for both together" (I.209). Athena promises the threefold gifts and expects a reconciliation between Achilles and Agamemnon. For Achilles, however, the quarrel has reached a point where the community must choose: either Agamemnon or himself. To attempt a reconciliation is in effect to choose Agamemnon, for a reconciliation would leave the king in place, unpunished for his unfairness to the greatest of the princes.

Achilles' great speech in Book Nine, then, is the speech of a man who feels himself evicted from his community. Furthermore, every attempt made by his friends to bring him back is felt by Achilles as a further eviction. This paradox gives the whole embassy scene in Book Nine its peculiar tone of passionate frustration and mutual incomprehension.

The hero, I have said, is a man on the margin between culture and nature. Achilles has, as it were, been pushed over the edge; he looks back at culture from the outside. He becomes a social critic, even a satirist. Menelaus' wife, it seems, was worth a whole war, but his own wife was not worth one murder. Now he is supposed to rejoice in the patronage of a man he despises. "Let him find some son-in-law *more kingly*," he says (IX.392), implying that these kings deserve each other, and that, as Agamemnon is valueless himself, so there is no value in Agamemnon's valuation of another.

In culture things have symbolic value as they function in social relations, as people believe in them and rely on them. Once belief and reliance are withdrawn, the flag is only a bit of cloth and the Constitution a scrap of paper. So Agamemnon's gifts, which when Agamemnon listed them had seemed a massive act of symbolic reparation, change in Achilles' hut back into mere things. Achilles heaps them up in his mind with all the other things in the world, heaps them into a heap of sand and dust. Achilles is driven back on the bare truth: that he himself is alive and strong. He can (in this sense) assert himself, but it remains a bare assertion; once he is excluded from the fabric of culture, Achilles can find no meaning in his life, no uses for his strength. He has become a mere creature in nature.

In the story of Achilles the poet dramatizes a fundamental contradiction: communities, in the interest of their own needs, produce figures who are unassimilable, men they cannot live with and who cannot live with them. This contradiction is not less puzzling for being familiar. It is a theme in many stories; Plutarch, for example, built on it his paired stories of Alcibiades and Coriolanus.[5] Of Alcibiades, another poet wrote: "They love him, they hate him, they cannot do without him" (Aristophanes *Frogs* 1425). In such stories the hero and his community stand as problems to each other. The hero behaves in a way he has been told is admirable and then is baffled to find that, in meeting the declared expectations of his community, he comes into conflict with it. Thus Shakespeare's Coriolanus, like Achilles, constantly asserts that he is acting only as he has been taught to act. Both heroes are led to the conviction that not they themselves but their communities have been faithless to the communal norm. Banished by the Roman state, Coriolanus responds: "I banish you." So also Achilles, in the picture he draws of the Greek army in his absence, implicitly asserts: It is not I who have been deprived of your company, but you of mine.

The warrior's role, as I have said, generates the warrior ethic. The community asks of some members that they leave the community and enter the anticommunity of combat. There they must overcome mercy and terror and learn to value their honor above their own lives or another's. The community praises and honors those who have this capacity. As this praise is internalized, it becomes a self-definition. Achilles is trapped by this self-definition, which permits him neither reconciliation nor retreat.

Achilles in his great speech in Book Nine draws a picture of two communities; against his satiric picture of Agamemnon's army he sets a romantic picture of Phthia at peace and himself at home there as son, husband, and man of property. But this picture of a peaceful Achilles is a fantasy. There is no path to Phthia from the place where Achilles is now; Achilles' quarrel with Agamemnon was founded on his claim to a warrior's honor, and to go home would be to abandon that claim and to admit that Agamemnon was right. To accept Agamemnon's gifts would equally be an admission that Agamemnon was right, since they would be given as the gifts of a superior to an inferior. Achilles' friends, in calling him back to the warrior's role, implicitly ask him to modify his commitment to the warrior ethic. Achilles' response to this contradictory demand can be only an out-cry—the baffled rage of the great speech.

The contradiction is further clarified—for us and for Achilles—by a contradiction in Phoenix' speech (IX.434–605). Phoenix tells the story of Meleager as an example of heroic reconciliation, but in fact the story tells us that Meleager, once wronged, refused all reconciliation, refused prayers and gifts, and was brought back to battle only by the helpless tears of his wife. Without wishing to, Phoenix gives the true pattern of heroic rage; the hero cannot choose to be reconciled, he can only come back under compulsion (*anangkēi*, XVIII.113 = XIX.66), overpowered by the irresistible claims of those closest to him. The next stage of the action is here foreshadowed; Meleager's weeping wife foreshadows the weeping Patroclus, who the next day appeals to Achilles like a little girl crying to her mother to be picked up (XVI.7–11).

Achilles' story, in fact, is not a departure from the heroic pattern but an enactment of that pattern; in his great speech Achilles states the heroic ethic as it appears to a hero for whom it cannot be made to function. The result is, as it were, Sarpedon's speech inside-out or in negative print. Sarpedon says that only honor can soften the necessity of death. Achilles says, first, that honor cannot be conferred by a mere heap of objects and, second, that when true honor is absent, nothing can soften the necessity of death. Achilles' refusal of the warrior's role is an affirmation of the warrior ethic; the absoluteness of that affirma-tion makes Achilles the greatest of the heroes. Achilles, then, is a marginal figure in his society, but a hero's place is on the margins; as so often happens in social systems, Achilles' uncertain status makes possible for him a kind of ethical fundamentalism and purity of spirit.

In what sense, then, does Achilles do wrong in refusing the gifts? Both Ajax and Diomedes (IX.628–42, 697–703) are certain that he is wrong. And of course he *is* wrong: a norm is supposed to function. Adherence to principle cannot be right when it brings disaster on both the actor himself and those to whom he is obligated. Achilles has no transcendent God or next life to which he can appeal; his act must be justified in terms of this world, and in this world his moral absolutism is disastrous. Ajax (IX.624–42) does not quite know how to say this; he can only bring into play the counternorm of *philotēs*, of loyalty to one's friends. This also is part of the heroic norm, and Achilles is shaken. Ajax' speech provokes from Achilles his ill-considered vow to wait until Hector reaches his own ships. More than that he cannot do, says Achilles; he is helpless (IX.644–47). Achilles is the victim of his own ethic.

ACHILLES AS TRAGIC HERO

Achilles' story is certainly a tragedy in several meanings of that polyvalent term. It is a story of suffering and insight. But it is not a tragic action in the narrow Aristotelian sense. We can clarify this point if we ask: Where is Achilles' error? In calling the assembly? But he is simply doing what Hera had told him to do. In his rage with Agamemnon? But everyone in the story, from Thersites to Athena, and including Agamemnon himself, agrees that Agamemnon was in the wrong and Achilles in the right. Was it then in failing to kill Agamemnon? Again Hera—and Athena—made that choice for him. Was it an error to refuse the gifts? Perhaps—but we should notice that this particular error, if error it was, did not advance the catastrophe. It simply left things as they were. Perhaps Achilles was in error in not going home, but we have seen that this was not a real choice. Perhaps he was in error in his ill-considered vow. But here again the connection with the catastrophe is indirect. Achilles brought the catastrophe down upon himself by sending Patroclus into battle—but here we should remember, first, that this plan was suggested by wise Nestor and, second, that the proximate cause of Patroclus' death was Patroclus' own error (carefully marked by the poet: XVI.685–87), against which Achilles had explicitly warned him (XVI.80–96). Surely Achilles makes errors, and surely Achilles suffers; but the poet has not been at pains to construct a clear relation of cause and effect.

Homer, in fact, marks only one error in Achilles' story, in a scene which otherwise would seem rather casually included. Machaon is being carried by, wounded, at some distance, and Achilles, curious, sends Patroclus for news—"and this was the beginning of trouble for him" (XI.604). On this errand Patroclus meets Nestor, and the fatal scheme is proposed. Achilles (who in this point also resembles Coriolanus) brings the catastrophe upon himself because he is not, after all, as detached from his community as he had supposed.

The crucial errors in Achilles' story, however, are the errors of others—of Agamemnon, of Nestor, of Patroclus. The tragedy is Achilles' own in that another man—a man less purely a hero—would not have allowed these errors to bring him destruction. But the tragedy of Achilles is not so much a tragedy of action as of reaction. Achilles is the central figure as a kind of arena of forces, a focus of the contradictions of his world. And his story, from this point of view, is a profound revaluation of the heroic ethic.

The tragedy of Achilles is in a sense complete by the beginning of Book Eighteen. Achilles, when he hears of Patroclus' death, speaks and acts as if his own life were over.[6] There remains one more task: to bury Patroclus and, as part of that burial, to kill Hector. This task Achilles single-mindedly completes through the rest of the poem; having killed Hector, he tries, as it were, to kill him again by despoiling and mutilating and befouling his body.

Throughout these scenes of action Achilles remains, oddly, a kind of victim. The intensity of his suffering is only partly hidden by the brilliance of his act. He achieves in his *aristeia* what for any other hero or for himself at another moment would have been the summit of happiness yet for him now is only an act of mourning.

In Book Sixteen, when Achilles first decides to send Patroclus to the battle, he concludes his speech with a strange prayer:

> If only, father Zeus and Athena and Apollo,
> No Trojan would flee death, of all there are,
> Nor any Argive, but we two escape destruction
> So that we alone could loose the crown of Troy.
>
> (XVI.97–100)

This prayer is so strange that most of the Hellenistic grammarians omitted it from their texts. But we should notice that it is in a way granted. When Patroclus dies, Achilles in a way dies with him. When Achilles returns to battle, it is on behalf of Patroclus, not the Greeks; he speaks to his mother only of his obligation to his dead friend. In Book Nineteen Achilles undergoes a ceremony of reconciliation; he says a few frigid words (XIX.56–73) and thereafter remains uninterested in Agamemnon's apology and gifts.[7] He refuses to eat, and with difficulty Odysseus gets him to allow the rest of the army to be fed:

> These things are of no concern to my heart,
> But murder and blood and the harsh crying of men.
>
> (XIX.213–14)

On the battlefield Achilles appears not as a leader of men but as an isolated destroyer—a kind of natural force, like fire or flood. Once, after Hector's death, he thinks of the battle as part of a war between cities; but then he calls himself back:

> Come, let us make trial of this city with arms,
> That we may know the intent the Trojans have:
> Whether they will leave their citadel, now he is fallen,
> Or be ready to stay, although Hector is no more.   .
> But why does my own heart speak with me thus?
> There lies by the ships a corpse unwept, unburied—
> Patroclus. I'll not forget him, not while I
> Stay with the living and my own limbs bear me.
> Yet if the dead forget, down there in Hades,
> I for my part will remember my friend even there.
>
> (XXII.381–90)

Achilles speaks as if he were already among the dead, alone with the dead Patroclus.

In Book Twenty-three Achilles celebrates the complex ceremony of funeral and funeral games. These ceremonies do not serve to reunite Achilles with his community. At the beginning he refuses to wash and calls the necessary feast *stugerē*, "hateful" (XXIII.48). At the end, when everyone else sleeps, Achilles is still awake, restless in his grief (XXIV.2–12). The final reconciliation with Priam, I shall argue later, does not take place within human community but in a sphere apart. Achilles, once evicted, does not return.

In the often-quoted phrase of Aristotle, the man without a city becomes "either a beast or a god." Achilles, as we shall see, becomes both. He gives himself to battle with such a whole heart that his acts cannot be called courageous; they are too easy and spontaneous. He has become a natural warrior and kills men as a weasel kills ducks, for sport. At the same time he looks on at his own scene and describes it with dispassionate clarity; nothing there is of any special value to him any more. Achilles thus achieves the perfection of the heroic consciousness. He sees the cultural world only to see through it, to see its insignificance, and his own insignificance, against the ground of nature.

In Achilles the poet has created a figure who by the end of the poem can function as hero and chorus at once, who dominates the action and yet remains detached from it. Achilles is himself a tragic figure and is the cause of tragedy to others, but he remains with us most as a voice, as a prophet of the tragic vision.

That vision, I have suggested, implies a revaluation of the heroic. We shall return to this revaluation at the end, where we speak of the mingling in the heroic of beast and god together. Here it is appropriate to note that if we are to revalue the heroic, we must know what it is; and if that revaluation is to be serious, we must know why the heroic is, after all, necessary. These themes are conveyed in the poem primarily through the story of Hector.

Hector's story, I shall argue, is a tragic action in the classic mold; it is the story of a man somewhat better than ourselves who falls through his own error. It is a mark of the ethical complexity of the *Iliad* that the true tragic hero of the poem is a secondary character; the poet of the *Iliad* has set a finished tragedy as a subplot within a design yet more ambitious and grand.

HECTOR

The hero, we said, tests the limits of life and experiences the contradictions of life with heightened awareness. For Achilles this heightened awareness entails the rejection of community and culture, the rejection of life itself. In this way Achilles survives, though his survival lacks meaning for himself. Hector, on the other hand, tests the limits of loyalty. His loyalty, like Achilles' wrath, leads him into an impasse, and when he can no longer solve the riddle of his situation, he ceases to live. In asserting the value and meaning of human things, he finds death. The resolution of the conflict between these opposite figures is the impossible task which the poet has set himself; at the end of his poem he achieves (as is the way of poets) the impossible. But to understand this achievement will require of us close and extended attention, particularly to the figure of Hector.

In contrast with the monstrous potencies of Achilles, a human creature like Hector might easily seem trivial. In fact the poet has taken great trouble with his secondary hero, compensating for his secondary status with a profusion of detail. Achilles' heroic consciousness sets him against his community; he passes judgment on it *en bloc.* He therefore does not have to make distinctions among its members. Hector remains within his community; his story is shaped by a delicate structure of diverse relations—with father and mother, wife and brother's wife, brother and cousin, kinsman and ally. In Hector's story we see that "the heroic" is not a single thing but a set of virtues and obligations—diverse relations sometimes in conflict with one another.

The poet brings Hector on the scene very slowly. We are well into Book Six before it becomes clear to us that Hector is going to be an important character. His story does not properly begin until Book Seven. With respect to his character, the first six books of the epic are an extended introduction, showing Hector first among men, then among women.

The first to mention "man-killing" Hector's name is Achilles (I.242), for whom he is simply the leading adversary. Similarly, Pandarus, on the other side, says that he came to Troy "doing a favor to Hector" (V.211), while Sarpedon addresses him as the supreme commander, responsible for the Trojans and the allies alike (V.472–92). In the Catalogue of Ships, Hector is named first, as the commander of the finest detachment (II.816–18), yet at the same time he is one commander among many, at most *primus inter pares*. In the battle scenes of Books Four and Five, Hector is the most important warrior on the Trojan side, and his power is marked by a notable simile when he confronts Diomedes:

> As when a man is baffled, crossing a plain,
> And he stands by a fast-flowing river that flows on seaward;
> He sees it swirl with foam, and steps backward—
> So Diomedes drew back.

(V.597–600)

Yet, for all his force, Hector says little in these books and does little on his own initiative. Iris tells him to marshal the troops, and he does so (II.802. ff.); Paris proposes a duel, and Hector arranges it (III.67 ff); Sarpedon calls upon him, and he goes where he is needed (V.472 ff., 683 ff.); Helenus sends him to the city (VI.77 ff.). Hector's heroism in these books is primarily responsive; he appears as a hero of responsibilities.

There is a certain modesty in Hector which reflects his role in the war. Hector is the field commander, but he is still subject to his father, Priam, who is king. The relation between father and son is presented as cooperative. Hector first appears on the scene in the assembly at Troy; Priam presides at this assembly, but Hector adjourns it (II.786–808). Later, when Hector arranges the duel between Paris and Menelaus, he sends for his father from the city (III.116–17). Priam and Agamemnon exchange the oath, while Hector and Odysseus make the practical arrangements (III.264–317). Hector does not ask his father's consent, but in the formal working-out of the occasion he steps down to the second rank.

FATHER AND SON

It is perhaps a feature of preurban societies that the ethical system is age-graded, so that different virtues are expected at different life stages.[8] In Homeric society a distinction is made between the young man and the mature man, a distinction correlated with the distinction between council and battle as arenas of excellence and with the contrast between the word and the deed. Excellence in both speech and combat are required of the perfect hero (IX.443; cf. xi.510–16), but speech develops later in life (IX.53–61). In a culture where physical strength and beauty are so important, old age can only be hateful— *stugeros, lugros,* or *oloos*—but there are certain partially compensating advantages. The young man's mind is hasty, and his wits are slight (XXIII.590). The elder "knows more" (XIII.355, XXI.440); there is an authority which belongs to age (I.259, IX.160–61). The contrast between the mind which plans and the hand which executes gives rise to the diverse public roles of king and warrior—a diversity which in the Greek army generates the quarrel between Agamemnon and Achilles (cf. I.280–81) but at Troy generates the cooperative division of roles between Priam and Hector.

The cooperative relation between father and son is an outgrowth of the special character of inheritance in the Homeric world. Inheritance secures the continuity of the household, which is the fundamental social institution. Through the continuity of institutions, culture rescues some stability from the flux of nature; the household continues, and each householder has his household, as it were, in trust for his heirs.[9] Thus Odysseus speaks the private prayer of each Phaeacian householder when he asks the gods to give them prosperity in their lifetime, and "that each should commit to his sons the possessions in their halls and the *geras* the folk have granted" (vii.148–50)—as we would say, their property and status. Because successful inheritance is the completion of the householder's social task, each householder is (in effect) dependent on his heir. The most powerful type of affection in the poems is that felt by a father for his sole grown son (XXIII.222– 23, xvi.17–21), especially the son who has been raised "among many possessions" (IX.481–82; cf. 143=285). The father's greatest hope is that his son will surpass him.[10]

In Homeric society, property can hardly be distinguished from possessions; the householder's economic status depends on his authority over *dmōes,* "servitors," and dependent smallholders, and these latter respect his authority out of personal loyalty and the habit of obedience.[11] Under these conditions the transfer of property is secure only when it occurs *inter vivos,* so that the father can use his authority to establish the authority of the son. This pattern gives us three roles for adult males of the propertied class: the son who has not yet inherited, the active householder, and the father who has retired from possession— Telemachus, Odysseus, Laertes. All three are *hērōes,* but only in the second is heroism actual. The old, however great their wisdom, lack the strength for those deeds which assert the validity of usage. They thus become dependent on the young for their livelihood (the *threptra*: IV.478=XVII.302) and their status. Thus Achilles in the underworld asks after Peleus (xi.494–502), and Odysseus inquires:

> Tell me of my father and son, whom I left,
> Whether they still hold my *geras*, or already
> Some other man has it, since they say I won't return.
>
> (xi.174–76)

Laertes cannot convey the inheritance to Telemachus; both are dependent on the acts of the vigorous, established Odysseus.

Hector is Priam's heir (XX.240). This is not a statement about property, for where there are many brothers, the property is shared among them equally (xiv.208–9).[12] Hector is heir to Priam's kingship, as Aeneas is heir to Anchises; both have in a sense inherited the *geras* of king *inter vivos*, in that each acts as field commander of troops during his father's lifetime. Kingship, however, is a public role, and the succession to it is determined by factors beyond the relations within the family.

Among brothers, the eldest is "attended by Erinyes" (XV.204). He is equal in property, but his greater authority is marked by the power to curse—a power which also belongs to the parent (IX.454, 571, XXI.412, ii.135, xi.280). Other things being equal, the eldest son will inherit the *geras* of kingship. Priam is the eldest (legitimate: VI.23–26) son of Laomedon (except for Tithonus, who is otherwise occupied: XX.237, XI.1). Priam is king in Troy, with his brothers around him in council (III.148). It may be that Hector is the eldest of Priam's sons, but this point is not made about him. Hector is not the favorite son; that status belongs to his half-brother, the youngest, Polydorus (XX.407–10). We are told that the people called Hector's son "prince" because "Hector alone protected Ilium" (VI.403; cf. XXII.507). Hector is heir because he has earned the succession.

The *geras* of kingship is in the gift of one king to the next, and he can give it to anyone he wishes (XX.182). It is no easy matter to be king; the king is father to the whole folk (ii.47, 234, v.12), and they honor him as a god. A good king brings prosperity (xix.109–14); a bad king can bring down divine destruction (XVI.384–92). The king must be wise and strong; in order to find such an heir, a king may even consider going outside his own community and adopting an heir from elsewhere, as Alcinous considers adopting Odysseus (vii.309–16). When Alcinous receives Odysseus, he moves Laodamas aside, his favorite son (vii.170–71). No wonder Laodamas later tests Odysseus and provokes a friend to insult him (viii.145–64). The kingship will go, by heredity or adoption, to a man judged qualified to hold it.

In his despair at the end of the poem, Priam says that the death of Hector has deprived him of his last qualified heir:

He called his sons in rebuke,
Angry with Helenus, Paris, bright Agathon,
Pammon, Antiphon, Polites good at the war cry,
Deiphobus, Hippothous, bright Agauus,
Rebuking the nine, the old man called them to him.
"Hurry, you wretched sons, you disgraces. If only
You all could have died by the ships in exchange for Hector.
I am left with nothing, since the best sons I bore
In broad Troy—not one of them is left,
Not godlike Mestor or Troilus, lover of horses,
Or Hector, who was a god among men—not like
The child of a mortal man, but of god.
Ares killed him, and left me with this refuse,
Liars and dancers, foot-tappers in the chorus,
Filchers of lambs and kids among the folk."

(XXIV.248–62)

Priam's line is being slowly exterminated; finally his inheritance will pass to Aeneas in the collateral line (XX.303). While Hector lives, he is the hope of Ilium; as future king, he embodies the continuity of the state. As such he is also his father's hope for the maintenance of royal privileges within the family.

Nemesis AND *Aidōs*

Hector's primary social role is that of the worthy son. As such, he is most clearly defined in contrast with Priam's most worthless son, Paris. Paris' crime has made the defense of Troy necessary; Hector's virtues make the defense possible. The poet seems to have intended the contrast between them and to have marked it by certain parallel features. The two men share one simile (VI.506–11=XV.263–68) and part of a speech (VII.357–60=XII.231–34). Both fight duels with picked Greek heroes in the arena between the two armies. The two first speak in the poem in conversation with each other; they are introduced as a sort of pair. Their likeness, however, is that of opposites.

Hector never speaks to Paris except to denounce him; Paris always replies with respect and admiration. In Book Three, their first conversation, Hector accuses Paris of cowardice; this accusation is quite unjustified,[13] as Paris proves by offering to fight in single combat with Menelaus. In this interchange Paris defines the difference between them:

> Hector, you fitly abuse me, not unfitly.
> Ever your heart is like an ax, hard-tempered,
> Which a man drives through a board, who with art
> Cuts ship timber, and it fulfills his blow—
> So, within you, unflinching is your mind.
> Do not throw up against me the gifts of Aphrodite.
> The gifts of the gods are not to be rejected,
> Whatever they give, and a man does not take them freely.
>
> (III.59–66)

Hector's hard-driving, focused energy is contrasted with the easy spirit of Paris, who accepts situations, however they develop. Later, after Aphrodite has transferred him from the battlefield to his wife's bedroom, Paris responds with similar calm to his wife's contumely:

> Wife, do not scold my heart with bitter insults.
> This time Menelaus beat me, he and Athena;
> Next time I'll beat him—we have gods on our side too.
> But now, let us make love in bed together.
>
> (III.438–41)

In the battle by the ships, Hector, full of impatient rage, comes upon Paris, who is "encouraging his companions and urging them on to fight" (XIII.767). Hector speaks to him wildly, and Paris responds mildly that Hector likes "to accuse the guiltless" (XIII.775):

> I deny
> Any lack of valor, as far as my powers extend.
> One can't fight past his power, try as he may.
>
> (XIII.785–87)

Paris accepts himself as he is; he did not make himself, he says, and he cannot be otherwise. For the poet of the *Iliad* such an attitude is fundamentally unheroic—because it is unsocialized. Paris, content with his own knowledge of himself, is unaffected by other people's opinion of him; he is aware of their contempt, but it does not touch him. Helen says of him to Hector:

> Since the gods ordained these evils to me thus,
> Would that I'd been the wife of a better man,
> Who knew the outrage and many shames of men.
> His wits are not steady, nor in time to come
> Will they ever be.
>
> (VI.349–53)

Paris is insensitive to *nemesis*, the moral disapproval of others, and has no sense of *aischos*, shame. Hector feels both acutely; thus his "wits are steady," he is held to his obligations by his feeling for the feelings of others. He says of himself:

> Most dreadfully
> I shrink [*aideomai*] from the Trojan men and long-robed women
> If, like a coward, I draw back from the battle.
> Nor does my heart so instruct me; I've learned to be good
> And ever to fight with the foremost of the Trojans,
> Winning great fame for my father and myself.
>
> (VI.441–46)

Hector inherited his warrior's role "among the foremost," and he has schooled himself to play it. His virtues are the outcome of his responsiveness to society. Paris, in his duel with Menelaus, goes cheerfully to combat and cheerfully accepts his defeat and his salvation by Aphrodite. Hector in his duel with Ajax shows no such spontaneity:

> A dread trembling in his limbs came over each Trojan;
> As for Hector, his heart cowered within him,
> But not even so could he tremble or shrink back
> Into the crowded folk, since he'd invited to battle.
>
> (VII.215–18)

Hector's fear of death is overcome by his greater fear of disgrace.

The fear of injury and the fear of disgrace are of course quite different kinds of fear, and in Homeric Greek they have different names—*deos* and *aidōs*.[14] *Aidōs* is the most pervasive ethical emotion in Homeric society; it is basically a responsiveness to social situations and to the judgments of others.[15] Thus *aidōs* can manifest itself as simple shyness; Thetis says that she feels *aidōs* to go among the immortals, "for I have not sorted out my own feelings" (XXIV.90–91).[16] Odysseus feels *aidōs* to be seen naked by young girls (vi.221); the goddess feels *aidōs* to see the lovers caught in the act of love (viii.324); Nausicaa's *aidōs* prevents her from mentioning her marriage to her father (vi.66); because of *aidōs* Penelope does not want to appear alone among men (xviii.184), and Odysseus does not want to be seen crying (viii.86).

In contrast with *aidōs* is the feeling of *nemesis*. *Aidōs* shrinks away and draws back; *nemesis* is an invasive passion that drives one to intervene in the affairs of others. When Hera feels *nemesis*, she rocks in her chair and makes Olympus shake, she smiles with her lips but not with her eyes, and she speaks maliciously and without proper control (VIII.198–200, XV.101–3). *Nemesis* is an excited condition, a feeling of outrage.

Aidōs and *nemesis* are a reflexive pair (cf. XI.649, XIII.122). The *nemesis* of others evokes *aidōs* in oneself (XVII.91–95). Just as Odysseus feels *aidōs* to weep, so also he fears lest his excessive weeping provoke the *nemesis* of others (xix.121). The *aidōs* Diomedes feels before Agamemnon inhibits his feeling of *nemesis* in response to Agamemnon's rebuke (IV.402, 413). Diomedes' annoyance with Agamemnon the man is inhibited by his respect for the royal office.

Aidōs inhibits action by making the heroes feel that if they acted thus they would be out of place or in the wrong. *Nemesis* drives one to attack those who have shown themselves lacking a proper *aidōs*.[17] *Aidōs* is thus a kind of hypothetical anticipation of *nemesis*. One often acts in order to avoid *nemesis*; thus Penelope says she must complete her father's shroud "lest someone among the folk should feel *nemesis* against me" (ii.101 = xix.146 = xxiv.136). One can put oneself in the position of others and ask how one's own action is likely to look; thus Nausicaa says: "I would feel *nemesis* toward another girl who acted in that way" (vi.286). One can even feel *nemesis* toward oneself, considering one's own acts (as it were) from the outside (cf. ii.64, iv.158–60).

The Homeric culture, in other words, is a "shame culture."[18] The heroes do not distinguish personal morality from conformity; in a world where "what people will say" is the most reliable guide to right and wrong, the two are practically identical. The feeling of *aidōs* is reinforced by the *dēmou phēmis*, the "voice of the folk" (xvi.75 = xix.527). *Aidōs* is thus nothing like conscience—a concept which is certainly post-Homeric and perhaps makes its first tentative appearance in the fragments of Heraclitus. *Aidōs* is a vulnerability to the expressed ideal norm of the society; the ideal norm is directly experienced within the self, as a man internalizes the anticipated judgments of others on himself. As such, *aidōs* is the affective or emotional foundation of virtue.

The Homeric Greeks, further, make no distinction between propriety and morality. *Nemesis* can be used to describe the petty strains of social intercourse; thus Athena (disguised as Mentes) says, "Are you going to feel *nemesis* at what I will say?" (i.158)—as we might say: "I hope you won't think me out of line" (cf. ii.138). The application of the ideal norm, furthermore, is modified by the descriptive norm; some behavior is *ou nemesis* (does not invite *nemesis*) in that, while unfortunate, it is within the pattern of social expectation—as we would say, it is "perfectly understandable." It is *ou nemesis* to weep when a

dear one dies (iv.195, xix.264); "no one could hold it against you."
Ares tells the other gods not to feel *nemesis* when he goes off to
avenge his son; it is as if he were asking, "What do you expect me to
do?"[19] Odysseus explains that even to stay away from home for a
month provokes impatience; therefore he feels no *nemesis* against the
army for rioting (II.296; cf. III.156–57). Agamemnon says (perhaps
employing a proverb), "There is no *nemesis* in running from trouble,
even by night" (XIV.80). But *nemesis* is provoked by any act which is
both improper and unexpected, ranging from failures of tact to
cowardice and betrayal.

Aidōs and *nemesis* (which, as we have seen, are inner and outer
aspects of the same thing) have a specific relation to the other emotions. *Nemesis* is closely connected with anger, and the two emotions
can be felt at the same time (II.223, VI.335, VIII.407, 421, xxiii.213).
Nemesis is in fact a specific kind of anger; we might call it "righteous
indignation." *Nemesis* is thus different from *achos* or *cholos*; those
pathēmata come upon a man immediately, as pain comes with a blow.
Nemesis is anger mediated by the social sense; a man not only feels it
but feels himself correct in feeling it.

When two parties quarrel, *nemesis* is evoked, not in the parties, but
in the bystander who disapproves of the whole quarrel (V.872, XXIII.
494). Justified anger does not provoke *nemesis*; but as soon as anger
goes beyond the point of justification, *nemesis* arises (IX.523, xviii.227,
xxii.59). *Nemesis* may be felt for actions which are simply foolish, like
wandering about in the dark (X.145), or negligent, such as standing
about talking when there is fighting to be done (XIII.293). But there
is always some implication of categorical judgment: the behavior is
not merely annoying but wrong. The suitors feel *nemesis* when Odysseus, disguised as a beggar, offers to draw the bow (xxi.285), for a
beggar is an improper person to take part in such a contest; it would
also be *nemessēton*, a cause of *nemesis*, for Odysseus to appear before
his wife in rags (xxii.489). The behavior of the suitors is generally
nemessēton (ii.64, xxi.147, xxii.40). They are also lacking in *aidōs*
(xx.171). The folk are subject to *nemesis* for not resisting the suitors
(ii.239). It is *nemessēton* for a common man to speak in the assembly
(II.223) or for a god to appear too friendly with a mortal (XXIV.463).
It is *nemessēton* to send one's mother away against her will (ii.136), to
give someone poison for arrows (i.263), or to commit wanton destruction (V.757). In all these cases there is some sense of crossing lines or
transgressing limits. On the other hand, annoying behavior is not subject to *nemesis* so long as it corresponds to some propriety; as long
as Telemachus had some hope of his father's return, it was *ou nemesis*

117

to put off the suitors (xx.330), and it is *ou nemesis* for Phemius to sing of the return of the Argives (i.350)—he is just doing his job. Only in the case of Achilles is *nemesis* purely personal; Achilles would feel *nemesis* toward Patroclus if Patroclus felt sorry for Achilles' enemies (XVI.22) or simply lingered about an errand (XI.649). Achilles has made of his own will a moral law.

To return to *aidōs*: *aidōs* accompanies a variety of other emotions. *Aidōs* may be joined to pity (XXII.82); *aidōs* and *eleos* cause one to accept the suppliant instead of killing him (XXI.74–75, XXII.123–24, v.447–50, ix.266–71, xxii.312–24; cf. vii.165=vii.181). Achilles' defilement of Hector shows Achilles to be lacking in *aidōs* and in pity (XXIV.44 [cf. XXII.419], 207–8, 503). *Aidōs* is thus specifically connected with restraint in treatment of the helpless.

But *aidōs* is also connected with fear, particularly with fear of one's superior officer (I.331; cf. XXIV.435, xvii.188–89). Hence the saying: "Where there is fear, there also is *aidōs* (quoted from the *Cypria* in Plato *Euthyphro* 12a). If *aidōs* is a shrinking from cruelty, it is also a shrinking from disobedience. Penury constitutes a claim on the *aidōs* of others, but so does wealth (xi.360, xiv.234).

Aidōs, finally, is connected with friendship and affection (X.114, XIV.210, XXIV.111, v.88). The close friend, especially the friend to whom one owes an obligation, is at once *philos, deinos,* and *aidoios*—dear, dread, and a source of *aidōs* (XVIII.386, 394, 425, viii.21–22; cf. III.172).

Thus we can see that *aidōs* is in general an emotion provoked by the perception of one's place in the social structure and of the obligations which accompany that place.[20] One should pity one's inferiors and shrink from mistreating them; one should fear one's superiors and shrink from disobeying them; one should treasure one's friends and shrink from disappointing them. *Aidōs* accompanies an immediate emotion when that emotion is mediated by the social sense.

Aidōs is in general felt toward persons in the exercise of their social roles or when they are perceived as having a social relation to oneself. *Aidōs* is felt toward one's uncle (XXI.468–69, vi.329–30), one's mother (xx.343), an elder (iii.24). *Aidoiē* is a fixed epithet of the *tamiē*, the senior female house servant. *Aidōs* is felt toward a king (IV.402), a bard (viii.480), a priest (I.23 = 377), and a dependent (xiv.505). Here again we see that the sense of rightness, of fitness, pervades the entire social order; it is morally right for a bard to be a bard—because he is one.

Aidōs and *nemesis* are most frequently mentioned in connection with the three types of social situation which most test the moral sense: situations involving sexuality, the entertainment of guests, and standing one's ground in battle.[21] In all three the worth of a man is tested by his power to overcome selfish impulses which might lead him to be self-indulgent, miserly, or cowardly. Of the three, the battlefield is the most testing and the most important.

Combat is the crucial social act, for in combat the survival of the collectivity is at stake. The *aidōs* felt in battle is an experience of the collectivity; a man stands his ground because he shrinks from betraying his fellows. Thus the bare word *aidōs* is a battle cry (V.787 = VIII.228, XIII.95, XV.502, XVI.422); the Homeric proverb says: "When men feel *aidōs*, more are saved than perish" (V.531, XV.563). Hector refers to *aidōs* in this sense when he tells Andromache that he has "learned to be good."[22]

Hector is a warrior not because he loves war but because he is before all else a hero of *aidōs*. He has devoted his life to its dictates and to the avoidance of *nemesis*. Hector thus embodies the ideal norm of Homeric society. In his story we see that norm tested, and we come to see its limits.

In his speech to Andromache, Hector says that he feels *aidōs* before both Trojan men and "the long-robed Trojan women." *Aidōs* is particularly associated with women (see II.514, for example), who, as structural inferiors, have the same sort of claim to *aidōs* as the guest, the suppliant, and the beggar. In order to understand Hector's *aidōs*, we must see Hector in relation to his women. This picture occupies the greater part of Book Six.

WOMEN

The battlefield is inhabited solely by men, and heroism is a superbly masculine role. Manly himself, the hero is also the son of heroes; in his breeding he recapitulates the masculinity of his fathers. Yet the hero is also born of woman, and there are in Homer traces of a notion that a person's innate qualities, as opposed to those conferred by his social role, are his inheritance from his mother (see, e.g., vi.25, xxi.172). It is as if the father were the social or cultural parent, the mother the natural parent; *mētēr* can be used of animal parents, while *patēr* cannot.[23] The son's social task is to replace his father; he may or may not have the natural capacity to do so (see IV.399–400, V.800–801). The mother is the source of these natural capacities. Thus Paris says: "My mother did not bear me (*geinato*) completely without valor (*alkē*)" (XIII.777). When Achilles boasts of his high lineage, he traces his origins through Peleus back to Zeus (XXI.184–91); but his personal greatness comes to him from his divine mother (I.280, XXI.109). Aeneas has his status among the Dardanidae by his descent from Anchises, but it is his descent from his divine mother Aphrodite that will preserve him through the war (see XX.300–305).

A woman cannot be a hero, but she can be the mother of heroes. Her participation in combat is thereby vicarious. When the warrior "has killed his man in battle, his mother would joy in her heart" (VI.481). Thus, in terms of his audience or social referent, the hero has a double sense of his role; while his bravery in battle is *like* that of his father and his other menfolk, it is *from* his mother and *for* her and his other women. When Meleager's wife roused him to action,

> she told him all
> The sufferings of a people whose city is taken:
> They kill the men, the city is razed with fire,
> The children go to others, and the handsome women.
> And his spirit rose as he heard of these evil acts;
> He went forth.
>
> (IX.591–96)

The men are killed, the women and children enslaved. A grown man cannot be enslaved;[24] if he is taken prisoner, he may undergo a fiction of slavery (XXIV.751–53), but he is in fact held to be resold to his own people; his price is a ransom (VI.46–50 = XI.131–35; X.378–81; XXI. 34–44, with 80). A child can be enslaved (XXIV.732–34), as Eumaeus was enslaved; he was young and could be raised to the life (xv.363–70), but a grown man is no longer so pliant. But a woman is; she has been one man's and can be another's. In this limited sense the woman is a permanent child. Women, children, and slaves are alike in that all are dependent and thus differentiated from the active warrior on whom they must all rely. All together, along with his material possessions, are the warrior's property, and combat is on their behalf:

> It is not unfitting, defending one's homeland,
> To die. Then your wife is safe and your children after;
> Your house and lands are undespoiled.
>
> (XV.496–98)

The warrior defending his city obviously and "by necessity" (VIII.57) fights for those who cannot fight. But the invader fights for his women and children also; thus Nestor says:

> Friends, be men; put *aidōs* in your heart
> Of other people; remember each of you
> His children, wife, property, and parents,
> Both those who live and those who are with the dead.

On their behalf I beseech you, though they are absent,
Stand firm.

(XV.661–66)

The memory of the weak gives rise to *aidōs*; thus, by a basic principle
of social differentiation, the weakness of some generates strength in
others. The masculinity of the warriors has its source in the femininity
of the unwarlike. The very closeness of the relation between the warrior and his women, further, requires their separation in time of war.
Cowards turn into women (II.235, VII.96, VIII.163) or may run to the
arms of their women (VI.81). The worthless Paris is commonly found
among women (see XIII.769). The warrior's place is in the masculine
world of war. When Hector leaves the battlefield and enters the city,
he appears as a messenger from one world to the other:

Around him the wives of Troy ran, and the daughters,
Asking after their sons and brothers and kinsmen
And husbands. But he told them to pray to the gods,
As each came up. But sorrow was certain for many.

(VI.238–41)

Hector goes to the city on Helenus' instructions (which are specifically endorsed by the poet, so that we know that Hector is acting
rightly [VI.73–76]). Hector's mission is to the Trojan women, and he
carries it out. But when he speaks to his army before leaving, he also
says that he will speak "to the elders, the councilors" (VI.113–14); in
the event he makes no attempt to do so. It has been thought that this
anomaly is a trace of multiple authorship.[25] One may, however, prefer
to think that Hector, embarrassed to be seen going among the women
in time of war, therefore asserts that his mission is also to the men.

There is an undercurrent of tension in Hector throughout the book.
His mother assumes that he has come himself to pray to Zeus; she
offers him wine—"when a man is tired, wine much revives his force"
(VI.261). Hector replies:

Bring me not wine that honeys the heart, lady mother,
Lest you strip my limbs of force, and I forget valor.
With unwashed hands to pour the wine to Zeus—
I shrink from that. It's wrong to go in prayer
To cloudy Zeus when smirched with blood and gore.

(VI.264–68)

He tells her that, although he is present in her house, he still belongs
to the battlefield; he is only a messenger and cannot come home. If he
forgets and allows her to care for him, he will lose his *alkē*. So also

he says to Helen: "Don't ask me to sit down, Helen, though you love me. You will not persuade me" (VI.360). Any strong "no," in poetry as in life, is likely to conceal a "yes." Hector lingers a moment among the women, repeatedly asserting that he must not stay. He sees his mother on Helenus' instructions; he sees Helen because he improvises a need to speak to Paris. Finally, he searches the city until he finds his wife. The conversation between Hector and Andromache is the crown of Book Six. It is the one moment in Hector's story in which he acts, not from a sense of obligation, but from the fullness of desire.

As Hector and Paris are a kind of opposite pair, so are Helen and Andromache. Andromache is the faithful wife who completes and motivates the hero; Helen is woman as source of danger and social disorder (III.156–60). Yet Helen is no villainess; she does harm passively, it is not her fault. Helen and Hector are close; she, with his wife and mother, is the third mourner at his funeral, where she says that, of the Trojans, Hector and Priam alone were always kind to her (XXIV. 767–72). Helen does not think of herself as deserving kindness; she is filled with self-distaste and regret for all she has caused. In her weakness Helen reaches out to Hector. A woman must be dependent on some man or men; and as her own husband is weak, Helen reaches out along the chain of kinship to the next men over, to Priam and Hector. In effect she says to Hector: "If only you were my husband instead of Paris" (see VI.349–51).

In Homer's world a woman's social position is defined by her relations with men. These are of two kinds: consanguineal and affinal; more concretely, she has a father and can have a husband. A married woman remains a part of her father's family. If she is to be ransomed from captivity, her father will pay the ransom (I.13, VI.427). The father gives his married daughter a dowry, which is the mark of her continuing relations with him; if she is sent away, the dowry must be repaid (ii.132–33). The dowry belongs to the woman in trust for her sons (XXII.50–51). It gives a married woman some independent standing in her husband's house.

Helen and Andromache, however, are alike uprooted—Helen because her marriage with Paris was not a proper transaction, Andromache because Achilles has killed all her consanguine male kin and destroyed her father's house. Thus Andromache's words to Hector are, in a social sense, literally true:

> Hector, you are now my father and lady mother
> And brother; you are my strong-grown husband.
>
> (VI.429–30)

All of her relations have been reduced to one; Hector is her sole link with the fabric of kinship. As her dependence on Hector is absolute, so is his response:

> Well I know this in my heart and spirit:
> The day will come when sacred Troy will perish
> And Priam and ash-speared Priam's folk.
> Not for Troy do I care for the pain to come
> Nor for Hecuba herself nor Priam the king,
> Nor for my brothers, who so many and brave
> Shall roll in the dust before their enemies,
> As much as for you, when some armored Achaean
> Will take you in tears and strip you of your freedom.
>
> (VI.447–55)

HOUSEHOLD AND COMMUNITY

Hector's meeting with Andromache is a parting.[26] Her first words to him are a reproach:

> You strange creature, your strength will fail, you've
> No pity for your son, for me, ill-fated, soon your widow,
> As I shall be. Soon they will kill you, these Achaeans
> Massing against you. And then I'll find it better,
> Once I have lost you, to sink within the earth.
>
> (VI.407–11)

In the conversation between Hector and Andromache the poet dramatizes the pain of the warrior's role, of the man who, on behalf of his family, must leave his family, so that his very defense of them becomes a betrayal. The community can defend itself only with the loss of some of its members; the warrior when he goes to war immerses himself in the collectivity. There is thus a tension between obligations to household and to city, for in defending everyone the warrior must set aside his special obligations to those who are most truly his own. Hector in his armor is a terrifying, alien figure to his own son; for a moment he can set aside the costume of his role and play with the child, but he must then again put on his helmet and his task.[27]

The conflict between personal loyalty and collective loyalty is an element of the generic situation of the warrior; it arises in many epic stories, for instance in the stories of Meleager and Patroclus. Hector's situation is more complex; "a man of great reputation and prosperity," he is more than a member of the collective: he is its focal point. As the leading warrior, he protects his city for the present; as Priam's heir, he is its hope for the future. He thus has two conflicting sets of

Chapter 3

obligations. To meet the first set, he must be ready to die; he can meet the second set only if he survives.

The life of communities is in their continuity, but excellence in combat requires one to forget continuity. The warrior must be given over to immediacy, ready to stake everything on the success of the moment. The warrior ethic is therefore egoistic; it is an ethic of glorious victory or glorious death. The householder, the king, the commander—and the warrior may be all these things as well—must be able to look forward to another day. His ethic is one of communal responsibility. In Homeric society this contradiction was to some extent mediated by the age-grading of the virtues; planning and forethought belonged to the elders, immediate action to the young. Inheritance *inter vivos*, however, tends to produce an overlap of social roles. As battlefield commander, Hector is both king and warrior; he must be cautious and reckless at once, act well himself and direct the action of others. This contradiction is already dramatized, quietly, in Book Five, in Hector's two meetings with Sarpedon. First Sarpedon tells him that he is failing as a commander, that his own personal courage is not enough (V.485–86). A little later Sarpedon himself is wounded; he calls on Hector, who advances, "bringing terror to the Greeks, and Sarpedon rejoiced to see him" (V.682–83). In his own moment of need Sarpedon relies, not on Hector's leadership, but on his personal valor. In neither case does Hector say anything; he responds to the conflicting demands on him simply by doing his best to meet them. The contradiction latent here becomes increasingly explicit in the course of Hector's story, until at the end it leaves him, alone outside the walls, paralyzed before Achilles' advance.

In their parting in Book Six Hector and Andromache speak together of Hector's death. Andromache speaks of her personal loss; Hector speaks of the fall of Troy. Hector does not have the privilege of dying that his community may live; the burden on him is greater than that. When he dies, his community falls with him. The fall of Troy (like the death of Achilles) is not part of the story of the *Iliad*; it is, however, part of the fatality of the poem. We know that Troy will fall, and this knowledge is, for us, part of the meaning of the death of Hector. His death is not a private matter; it has its meaning in its effect on all those others who have relied on him and by their reliance have made him what he is.

There are many anticipations in the story of Hector, and they are not consistent with one another. Andromache in her mourning in Book Twenty-two speaks of Astyanax' orphanhood:

> You will not be for him,
> Hector, his blessing, since you're dead—nor he to you.
> Should he escape this wept-for war of Achaeans,
> Ever for him the toil and sorrow after
> Remain. For others will mark his fields.
> The day of orphanhood makes the child friendless;
> Ever he hangs his head, the tears run down;
> In lack the child goes to his father's friends,
> Plucking the cloak of one, and another's shirt.
> In pity one hands him a drop in a cup
> To moisten his lips, but his mouth it doesn't moisten.
> The man with parents mocks him from the feast.
> With a blow of the hand and the harsh sting of an insult:
> "Go along. *Your* father does not feast among us."
>
> (XXII.485–98)

This speech does not fit our picture of Priam's polygamous household, maintained by supporting bonds of extended kinship. Andromache does not make a realistic prediction of the future; rather she states with vivid concreteness the meaning of Hector to herself as the mother of a son. At the moment of loss her overpowering awareness is of the son's dependence on his father.

Hector in Book Six—just after he has described so vividly the fall of Troy—has a different vision of his son's future:

> Zeus and other gods, grant that he become,
> My son, as I am, famous to the Trojans,
> As great in force, by might the prince of Troy.
> Someone might say: "He far exceeds his father."
> Coming from war he'd carry the bloody armor
> When he's killed his man; his mother would joy in her heart.
>
> (VI.476–81)

But this speech is no realistic prediction of the future; Hector is simply stating the meaning of his son to himself. At a moment of deep affection his central awareness is of the son as a recapitulation of the father, of the son who, by continuing, completes the father's social task.

Hector's vision of the fall of Troy (VI.447–55, quoted above) is not a realistic prediction either; it appears so to us only because we know that it describes what (in legend) actually occurred. Hector is denied a knowledge of the future; the various anticipations which run through his story express various aspects of his present situation. These anticipations are inconsistent with one another because his obligations—and therefore his various definitions of himself—are self-contradictory. Hec-

125

tor is caught between household and city, between youth and age. He is both king and warrior; he is son and brother and also father and husband. In these contradictions the tragedy is latent. All of them, further, are aspects of the relation between nature and culture; or better, we could say that that relation is the general source of contradiction.

Nature is eternal; the things of culture are transient. But from another point of view it is also true that the creatures of nature are ephemeral, while the institutions of culture—its families, cities, traditions—are in principle immortal. They will survive as long as the generations of men maintain them. Culture therefore confers on finite life a meaning; it offers a man something to live for, something beyond himself.

But culture does not thereby redeem man from death. Rather it imposes on him the burden of choice. Society asks of a man much more than he can do; when some paths are chosen, others are rejected. At the moment of death much remains undone. Thus culture, precisely because it offers purposes to life, shows each life to itself as incomplete. In culture, in his relations with others, man encounters his own mortality. However much he lives for others, he must always fail them in the end.

As a free, choosing being, the hero looks to the future; as a mortal creature, he looks away from it. That is the inner contradiction of Hector's farewell to his wife. He leaves her to go toward action, heavy with consciousness of the limits of action. His parting words to her are words of submission--submission to the order of nature and to the determining force of his social role:

> You strange girl, do not grieve so for me;
> No one will send me to death beyond my portion.
> But the portion no man, I say, has escaped,
> Neither coward, nor brave man, from the moment he is born.
> But go into the house and take up your own works,
> The loom and the distaff, and direct the servants
> About their work. We men will care for war,
> All of us—I the most—men born to Troy.

(VI.486–93)

The contradiction remains unresolved; here it is merely set aside. Hector's social role requires of him more than submission; it requires initiative, leadership, and choice. Choice entails the possibility of error; and since man is mortal, his errors are irremediable. Without freedom, however, and thus the possibility of error, there is no heroism. The

Hector of the first six books—responsive, responsible, and submissive—
is as yet only a hero *in potentia.* He becomes actual in action.

Yet in a sense the end is present at the beginning; Hector's action
and his error are an enactment of his situation. The poet has taken
great care to show us that situation in its complexity, its inner conflicts, and its pathos before he sends his hero into action. We are on
Hector's side, we understand him well, and we are prepared to follow
his story. Each of his acts, even at his moments of greatest blindness,
rises exactly from the admirable kind of man he is. When Hector
departs, the women raise the keening.

> While he still lived, they mourned Hector in his household.
>
> (VI.500)

Hector's story begins, as it ends, with his funeral.

4

ERROR

The Problem of Heroic Balance

The hero's error, we said earlier, is really an error, yet it is the sort of error a good man would make. It is thus an act both free and conditioned. The hero's error is not forced upon him, but he makes it under conditions so adverse that we watch him with compassion. Tragedy is thus grounded in meditation on action and the conditions of action, and these two can be understood only in relation to each other. Hector's freedom can be understood only in relation to the imperfections of his power and knowledge; these define his acts.

Hector's story in the *Iliad*, properly speaking, is bounded within the space of three days. On the first day, which occupies Book Eight, the Trojan army is victorious. On the second day, which occupies Books Nine through Eighteen, the two armies contest the field in balanced strength. On the third day, which occupies Books Nineteen through Twenty-two, the Trojan army is routed and Hector dies. On each day he makes a clearly identifiable error: first, at the end of Book Eight, when he promises his army victory for the day which follows (VIII.489– 541); second, in Book Eighteen, when he refuses to withdraw his army from the battlefield (XVIII.243–313); third, in Book Twenty-two, when he himself refuses to withdraw within the walls (XXII.25–130). Each error is made reflectively, not in the heat of combat but at a moment of repose. The first is made with the consent of all around him; the second is made against the counsel of Polydamas; in the third he rejects the heart-searing appeals of his parents. There is thus a sequence in which Hector becomes gradually more isolated and more self-willed. Later we will examine each of these passages; here it is enough to observe that each error conditions its successor.

Error, as the term is here employed, must be contrasted with the mistakes made by animals. All creatures experience the consequences of their behavior; man in society *lives with* his error, in that it becomes a part of his history and thus defines what he is. The consciousness of error is a species of shame; error is thus a social fact. Man acts with men, and he knows himself to be known to other men through his acts; thus in action he makes for himself the situation of his action. Action, therefore, is linear and irredeemable; what is next done cannot undo what has been done; the next act must include past acts in an unfolding definition and assertion of self.

Action, it follows, is conditioned in two senses: externally and personally. The actor acts out of an understanding of *where* he is and *what* he is. Error also has a double sense. The actor copes with a situation, and it may be beyond him. But since this situation is in some part of his own making and thus his own responsibility, his error may also be a failure to come to terms with himself. In what follows we will examine Hector's situation from both points of view, first considering the externally imposed limits on his action, then following his acts in linear order; we will first describe the situation of his error and then tell the story of his error.

Action, with its potentiality for honor and shame, is *with* men; in our description of the hero's character we stated his social relations. These relations may be thought of as a set of mutual claims. For each actor the claims of others define his obligations and responsibilities; they tell him the things he ought to do. Since, however, "ought implies can," each claim is also implicitly a praise of the actor, to whom is attributed the power of meeting the claim. To the degree that the actor finds himself relied upon, he also finds himself admired. Honor, as we saw earlier, is the link between altruistic heroism and egoistic. The warrior, finding that others approve him, approves himself; he is therefore driven to act as others would approve. "Honor felt is honor claimed and honor claimed is honor paid."[1]

The hero can claim honor most effectively by honorable acts, primarily by success in combat. The essence of combat as a moral situation lies in the fact that both parties have a chance of victory; otherwise combat becomes mere massacre. "The rage of war is random" (xi.537), as the Homeric proverb has it. The hero goes to combat knowing that the honor he claims may be beyond his reach. His excellence is not so much a power which he has as a hypothesis on which he stakes his life. Combat is a kind of experiment which falsifies the hypothesis of one party or the other. In combat the hero reaches beyond himself and promises himself greatness; he makes himself by asserting himself. Hence the importance of boasting, both before and after combat. Before combat the hero announces that he will win; afterward, that he has won. He goes to action in order to prove in action that he is what he claims to be. Paris never boasts; this is another sign that, while no coward, he is no hero either.

The Homeric hero acts among men, but he also interacts with higher powers. *Euchesthai* means both "to boast" and "to pray."[2] Victory is promised and celebrated in the face of men; it is asked of the gods, in whose gift it is (XVII.498 ff.). The gods are always present in the action; they are not, however, a steadying influence. The gods come and go unpredictably; sometimes the god shows himself, sometimes not, and he may appear to be present when he is not. Any temporary success is probably due to some god, and the hero who hopes to succeed must press his advantages; but at the same time he must be prepared for a sudden shift in the currents of divine assistance and resistance:

> There was a turmoil; incredible acts were done;
> Then they'd have been penned in Ilium like sheep
> But the father of gods and men took instant note.
> With a dread thundering he cast the shining lightning,
> And before the horses of Diomedes it pierced the ground;
> Dread the flicker arose of kindled sulfur,
> And the horses, frightened, shied against the car.
> The shining reins fell from Nestor's hands;
> He feared in his heart, and spoke to Diomedes:
> "Tydeides, turn back in flight your horses.
> Don't you see that Zeus does not grant you valor?
> To him, for now, Cronian Zeus gives fame—
> For today; later to us in our turn, if he likes,
> He will give it. No man can restrain the mind of Zeus,
> Not even the strongest, for he is far the greater."
> There answered him then good-at-the-cry Diomedes:
> "Yes, old man, all that you've said in measure;
> But this dread pain comes on my heart and spirit.
> Hector will one day say to the Trojans assembled:
> 'Tydeides in terror of me went back to the ships.'
> Thus he will boast. May the earth swallow me then."
> There answered him then Gerenian horseman Nestor:
> "Ah, son of bright-hearted Tydeus, what have you said!
> If Hector really calls you a worthless coward,
> The men of Troy and Dardanus will not believe him
> Nor the women of the Trojan noble shieldmen,
> Whose well-grown husbands you have cast in the dust."
>
> (VIII.130–56)

Nestor, the wise elder, states the principle of heroic balance: the hero becomes great by insisting on his own greatness while preserving a proper modesty before the far-greater gods. So long as the god is on his side, this combination is easy; the power of the god flows through the hero and makes him great. When the god withdraws his help, however, the hero is left with his boast without the power to fulfill it. He "gives his boast to another." When victory is no longer possible, he can only withdraw and remember his past victories. The hero who remembers this balance has a chance both to fight and survive. The loss of this balance—as by Patroclus—is the characteristic heroic error. The central ethical problem of the hero is thus a problem of rational knowledge: the hero must continue to act while guided by an exact awareness of how little of his action is truly his own.

GODS AND FATE

We, the audience of the epic, are far better informed about the gods than the heroes are. This inequality of knowledge can give rise to ironies, as when Agamemnon, after Pandarus has broken the truce, speaks of how Zeus hates and punishes those who break treaties (IV. 155–68). We know that this particular truce was broken at the instigation of Athena under the direction of Zeus. For the heroes the divine interventions are erratic and unclear; correlatively, they are able to maintain a hope that the divine power is an ally of human norms. We, who see the gods among themselves, can follow the shifting but coherent process which gives rise to their interventions: we find the gods less erratic but more willful, more frivolous [3] It is part of the terror of the *Iliad* that it shows us a world in which human action is conditioned by powers and purposes even less serious and less moral than our own.

The Homeric gods are, like animals, incapable of error—but for a different reason. The gods are conscious creatures, and, in a sense, are even social; but, since they live forever, no mistake of theirs is irremediable. Whatever they have done or experienced can always be done over or experienced again in some other way. Their mistakes are like their wounds, which heal "as the fig-juice curdles the white milk" (V.902). The gods are defined by their powers and qualities, not by their acts; for in the infinity of time any particular act sinks to insignificance. This point is established early in the *Iliad*, in the conversation between Zeus and Hera which follows Zeus's suggestion that Troy should be spared after all and the Greeks sent home:

> "Dread son of Cronos, what a word you have spoken!
> How are you ready to make labor vain and for nothing,
> The sweat I sweated in toil, and my horses strained,
> Gathering the folk, to Priam's harm and his sons'?
> Do it. But all we other gods will not praise you."
> Then in his anger spoke cloud-gathering Zeus:
> "Strange creature, what harm have Priam and his sons
> Done to you, that your raging is unbroken
> To sack the well-built castle of Ilium?
> If you could but enter their gates and high walls
> And eat them raw, Priam and his sons

And the rest of Troy, that would appease your choler.
Well, do what you like. Let us not start a quarrel,
You and I, some point of strife between us.
But I'll tell you something else, and you remember:
Whenever, driving ahead to sack some city,
I want one where the men have become your friends,
You're not to restrain my choler; you must let me—
For I gave you this willingly, though with unwilling heart.
In fact, beneath the sun and star-set heaven,
Of all the cities where men live on earth
My honors most suit my spirit at sacred Ilium
With Priam and with ash-speared Priam's folk.
My altar was never wanting at their feasts
For wine and fat-steam. That is our share and privilege."
   Then answered him the cow-eyed lady Hera:
"There are three cities much the dearest to me,
Argos and Sparta and wide-wayed Mycenae.
Well, you sack these, if ever you hate them so;
I will not stand before you or begrudge you.
If I were ungenerous and didn't let you sack them,
I'd be forced to be generous, since you are stronger.
So now my labor should not be for nothing;
I am a god too, my breeding is just like yours."

(IV.25–58)

Men and cities are the counters in a game played between the gods. The game can become absorbing, but it is never really worth a quarrel. The gods can always repair their differences by allowing the destruction of another ephemeral human thing. The fall of Troy thus becomes an emblem of the fall of Mycenaean civilization; all the cities will perish as, one after another, they happen to become the objects of divine anger. Whatever man does, in prayer and sacrifice, temples and feasting, is in the end not enough.

Nietzsche wrote, in *The Birth of Tragedy,* "The gods justified human life by living it themselves—the only satisfactory theodicy ever invented." Perhaps; but one could also say that the Homeric gods, by living human life *forever*, reduce our lives to insignificance or remind us that its significance is something privately shared among ourselves. Man, a conscious mortal creature, is between gods and nature. The divine is a sphere of continuous being, nature, of continual becoming. These are spheres of power but not of significance. On this middle earth between the powers men become significant, even godlike, in the eyes of other men. The community creates heroes, who are thus cultural products. From the point of view of the gods, however, the greatest hero is an ephemeral thing of nature.

The Homeric theology is a poet's theology. These gods complete the poem by providing the poet with actors who are outside the action —involved in it and yet finally unconcerned. The gods belong to tragedy not because their intervention is necessary to generate a tragic action—for this, the conflict between man and nature is enough—but because they provide a point of view from which the tragic action can be comprehended. The gods intervene on this side or that and therefore appear as man's allies; yet by their detachment they must always in the end prove themselves his adversaries. Man has achieved a historic existence in spite of nature and the gods.[4]

Beyond the gods there is fate—*moira, aisa,* that which is *peprōmenon.* Fate, however, is not a condition of action nor is it a cause. Everything which happens is according to fate.[5] This is by definition and involves us in a circularity, since what was truly fated is apparent only after the fact. To say that what will be, will be is only a way of saying in the future tense that occurrences occur. Fatalism (as in Hector's last speech to Andromache) is not a view of the future but a way of not thinking about the future.

Fate in fiction, however, has a special sense. The meaning of a work of fiction lies in its unity, in the probability that unites the parts and constitutes a *praxis.* The end is thus implicit in the beginning, and the action is an enactment of the initial situation. It follows that the events are necessary: no other events could so well complete this particular story. In this sense, fate is plot; it may well be that we see events in ordinary life as having a fateful quality when they approximate to the aesthetic unity of a well-made story and thus seem to reveal an implicit meaning.[6]

For the audience of the epic, the outcome is fated in a special sense, for the outline of the story is known before the poem begins. In this sense, fate is history. "We do not deliberate about the fall of Troy," says Aristotle. It is already over, and there is nothing we can do about it. Troy certainly fell; Homer's story of its fall does not tell us *that* it fell but how and by whom it fell.

The epic, as the imitation of an action, is a story of "how" and "by whom." It is therefore a story of free actors and their free choices. Some of these actors (especially if they are gods) at some moments know part of the fated outcome of the action, but this is curiously irrelevant. They are in the position of characters in a play who are aware that they are characters in a play and have been told how the play comes out. The effect is fascinating precisely because it is self-contradictory. They cannot stop being characters in a play, and they cannot stop doing what characters do, namely, making free choices and discovering the consequences. It makes no difference to their activity if they realize that, from the author's point of view, their free choices are determined by the needs of the plot and point toward a predetermined conclusion.[7] Knowledge of fate (since it is knowledge of what cannot be otherwise) is by definition useless knowledge; it adds a dimension of awareness to characters who can do nothing with it in practice.

There is a paradox here which comes to the surface whenever the characters imagine that they could, after all, make the poem come out in some other way. Such imaginings are frequent in the earlier parts of the poem; they drop away as the action gains momentum. Such is Agamemnon's suggestion that the army withdraw, which, while frivolous in Book Two (II.110–41), is perfectly serious in Books Nine and Fourteen (IX.17–28, XIV.65–81). Such is the attempt in Book Three to settle the war by a duel between Menelaus and Paris, and such is the Trojan proposal of a settlement in Book Seven (VII.345–411). Such also is Achilles' notion that he might go home, and here the paradox is made even greater by the strange story of his twin *kēres* (IX.410–16). He says that he has a choice, yet we know that his choice is also determined. In all these attempts "to deliberate about the fall of Troy" there is a certain pathos; we see free characters struggling against the necessities of plot. And to some extent the characters know what we know and see themselves as we see them; they often speak of the fall of Troy as promised or ordained, and they return always with stoic dignity to the enactment of the story in which they find themselves.

It is not really different for the gods, although, since their knowledge (like their power) is greater than man's, the paradox is sharper in their case. Thus when Zeus, in Book Sixteen, proposes to rescue Sarpedon, Hera replies, in a speech which has many echoes of their conversation previously quoted:

> Dread son of Cronos, what a word you have spoken!
> A man who is mortal, long set down to his portion,
> Do you wish to send back, freed from clashing death?
> Do it. But all we other gods will not praise you.
> I'll tell you something else, and you remember:
> If you send Sarpedon alive to his own house,
> Take thought lest some other one of the gods should wish
> To send his own son out of resistless combat.
> Many fight around the great city of Priam,

Sons of immortals; you will raise in them sharp anger.
But if he belongs to you, and your heart cries out,
Still allow him, in the resistless combat,
To fall to the hands of Menoetian Patroclus.
But when the shade has left him and his life,
Then send, to bear him, Death and painless Sleep
Until they come to his house on the Lycian plain.
There his brothers and kinsmen will inter him
With tomb and tombstone—dead men's share and privilege.

                                        (XVI.440–57)

The gods are actors in the *Iliad*, like men, and like men their acts
are conditioned by the order of nature and by the order of the poem.
Gods often save warriors from death in combat, but Sarpedon's death
is not a casual event. In killing Sarpedon, Patroclus passes the limit
set by Achilles and starts the chain of deaths which leads on, through
Patroclus himself, to Hector and, finally, beyond the poem, to Achilles
and the fall of Troy. Does Zeus really propose to break this chain?
Hera does not say that such an act is impossible but that it would be
senseless—*ultra vires*, as it were.[8] Such an irrational intervention would
shatter the plot of the poem; it would also disrupt the relation between
mortals and immortals—in itself a kind of social structure—on which
that plot is based. Sarpedon, she says, can be given a funeral; that is
the proper ending to his story and the fitting close of a life. Zeus
consents, as we, and even he, knew he would. In the sense that it could
not be otherwise, his consent is fated. Fate, however, is not one condition among many; it is the sum of all the conditions of action at the
moments when those conditions combine to give events a definite
direction and form.

In this sense, fate is nature, is the order of the world. The Homeric
gods did not create this world. They too have a *genos*, a "breeding,"
a nature and a place in nature. Not having made the world, the gods
are not responsible for it and have no special obligations toward it.
Being unconcerned, they are free; and, since they are powerful, their
unconcerned freedom is a source of danger to man.

At the same time, the gods are creatures of superior knowledge; they
are thus involved in the action both as actors and as audience. In the
first sense the divine activity is a cause of events; in the second sense
divine activity reflects events and the direction of events. Divine knowledge is returned to the world in the form of signs and omens. When
Zeus in Book Eight lifts his balance, the pan which stands for the
Greeks goes down to the earth. Zeus thunders, and the Greeks are
struck with fear (VIII.66–77). Zeus had planned this defeat for the

Greeks and had put his plan into force at the assembly of the gods (VIII.1–27)—acting, throughout, just as a human king acts. He then looks down on the field and raises his balance in order, as it were, to test whether his plan is being fulfilled. His thunder is a sign of his finding that it is so.

From signs and omens men can learn something about the direction of the events in which they find themselves. But just as the material help provided by divine interventions is temporary and unreliable, so the knowledge provided by signs and omens is unclear and partial. Since the poet shows us the gods among themselves, we can interpret these facts, as the heroes cannot. We see that the divine interventions are erratic because the relations of the gods among themselves are unstable; we see that signs and omens are unclear because the knowledge of the gods themselves is imperfect. They are represented not as full of foreknowledge but as eager spectators of the event as it unfolds. Even Zeus, who never admits to ignorance of the future, does not display much knowledge; he keeps his own counsel.

In all this, the poet protects the dignity of his heroes. No doubt they are less than the gods in power and knowledge, but the difference is one of degree and not of kind. Man has no special obligation to the gods; they are to be feared and, when possible, placated or even enlisted as allies, but they do not deserve much respect. When Asius cries out to Zeus, "So it turns out that you too are a lover of lies" (XII. 164), our sympathies are with Asius. The gods do not provide man with guidance or solutions; they are rather an objectification of his problem. Vis-à-vis the gods, humanity appears as an embattled species defending an uncertain perimeter with inferior forces. The gods are not outside the world; they are, like us, creatures within the world, with whom we contend.

THE PLAN OF ZEUS

Hector also contends with the god; the originating source of Hector's story in the *Iliad* is the Plan of Zeus.[9] Yet the Plan of Zeus is not directed at Hector; Hector is merely a convenient agent of Zeus's purposes. The Plan of Zeus originates in the inhibition of Achilles' act. The *Iliad* is not two hundred lines old when Achilles is ready to kill Agamemnon; Athena appears behind Achilles, takes him by the hair, and prevents him. She promises Achilles "threefold gifts" (I.212) in recompense for Agamemnon's *hubris*. From this promise, and the gods' attempt to fulfill it, springs the whole action of the *Iliad*.

At the end of Book One, Thetis appeals to Zeus to fulfill her *eeldōr*, her claimed recompense for past service. Thetis asks for a Trojan victory. By this means, the Greeks will be forced to offer Achilles the "threefold gifts." Zeus secretly grants this petition and thus provokes Hera to rage. But it was Hera who had instigated Athena's original intervention and promise (I.208). The *Iliad* thus begins with a certain confusion of purpose among the gods. Hera and Athena want Achilles and Agamemnon reconciled, but not at the price of a Trojan victory. There is no sign that they have an alternative plan.

The Plan of Zeus is enacted in Book Eight. Hector gains the offensive and drives the Greeks back within their wall. All this takes place against the protests and resistance of Athena and Hera; Zeus, while he tries to keep them out of the action (at one point threatening to lame their horses, dump them from their chariot, and break it to pieces [VIII.402–3]), treats these goddesses rather carefully. He smiles on Athena (VIII.38), grants the *eeldōr* of Hera by saving the Greeks from total destruction (VIII.242–46), and goes to some trouble to explain to both of them exactly what he is doing (VIII.438–82). Zeus blusters, but he gives the impression of a ruler who is trying to satisfy one part of his constituency without losing the support of the other. We, as audience, know that Zeus is supporting the Trojans for special reasons, that his support is temporary, and that the powerful forces ranged against Troy are only just barely being kept in check.

None of this, of course, is known to Hector. He knows only that Zeus has given the victory and that night has come before he could make his victory complete. This difference between our knowledge and his provides an ironic setting for Hector's speech in the assembly, concluding Book Eight:

> Hear me, Trojans, Dardanoi, and allies:
> I thought we'd destroy the ships and the Achaeans
> And then return to wind-swept Ilium.
> But the dark night fell first, which chiefly saved
> The Argives and the ships by the ocean strand.
> So now let us trust ourselves to the dark night
> And make ready a meal. The fair-maned horses
> We'll unhitch from the chariots; we'll give them fodder.
> From the city bring oxen and fat sheep
> Quickly; supply us with wine that honeys the heart
> And bread from your halls; collect wood in plenty
> So that all the night, until early-breaking dawn
> We may kindle many fires, and their flash reach heaven,
> Lest somehow even by night the long-haired Achaeans
> Set off in flight across the broad-backed ocean.
> Not without struggle or contest they'll board their ships,
> But one or another can nurse his wound at home

When he's stuck by an arrow or the whetted spear
As he jumps for his boat; the next time men will shrink
From raising tear-filled war against Trojan horsemen.
Let the heralds, agents of Zeus, instruct the town
That the boys just grown and the elders gray at the temples
Collect in the city by the god-built gates,
And the women, too, the wives—let each in her halls
Kindle a great fire; let the watch be steady,
Lest raiders enter the town while the host is gone.
So be it, great-hearted Trojans, as I instruct you.
Let this be the speech which is soundly said for now;
At dawn I will further instruct the Trojan horsemen.
I claim my hope from Zeus and the other gods:
To drive from here these dogs borne by the death-bringers,
Whom the death-bringers brought here on their black ships.
So for the night we'll stand guard for ourselves;
In the morning, early, we'll clothe ourselves in armor
And by the hollow ships wake whetted war.
I'll see if Tydean mighty Diomedes
Can drive me from his ship-wall, or if I
Subdue him with bronze and fetch the bloody armor.
Tomorrow he comes to the test of prowess, if only
He waits for my spear, as it comes. In the foremost
I see him lying wounded, and around him many companions
As the sun rises tomorrow. If only I
Could be immortal and ageless all my days,
Honored as are honored Athena, Apollo,
So surely this day brings evil upon the Argives.

(VIII.497–541)

This is a balanced and rational speech; Hector shows himself a thoughtful commander. He pays proper attention to logistics, secures his camp, and takes steps to avoid being outflanked. At the same time, the speech, while rational, is superbly confident. Hector's only fear is that the Greeks will escape insufficiently punished. "I claim my hope," he says—*euchomai elpomenos*; this may also be translated "I hopefully pray" or "I confidently boast." Hector promises himself the godlike standing of the victor.

We know that Hector is fated to fail; the pathos of the speech, however, does not lie in his boasting, for boasting, as we saw, is the proper prelude to battle. Hector sees a chance of victory, and he boldly reaches out for it. As in single combat the combatant stakes his life on the hypothesis of victory, so Hector here stakes his whole army. It is the task of the good commander to find a favorable moment for such risks.

The pathos of the speech lies in Hector's relation to the gods. He has won with god's help, and the gods are always fickle, but this truth has a special meaning in his case. Hector is being used as Zeus's instrument in order to prepare for Achilles' return to battle, and Achilles, when he returns, will drive the Trojans back. It is not, therefore, simply that Zeus's help is temporary; Zeus's intention is fundamentally hostile to the Trojans. Hector is in a trap, and the Trojans with him; every success brings them closer to disaster.

Hector's mistake here is made from ignorance, an ignorance which he has no means of improving. There is no failure within his own character; his mistake is therefore not a tragic error, although it prepares for the tragic error to come.

In the battles of Book Eight and the Greek assembly and council, the Plan of Zeus is brought to completion. The Greeks are defeated; Agamemnon is forced to humble himself and appeal to Achilles. Thetis' original prayer has been fulfilled. Its object, however, is left unfulfilled —for Achilles refuses the reconciliation.

We have considered the place of this refusal in the story of Achilles. In the wider story of the armies, also, Achilles' refusal of the embassy is the master stroke of plot-making by the poet of the *Iliad*; for when the intention even of Zeus is left incomplete, the action passes beyond the will of any of the actors, even of the gods; the unfolding situation comes to dominate all those involved in it.

Achilles' rejection of the embassy has the effect of postponing his return to battle for twenty-four hours. These twenty-four hours fill ten books of the poem, from the end of Book Eight to the end of Book Eighteen. This day is the Great Day of Battle of the *Iliad*; first come the eve-of-battle preliminaries, then the slow unfolding of the battle itself. This part of the poem is long and difficult; the poet makes his effects by massive accumulation of detail and slightly varied repetitions. At the same time, we begin to get a sense of the war as a single event; battle is more than a succession of hand-to-hand combats and comes to have a disciplined, tactical character. The armies rely less on the valor of individuals and more on the organization of their troops. For this one day, the forces are balanced and the outcome seems really in doubt. The Greeks are defeated on the plain and organize a defense of their wall; this defense is also defeated, and the Trojans drive into the ships; the Greeks counterattack, and their counterattack is in turn defeated. Patroclus and the Myrmidons enter the battle and drive the Trojans out of the ships and across the plain, but before the walls of Troy the advantage inclines once more to the Trojans. Night falls on the two armies in much the same situation in which first light had found them; the Trojans have again recovered the initiative but through the whole day have not really gained a yard of ground.

The Great Day of Battle is the middle of the *Iliad*, the time between the stating of the situation and its resolution.[10] Hector is the central figure of this day; the fortunes of war shift as Hector advances and retreats. Both the death of Asius (XII.174) and the valor of Sarpedon are in the service of Hector's success (XII.436–37). Hector repeats to Ajax on the battlefield the boast he had made to the Trojan assembly (XIII.825–28). Nor is it clear that his boast is irrational. Agamemnon, for one, believes that it is about to be accomplished (XIV.44–48). Zeus is on Hector's side; early in the day he saves Hector from harm (XI. 163–64) and then sends him a message, promising him success until dark (XI.181–209). Hera beguiles Zeus in order to make possible the wounding of Hector; when Zeus returns to his senses, he immediately orders Hector healed and returned to battle. Zeus has promised Hector one more day of victory, and he keeps this promise.

In all this, Zeus's motives are unclear. Obviously, his support of Hector is a continuation of the Plan of Zeus, but the Plan of Zeus has already failed. Zeus is continuing a policy which has become aimless and, being aimless, without definite limits. Does he really propose to continue Hector's victories until Achilles returns to the war? But Achilles, by saying that he would wait until battle reached his own ships, has committed himself to inaction (XVI.61–63). Hector can destroy the whole Greek army providing he stays away from Achilles' Myrmidons, and Achilles grants him that much intelligence or caution (IX.654–55). Thus the Plan of Zeus, in unexpected combination with Achilles' refusal of the embassy, has given Hector a real opportunity to defeat the Greeks—an opportunity vitiated only by the intervention of Patroclus.

Already in Book Eight Zeus refers to Patroclus' death:

> He will not cease from war, this mighty Hector,
> Until he has raised by the ships swift-footed Achilles
> On that day when they fight by the sterns of his ships
> In the dread narrows around the dead Patroclus.
> So it is fixed and spoken.
>
> (VIII.473–77)

These lines should shock us. The death of Patroclus cannot have been part of the Plan of Zeus, for that plan was a response to the prayers of Thetis and Achilles, and the death of Patroclus was desired by neither. Through the death of Patroclus the Plan of Zeus is fulfilled, but not as Achilles, Thetis, or Zeus had willed it. Patroclus' death is a consequence of the free choices of Achilles, of Nestor, and of Patroclus himself. While it is part of the story of the *Iliad.* and therefore of the fatality of the poem as known to Zeus, Patroclus' death is a consequence, not of the success of the Plan of Zeus, but rather of its failure.

Late in the Great Day of Battle, Zeus, making his peace with Hera, restates his Plan:

> Let Phoebus Apollo urge on Hector to battle,
> Breathing force in him, forgetful of pain,
> Which now afflicts his heart; let the Achaeans
> Be turned in the press of cowardly rout;
> And as they fly, let them fall on the benched ships
> Of Achilles. He will send forth his companion,
> Patroclus. Shining Hector's spear will kill him
> Before Ilium, when he's killed many vigorous men
> And especially among them my own son Sarpedon.
> In his rage for this, Achilles will kill Hector,
> And from then on a retreat away from the ships
> I would contrive, right through, until Achaeans
> Take steep Ilium through Athena's council.
> Until then I'll not stop my rage, nor allow
> Any immortal to come to the help of the Danaoi
> Until Achilles' desire has come to pass
> As I promised first, and nodded with my head
> On the day when goddess Thetis took my knees
> Imploring honor for city-sacking Achilles.

> (XV.59–77)

There is a harsh irony here, for Achilles' desire (*eeldōr*) is fulfilled in the way in which he least desired it. Zeus's knowledge of the future seems to become fuller as the situation unfolds; correlatively, he seems less in control of events. He grants Thetis what she asked for but not what she wanted, and the fulfillment of his Plan brings disaster on both Thetis and Achilles. "The Olympian has brought it all to pass," says Achilles, "but what pleasure can I take in it?" (XVIII.79–80). Achilles returns to battle, not because his quarrel with Agamemnon is resolved, but because something far worse has happened to him. Achilles' earlier vow, to wait until the Greeks reached his own ships, has become irrelevant. Probably it is significant that Zeus, in both passages quoted, refers to a rout or battle actually among the ships of Achilles, as if, in some form, Achilles were to keep his earlier vow. Even Zeus's foreknowledge is slightly in error, slightly simplified. The knowledge of the wisest is imperfect, the plans of the most powerful actors are distorted by circumstance. The story of the *Iliad* is not made by any actor, even by Zeus; all are within it, and the story unfolds through the interactions of the choices of gods and men.

As the forces against him—embodied in Achilles and Zeus—are seen to weaken, Hector becomes a stronger figure. The Great Day of Battle is for him a day of possibility and hope and also of ignorance and incipient failure. Hector, without knowing it, is engaged in a contest with Zeus. The tendency of the Plan of Zeus is to determine Hector's actions and reduce him to an instrument. As Zeus loses control of the action, Hector in a sense wins the contest. In another sense Hector loses, for the action sweeps him on to a disaster watched and consented to by Zeus. But neither is Zeus the victor. Hector kills Patroclus; this was not part of the Plan of Zeus. Hector's own death follows, and this was not part of the Plan of Zeus either. Thus the culminating event of the *Iliad*, while in a certain sense latent in the initial situation of the poem, comes to pass only as that situation unfolds through a complex chain of actions, reactions, and mistakes. Hector's own choices are links in that chain, so that his death, while in some general sense fated and necessary, is also, when and as it occurs, the consequence of his own errors and chosen by himself.

It follows that we can also read Hector's story as a contest with himself, a struggle to maintain his understanding of how small a part of his action is truly his own. As Hector becomes the central actor, the pressures of the situation focus on him; he finds it harder to think and becomes a reactor, an instrument of the situation. By a paradox, therefore, on this one day when events, more than anywhere else in the poem, are determined by Hector's free choice, Hector becomes less free. He gives himself over to the situation, and he changes. Already in Book Eight Hector's vaunting to Diomedes (VIII.161–66) strikes a new note. He has become less modest, and, more important, he becomes predictable. He does exactly what Diomedes a few lines earlier had said he would do. This predictability is later set forth in a simile:

> The Trojans struck ahead in a mass; Hector commanded,
> Pushing straight down, like a rolling stone from the crag
> Which a river in torrent carries away from the crest,
> With its flood breaking the props of the careless crag.
> It leaps and flies through the air, and crunches beneath it
> The brush. And it still rushes forward, until it comes
> To the plain. It rolls no more then, try as it may.
> Thus Hector threatened a while as far as the sea
> To sweep, with ease through Achaean huts and ships,

Killing. But when he met with the solid ranks,
He stopped, hard-pressed.

(XIII.136–46)

Earlier Hector was compared to a river (V.597–600); here he is compared to an object swept along by a river. Having made his choice, Hector commits himself to it and becomes the instrument of his own determination. He will go as far as the impetus of his charge takes him. In action he is free only as a dropped stone is free to follow the laws of gravitation.

HECTOR AND POLYDAMAS

Insofar as the tragic story turns on the ethical ambiguity of the hero, it is a story internal to the hero. In order to make it lucid, the poet may have to create a figure who will dramatize the hero's relation with himself. In the *Iliad* that figure is Polydamas.

Polydamas exists in the *Iliad* only on the Great Day of Battle. He makes his first appearance as that day begins and Zeus sends down his rain of blood (XI.57). In the books that follow he is frequently mentioned among the commanders, and when Hector is wounded he even makes one independent appearance as a warrior (XIV.449–74). But his most important appearances are those in which he gives Hector advice. Polydamas is the son of one of Priam's councillors (see III.146); he functions as Hector's *alter ego*, the voice in his ear of warning or restraint.

When Hector first drives the Greeks within their defenses, his horses neigh in fear, perched on the edge of the ditch (XII.51–52). Polydamas takes charge:

Hector, leaders among the Trojans and allies:
It is folly to drive swift horses through the ditch.
It is very hard to cross. The spikes within it
Stand up sharp; behind them is the wall.
There is no way to get through or to fight
With horses. It's narrow. I think we'll come to grief.
If in the fullness of malice thundering Zeus
Diminishes their strength and helps the Trojans,
Then I would wish to seek a quick result:
The Greeks should die here nameless, far from Argos.
But if they push us back, and we retreat
From the ships and become tangled in the ditch,
Not even the news of us, I think, will come
Back to the city when we've been trapped by the Greeks.
Come, I will state it, let us all obey:

143

Let the drivers hold the horses by the ditch
While we, on foot, clothed in all our armor,
All follow Hector together. Then the Greeks
Will stand no more, if the hour of destruction
Has reached them.

(XII.61–79)

Polydamas advises Hector much as Nestor had earlier advised Diomedes. The good commander must remember to read the currents of
divine favor and be prepared for a shift; an attack may at any moment
become a retreat, and the commander must see his way in both directions. This advice pleases Hector (XII.80), and he takes it, as he has
always taken advice before. Polydamas is still counseling an advance.
A few lines later Hector and Polydamas are no longer of one mind:

Still they struggled, stationed by the ditch,
And a bird came to them as they strove across it,
A high-flying eagle, skirting the army's left,
Holding a huge scarlet snake in its talons,
Alive still, twitching. Nor did it give up the fight.
It struck the one who held it between chest and neck,
Twisting backward. And he dropped it to the ground,
Hurting with pain, and it fell in the midst of the army
While he gave a cry and flew off down the wind.
The Trojans shivered to see the shining snake
Which lay among them, a portent from Zeus of the aegis.
　Polydamas then stood by bold Hector and spoke:
"Hector, you always chide me in the assemblies
For my good advice, since it suits you not at all
That our speeches differ among the folk, or in council
Or in battle, but your power should be ever increased.
Still, now I will tell you as I think it best.
Let us not go among the Greek ships to fight.
For thus it will come out, I think, if truly
This bird came to the Trojans, striving to cross,
A high-flying eagle, skirting the army's left,
Holding a huge scarlet snake in his talons,
Alive. But he dropped it before he could get it home,
Nor managed to carry it back to his own children.
So we, even if wall and gate of the Greeks
We break in the fullness of strength, and the Greeks give way,
Yet we'll retrace our path from the ships in no order,
Many Trojans we'll leave here, whom the Achaeans
With bronze will slaughter as they defend their ships.
That's what a seer would tell you, who clear in his heart
Knew about portents, and the host would obey him."

Then Hector scowled at him and spoke in answer:
"Polydamas, no longer do you speak to my taste.
You know how to make some other better statement.
But if you really speak this seriously,
Then it turns out the gods have crippled your wits,
Since you tell us to forget thundering Zeus
And his plans, which he promised to me himself and agreed to.
You there, you tell us to trust the fluttering birds;
But I don't let them turn me, nor do I note them,
Whether they go to the right, to the eastern sun,
Or to the left and the darkness of the west.
We will trust in the plan of mighty Zeus
Who of all the immortals and mortals is the king.
One ominous bird is best: to defend our country.
Why are you so afraid of war and battle?
Even if all the rest of us are killed here
By the Argive ships, there's no fear you will perish.
You have no heart for war or an enemy's charge.
But if you slack in battle, or anyone else
You seduce with your words and dissuade him from war,
With a quick blow of my spear you will lose your own life.

(XII.199–250)

This is the beginning of Hector's error. He is unable to hear Polydamas' advice; he is caught up in the momentum of his charge. Zeus
has promised him success; the omen (which is also from Zeus) warns
of failure. We know the meaning of the ambiguity: Zeus intends a
Trojan victory leading to a Trojan defeat. Hector is unable to resolve
the ambiguity and ignores it.

Polydamas accuses Hector of megalomania; Hector accuses Polydamas
of cowardice. Both are wrong, yet both see something true. Thought
is the necessary complement of action, yet thought and action are
antagonists. Deliberation can become an excuse for inaction; the actor
must be decisive, which means that at a certain moment he must stop
thinking and stop listening. He must rely on his hope that the determination he has already made is correct. This hope, since it is a form
of self-reliance, easily converts itself into a conviction that, since the
choice is his, it must be correct.

Hector and Polydamas are talking on a battlefield. In this context
even Hector's violence—his threat to kill Polydamas if he says another
word—is acceptable, in the sense that, if Hector's judgment of the
situation is correct, we will find his violence justified. Reason and
communication are necessary casualties of war. Hector is fated to fail,
and therefore his violence is an error. But it is a noble error and en-

gages our sympathy. Polydamas is right and Hector is wrong, but we are on Hector's side. Polydamas, after all, does not have some alternate plan for defeating the Greeks; he can only advise caution. He is not himself an actor; he is merely a counselor. Even if Hector takes his advice, the responsibility remains with Hector. In rejecting Polydamas, Hector is doing his best to meet his responsibilities. He makes the error that a good man would make.

Hector's charge takes him within the wall, and the battle sways this way and that. Polydamas intervenes again:

> Hector, there's no way to get you to trust advice.
> Because of your gifts from the god in works of war
> You want also to excel all men in counsel.
> But you haven't the power to take all things on yourself.
> One man has gifts from god in works of war,
> Another man in dance, another in music and song;
> Another has a mind within him from Zeus
> Which is good, and many men profit from it;
> It saves cities, but he knows it best himself.
> So I will speak as seems to me the best:
> The ring of war is round you every way.
> The warrior Trojans, now they've crossed the wall,
> Draw back in armor, while some others fight
> As less with more, scattered about the ships.
> But give some ground, and call the princes here;
> Then we can discuss some general plan:
> Either to throw ourselves among the many-benched ships
> If the god would give us power, or else
> Withdraw from the ships unharmed. I for my part
> Fear the Achaeans yet will even the score
> From yesterday. By the ships a man hungry for war
> Lingers; not long do I think he'll hold from battle.

(XIII.726–47)

This is the first reference in Trojan councils to the return of Achilles to battle. Polydamas cannot see the whole Plan of Zeus, but he can, so to speak, see around the corner of it. Hector does not respond to this point, but Polydamas' speech pleases him; he goes off to organize the council. The officers he is seeking, however, are all dead or wounded; no council takes place, because none is possible. Thus we are reminded that Hector cannot act well simply by taking advice. Polydamas' advice is always rational, but it is not always correct. The poet dramatizes his point with some subtlety. He has created Polydamas in order to show us that Hector's noble strength and authority carry with them certain characteristic weaknesses. Then (lest we take him too simply) he undercuts Polydamas as well. Action is conditioned by the limits of power; it is the task of deliberation to determine these limits, to find what is possible. But deliberation, also, is conditioned—by the limits of knowledge; it also is situated in the world and therefore liable to imperfection.

HECTOR'S ERROR

When Hector is wounded, the Greeks rally; when Zeus heals Hector, the Trojans return to the charge. Their renewed momentum carries them among the ships; Hector holds tight to a stern and shouts to his army. His words mark a new stage in his error:

> Bring fire, and hurl yourselves in a mass into the fray!
> Now Zeus gives us the one day that pays for all;
> To seize the ships which came here against gods' will
> And brought us so much pain, by the cowardice of elders
> Who, when I wanted to fight by the ships' sterns,
> Held me back before and restrained the folk.
> But even if then Zeus crippled these wits
> Of ours, today he himself sends and instructs us.
>
> (XV.718–25)

The novelty here is not in the flat misreading of fatality but in Hector's scornful words about the elders. The megalomania which Polydamas saw in him is becoming actual; he, who has acted always as his community's guard and servant, here for a moment sets himself up against it. This is the moment of Hector's greatest success and greatest pride; but since it is also a moment in which he isolates himself, we see it as a moment of great vulnerability. We are not carried with him in his joy of conquest; we watch him with compassion because we can see the outlines of the coming catastrophe.

At this point the Plan of Zeus turns its corner, and Achilles' Myrmidons come into battle. Hector knows that victory has shifted sides, "but even so he stayed to save his companions" (XVI.362–63). The Trojans are gradually pushed back; in the struggle around Sarpedon's body Zeus intervenes:

> Into Hector first he put an unvalorous heart;
> He mounted his chariot and retreated, calling
> The Trojans to fly—for he knew the balance of Zeus.
>
> (XVI.656–58)

Here Hector is acting as Polydamas would have him act. He has gone forward with divine favor as far as he could; when that favor leaves him, he leads his troops in retreat.

147

So far Hector has not made any objective error. We have seen him change from a state of simple ignorance (at the end of Book Eight) to a condition of ignorance become dogmatic, self-confirming. We have seen him become less modest, less responsive, and more harsh, as when he threatens to feed his own troops to the dogs (XV.351). The potentiality for error is there—but there is a further transition, centering on the death of Patroclus.

In killing Patroclus, Hector is the instrument of Apollo. Patroclus, "greatly deluded" (XVI.685) and forgetting Achilles' instructions, attacks the wall of Troy. Three times Apollo beats him back and the fourth time warns him to stand clear; Patroclus withdraws (XVI.702–11). Apollo then goes to Hector and, taking the shape of Asius, his mother's brother, urges him to attack Patroclus, promising him Apollo's help. Hector pursues Patroclus, and Patroclus kills Hector's brother, Cebriones, who has been serving as Hector's charioteer since the previous day (see VIII.318–19). Patroclus and Hector contend over Cebriones' body. Three times Patroclus drives forward, each time killing nine of his enemies (XVI.785);[11] on his fourth charge, Apollo, invisible, strikes him across the back:

> His helmet he struck from his head, did Phoebus Apollo;
> It rolled with a clang under the feet of the horses,
> With its eyeholes and sockets; the plumes were all begrimed
> With blood and dust. Before it was not permitted
> That the horse-plumed helmet be begrimed with dust.
> It protected the head and face of a divine man,
> Handsome Achilles. But then god gave it to Hector
> To wear on his head, for his own destruction was close.
>
> (XVI.793–800)

There is a tone of magic and mystery in this scene—a touch of ritualization in the repetition of "three times . . . and on the fourth . . . ," and a special touch of divine deception in Apollo's reference to himself while disguised as a mortal: Apollo-Asius, saying that he is weak while Hector is strong, appeals to Hector to use his strength as he ought (XVI.721–23); Apollo thus uses Hector's moral sense to trap him. Achilles' helmet, worn into battle by Patroclus, was before not permitted—*ou themis*—to be defiled; now the line of *themis*, propriety, is crossed, in preparation for the destruction of Hector. The whole scene is a brief, dramatic recapitulation of the Plan of Zeus: Hector is granted a victory which entails his own death.

Euphorbus runs out of the crowd and wounds Patroclus, then runs back. Hector, following close behind, runs Patroclus through with his spear and boasts over his dying enemy:

"Patroclus, it seems you said you would sack my city,
The Trojan women you would make your slaves
And carry them in your ships to your own country.
Fool. Before that happened the horses of Hector
Brought him into the war. I with my spear
Excel among warlike Trojans; I keep off
The day of compulsion. The vultures can eat you here.
Poor thing. Great though he is, Achilles failed,
Who stayed behind and gave you so many instructions:
'Don't come back to me here, Patroclus, horse-ruler,
To the hollow ships, until from man-killing Hector
You've stripped the bloody shirt from off his chest.'
So he told you, and you in your folly believed him."
    Then feebly you gave him answer, Patroclus, horseman:
"For the moment, Hector, boast as you will; he gave you
Victory, Cronian Zeus, and Apollo who slays,
Easily. Those two took my armor from me.
Such as *you* are, if twenty men had attacked me,
They all would have died before my slaying spear—
But the portion that destroys and Apollo killed me
And, of men, Euphorbus; you come as the third to despoil me.
I'll tell you something else, and you remember:
Not for you either will life be long; right now
Death stands close by you, and your ruling fate,
To be slain by the hands of blameless Aeacid Achilles."
    So he spoke, and finished death concealed him.
His image went from his face down into Hades,
Wailing its fate, leaving his youth and manhood.
And to him dead there answered shining Hector:
"Patroclus, why do you prophesy sharp destruction?
Who knows if Achilles, son of fair-tressed Thetis,
Will not go before, his life struck down by my spear?"

                                                (XVI.830–61)

Hector, of course, is exactly wrong about Achilles' instructions to Patroclus; his boast, therefore, has an entirely hollow ring. Hector does not act in error when he kills Patroclus—to kill Patroclus is his task—but he is acting blindly. Through Patroclus his fate comes to meet him; we see it, but Hector does not. He does not hear the knowl-‘ edge in Patroclus' dying voice; he still speaks of combat as a testing ground for balanced forces. But as the story gathers momentum, the battlefield becomes the stage where fated outcomes are enacted. As Hector puts on the arms of Patroclus, Zeus looks down on him and speaks:

Poor fool, you're not so desirous of this death
Which is close to you now. But you wear the immortal arms
Of the best man, whom others also fear.
You killed his comrade, who was gentle and forceful,
And wrongly you took the arms from his head and shoulders;
In return I now guarantee great force against you
In payment for that. You'll not return from the battle,
Nor will your wife receive the arms of Achilles.

(XVII.201–8)

The story proceeds by the interplay of character and action. In action Hector's character changes. The Plan of Zeus sets him in motion; once in motion, he is possessed by his own action. He is, as it were, pinned to the battle line, committed to accept what comes his way. Patroclus comes, and in killing Patroclus Hector seals his own fate. There is a tragic irony here, for what seems to him a victory both easy and glorious in fact brings Hector to his own death.[12]

On the Great Day of Battle Hector becomes incapable of retreat. This incapability is Hector's error, which is thus not embodied in any one act but in the change in his character. To be incapable of retreat is in a certain way noble, but it is also, like any incapacity, a weakness, a loss of the fullness of human potentiality. And since retreat, for Hector, means also going home, going back to the city for which he is fighting, the Hector who is incapable of retreat is also a Hector who has lost contact with that social order which defined and generated his heroism. Having become isolated, Hector becomes expendable. Thus the poet, while maintaining our compassion for Hector, at the same time elicits our consent to his death. It is not that we find that Hector deserves to die but that we see a probability and a necessity in it.

At the end of the Great Day of Battle Achilles appears at the wall and looks out on the field. A flash shines from him like the fire of a burning city; he shouts three times, in a voice like the trumpet of a besieging army, and the sheer force of his voice drives the Trojans back. The catastrophe of the following day is foreshadowed. This day ends, like its predecessor, with a Trojan assembly; here Hector and Polydamas have their last encounter, and the *alter ego* quality of Polydamas is stressed:

They held their assembly standing, nor did anyone dare
To sit. Fear held them all, since Achilles
Had shown himself, though he'd long withdrawn from battle;
Then Polydamas took breath and began to speak,

Panthous' son. He alone looked forward and back.
He was Hector's companion, born on the same night;
He excelled in words, as Hector excelled with the spear.
In the fullness of his mind he spoke and addressed them.
"Think it through both ways, friends. Here is my advice:
Go back to the city, don't wait here for dawn
In the plain, by the ships. We are far, here, from the wall.
While that man was still angry with Agamemnon,
The Argives, then, were easier to war with;
I myself was pleased to camp by the swift ships,
Hoping we'd take the ships with curving sides.
Now I'm in terrible fear of swift-footed Achilles.
The heart in him is so forceful, nor will he wish
To stay in the plain, there where the Greeks and Trojans
Divide and share the force of Ares between them—
He would rather fight for our city and our women.
Let's go to the city. Trust me. For thus it will be:
Just now the night holds back swift-footed Achilles,
Sweet-smelling night. But if he finds us here
Tomorrow, coming in armor, each of you
Will know him. You'll be glad to come to Troy,
Whoever escapes, and many the dogs and vultures
Will eat. God spare me from such news.
If we trust my words, unpleasing though they are,
All night we'll assemble our strength; the city towers
And the high gates and the doors that are fixed upon them,
Tall and well polished, we'll keep tightly bolted.
In the morning, early, we'll clothe ourselves in armor
And stand to the towers. It will be the worse for him
Should he leave the ships and fight us by the walls.
Back he will go to the ships, when his high-necked horses
Have had their fill of racing about the city.
His heart will not let him force his way within it,
Nor will he sack it thus. But the dogs would eat him."
    Then Hector scowled at him and spoke in answer:
"Polydamas, no more do you speak to my taste,
Since you tell us to huddle together, back in the city.
Have you not had enough of huddling within the towers?
One time the men of this earth called Priam's city
Always by the name of 'gold-rich,' 'bronze-rich';
Now the laid-away treasures are gone from the buildings.
Much has gone to Phrygia and Maeonia,
Sold property, since Zeus in his malice harmed us.
Now, just when the son of wily Cronos gave me
Renown by the ships, and to drive the Greeks in the sea,

You fool, you're not to show these thoughts to the folk.
No Trojan will trust you. I will not allow it.
Come: I will state it, let us all obey:
Take your meal throughout the host in order;
Post the sentries, and each of you stay awake.
Any Trojan distressed beyond bounds for his goods
Should pass them out to the folk for public consumption.
Better that *they* should have them than the Achaeans.
In the morning, early, we'll clothe ourselves in armor
And by the hollow ships wake whetted war.
If, truly, bright Achilles is roused by the ships,
The worse for him, if he likes, it'll be. I at least
Won't run from the sound of war, but face to face
I'll stand, to know if his power is greater, or mine.
War strikes both ways, and the slayer becomes the slain."
    So Hector spoke, and the Trojans shouted assent,
Fools. For Athena took from them their wits.
They approved of Hector, though his plan was wrong.
Not one man heard Polydamas' good advice.

(XVIII.246–313)

This is error pure and simple, and the poet makes sure that we know it. Hector has been overtaken by the disease diagnosed by Thucydides: "Hope and desire, one pushing and the other pulling . . . do the greatest harm. . . . And chance also counsels them to make the attempt, for sometimes unexpectedly she takes a hand and so leads people to run risks with inferior resources, especially when cities are fighting for the greatest stakes. Each man, supported by the rest, has an irrationally exaggerated opinion of himself" (Thucydides 3.45). There is something suicidal in Hector's talk of giving away property to keep it from enemy hands; he proposes a desperate gamble against the odds.

Yet Hector is not being merely irrational. At this late moment the poet suddenly shows us why the Trojans cannot remain on the defensive, why Andromache's appeal—to "station the folk by the fig tree" (VI.433) and hold the walls—is mere women's words. The Greek host outnumbers the warriors of Troy by a ratio of better than ten to one (II.123–28). Troy is defended by its allies; of these, many are descendants of Dardanus or linked with Priam's house through marriage, but many are not. When the implications of this fact sink in, we understand why Glaucus and Sarpedon are an appropriate chorus on the Trojan side; having come the greatest distance—"from far off Lycia, by twisting Xanthus" (II.877)—they are the most detached from the

Trojan cause. We understand why the poet puts such weight on Sarpedon's complaint to Hector in Book Five (ll.472–92) and Glaucus' complaint in Book Seventeen (ll.142–68). Hector's greatest strategic problem, like Agamemnon's, is that of keeping his allies in the field.[13] Agamemnon offers chiefly the incentive of the wealth of Troy, which is to go to those who sack it. Hector offers the same incentive, not for the future but in present distributions to the city's defenders—"gifts and maintenance" (XVII.225). The wealth of Troy is disappearing as it is being fought over (see IX.401–3, XXIV.543–48). Hector cannot hold the enemy off forever; he can save his city only if he defeats them while his resources last.

The poet, by saving this argument for such a late point in Hector's story, helps to maintain our sympathy with the hero. We see him going wrong and at the same moment see an important reason on his side. Yet it is also true that at this point in his story Hector's argument appears less as a reason than as a rationalization. With the death of Patroclus, Hector's future takes on a definite shape; his actions come to be ruled by fate. Whatever reasons he gives to himself and to others must appear to be justifications for what, in any case, cannot be otherwise.

If the poet had allowed Hector to know and state the whole rationale of his acts at the beginning, we would have had a quite different story. We can imagine an *Iliad* in which, at the end of Book Eight, Hector had described to his army the desperate gamble which lay before them and the necessity for taking such a gamble. Hector would then have gone into action with his eyes open, with the possibility of failure always before him and previously accounted for. Such a hero would have remained detached from the action in both success and failure, and his story would have had a very different pathos. There would have been no error, since to take a necessary risk and fail is simply misfortune.

THE DEATH OF HECTOR

The tragic hero does not engage our affections merely because his needs outrun his resources, or his problems their solutions. The hero's drama is, at least in part, internal to himself, and his failure is a failure of self-knowledge and self-definition. Our pity and terror are evoked partly by the realization that virtue can be inadequate to circumstance, but they are evoked much more deeply by the realization that virtue itself is not immune to circumstance, that in action it can turn to vice. In learning something about the interrelation between the virtues and their circumstances we learn something about the interaction between an individual and his community. The dilemmas of the hero are enactments of the contradictory cultural setting in which he finds himself. In our most abstract description of it, we can describe Hector's error as an enactment of the contradiction between the two heroisms: altruistic and egotistic.

The community, out of its collective needs and aspirations, creates heroes. It prescribes for certain men specific tasks, demands of them specific virtues, and offers specific rewards. The hero thus grows into a role and an identity; like all of us, he knows who he is, in that he is defined by others. Heroism, however, is not merely one social role among many; it has a special status because it demands risk. The hero is expected to prove himself in combat. His social role therefore always lies before him, as something to be achieved. His self-definition is a boast and a promise he makes to himself and to others.

In victory the hero's self-definition and his social task are a single thing; in defeat they break apart. The defeated hero has proved himself not to be what he claimed to be. He is (so long as his community survives) as necessary to it as ever; his capacities are not less merely because they have proved for the moment inadequate to circumstance. But the identity and self-definition which maintained him in his role have been undercut. The hero who can hold to heroic balance overcomes this moment of stress; he retreats and holds his identity in a state of potentiality, promising himself victory on another day. But the stress may be too great; the hero may find himself faced with a choice between his self-conception on the one hand and the continuation of his social task on the other. This is what happens to Hector. When Zeus gives Hector his moment of victory, he induces Hector to define himself as a victor. When the god's help fails him, Hector finds himself left with this self-definition but lacking the power to make it actual. The proud confidence which at the end of Book Eight had represented Hector's total coordination of his resources and capacities has, by the end of Book Eighteen, become mere self-assertion, a vain resistance to the current of events. Hector's fate thus has the effect of depriving Hector of himself. His action becomes ungrounded; he deserts his social task in his desperate efforts to fulfill it. The egoism which in success had marked Hector as the focal point of his community, the bearer and leader of its energies, in defeat becomes an egoism which isolates him from his world. This isolation is not moderated but rather made worse by Hector's rhetorical success; his troops shout assent, not to the world as it is (which Polydamas lays before them), but to Hector's willful misreading of events. Hector thus (for the moment, until the event brutally disproves him) takes his community with him into the nonworld his private self-assertion has created.

With the assembly of Book Eighteen the story of Hector's error is in one sense complete; by keeping his troops on the field, Hector makes his one catastrophic mistake, and from the way in which he makes it we see that the change in his character is irreversible. In another sense, however, this is only the first half of the story. Error is known by its consequences, and the tragic pathos is evoked, not by the fact of error, but as the meaning of error is experienced through consequences. With the return of Achilles to the battle, Hector ceases to be the leading actor, yet with Hector's death and funeral the poet brings his ethical design to a lucid conclusion.

From the beginning of Book Eighteen Achilles is looking for Hector (see, e.g., XVIII.114–16); in Book Twenty-two he finds him. All the events between—the description of the shield, the Greek assembly of reconciliation, Achilles' battles with the Trojans and the river—are incidents which stand in Achilles' path and delay the denouement. It is worth observing, however, that one of these incidents is an encounter between Achilles and Hector. Hector has been warned to stay out of Achilles' way (XX.371–80), but in rage at Polydorus' death he jumps in Achilles' path. Achilles is about to kill him when Apollo makes Hector invisible. There are echoes here of Hector's encounter with Agamemnon in Book Eleven (XI.362–67 = XX.449–54) and of Paris' duel with Menelaus (III.381 = XX.444). Hector, who might at this moment have died bravely and thoughtlessly, is saved by the god for another kind of death, less brave and more thoughtful. The whole incident is one of those nonevents which in poetry often serve to clarify later events. It is the special privilege of the tragic hero that he meets his own death in the fullness of reflective self-knowledge.

At the beginning of Book Twenty-two Hector stands alone outside the city; his parents call to him from the wall:

> The old man spoke of pity, arms outstretched:
> "Hector, please don't wait, dear child, for that man
> Alone, without others; or soon you'll meet with death,
> Brought down by Peleus' son, since he is much stronger,
> Merciless. If only the dogs would love him
> As I do. Soon the dogs and birds would eat him,
> Lying there. My searing pain would leave me.
> He has left me bereaved of so many sons—of brave ones—
> Killing or selling them to far-off islands;
> And now two sons, Lycaon and Polydorus,
> I cannot see huddled in here with the Trojans—

Laothoë bore them, queen she is among women—
But if they're alive in his camp, then in time to come
With bronze and gold we will ransom them. We have it,
For much he gave with his child, the old man Altes.
But if they're already dead in the house of Hades,
It will sorrow my heart and their mother's, we who
Bore them. But for the folk at large, it will sorrow
Them less unless *you* come to die, slain by Achilles.
Come into the wall, my child, so that you can save
The men and women of Troy; don't grant great honor
To Peleus' son, or squander your own life.
Have pity on me—I must live with my misfortune—
Ill-portioned. Father Zeus on the old-age threshold
Makes harsh my death, so great his gift of evil,
With sons that die and daughters dragged away,
Their chambers looted, and their infant children
Hurled to the ground in dreadful slaughter,
My sons' wives dragged away by Achaean hands,
Myself, at the end, the dogs before my doors
Will devour raw, when one with whetted bronze
By blow or cast will strip my limbs of life—
The dogs I raised, my table dogs and watchdogs,
They will grow rabid as they drink my blood,
Lying there in the forecourt. It fits a young man,
War-slain, rent apart by the whetted bronze,
To lie there. Even in death and exposed he is fair.
But when it's a man gray-haired, a man gray-bearded,
His genitals shamed by dogs, when an elder is killed,
This is most full of grief for wretched mortals."
   The old man spoke; his hands clutched his gray hair,
Tearing it from his head. Nor would Hector hear him.
In her turn his mother wept and poured out tears;
She opened her dress, and held out her breast with her hand,
And pouring out tears she spoke to him winged words:
"Hector, child, feel *aidōs* for this, and pity
For me, if ever I gave you the soothing breast.
Remember us, my child, and resist that foeman
From within the walls; don't stand out foremost to him,
Merciless. If he kills you, I will never
Weep at your bier, my sprig, not I who bore you
Nor your precious wife. But far away from us,
By the ships of the Argives, the swift dogs will eat you."
   So they both wept and spoke to their dear son
With many beseechings. Nor would Hector hear them.

(XXII.37–91)

The son's relation with his parents is both metaphoric and metonymic; the son is a repetition of the father, an extension of the mother.
Hector's father says: in dying, you are killing me. His mother says: in
dying, you are killing a part of myself.[14] Both threaten him with the
guilt of killing his parent. He remains unmoved. By the power of
their prayers we measure his isolation. "Like a snake coiled in his
lair" (XXII.95) he talks to himself:

> Alas for me. If I enter the gates and walls,
> Polydamas will be the first to reproach me,
> Who told me to bring the Trojans back to the city
> On that cursed night when Achilles roused himself.
> But I would not trust him. Surely it would have been better.
> Now, since I ruined the folk by my own folly,
> I shrink from the Trojan men and long-robed women
> Lest someone say—some worse man than I am—
> "Hector, trusting his own strength, ruined the folk."
> That's what they'll say. For me it would have been better
> To face Achilles, to kill him and then come back,
> Or myself to die in good fame before the city.
> Perhaps I could take my shield from off my back,
> And my bristling helm, and lean my spear by the wall—
> I could simply meet Achilles to his face.
> I'd offer him Helen and the property with her,
> All that Paris in his hollow ships
> Brought to Troy, which was the beginning of strife.
> We'd let the Atreidae take it, and with the Achaeans
> We'd divide the rest, as much as the city hides.
> Then from the Trojans I'd take the oath of the elders:
> They would hide nothing, but divide it all—
> So much wealth as the lovely castle holds.
> But why does my own heart talk within me thus?
> Suppose that I went—he would not pity me
> Nor shrink at all; he'd simply kill me naked,
> Like some woman, since I'd put off my armor.
> This is no time now, from an oak or a rock,
> For courting with him, like a boy and a maiden,
> A boy and a maiden courting with one another.
> Better to drive together in sudden combat;
> We will know to which man Zeus fulfills his boast.

(XXII.99–130)

There is an echo here of Hector's conversation with Andromache
(VI.442 = XXII.105). The same inner force that sent him into battle—
his *aidōs* before the men and women of Troy—prevents him from re-

157

turning home. There is a balance between Andromache's appeal in Book Six and his parents' appeal in Book Twenty-two. Hector's isolation here is thus not a lack of relation to his community but a negative relation with it; he is sure that his community—embodied in Polydamas and the anonymous "man worse than I am"—rejects him. Community takes precedence over family.

Aidōs, as we saw, is a socializing emotion, or rather the characteristic emotion of the social man. Through *aidōs* the ethical judgment of others is perceived and experienced directly in the self. *Aidōs* is usually a good thing—but not always.[15] Since *aidōs* is not a virtue but a *pathos*, an emotion, it is not perfectly trustworthy.[16] *Aidōs* is out of place, for instance, in a beggar, or in a boy when it is time for him to become a man.[17] One can become the victim of *aidōs*; that is what happens to Hector. A hero who is preeminently responsive and responsible, he is here defeated by his own characteristic goodness.

In his paralysis, Hector takes refuge in fantasy; the notion of a settlement, which, as we saw, runs through the earlier parts of the poem, comes to his mind here. He plays with the fantasy a moment and then lets it drop. Hector has long acted blindly, but at the end he can see his fate coming toward him and resolves to go to meet it.

Hector as a warrior had drawn his power from his fellows; his strength lay in his status as a representative figure. Here he is isolated and therefore weak. There is thus another echo of Book Six in the verb *oarizemenai*, "to court," used elsewhere in Homer only of Hector's conversation with Andromache (VI.516). Having lost the power of his social role, Hector feels himself no longer a warrior but a woman—or a child. Achilles' armor flashes, and Hector is terrified (XXII.134–36), just as his own son had been terrified of his helmet (VI.467–69). His nerve breaks, and he runs.

Hector is alone with his enemy, and in the language of his soliloquy —with its talk of naked courting—he expresses the curious intimacy of his encounter with Achilles. But this is not an intimacy of love or protection; it is the intimacy of slayer and victim. Hector's fantasies thus turn to a nightmare of panic:

> As in a dream one can't overtake the escaper,
> Nor can he escape the other, who can't overtake him,
> So the one couldn't catch him running, nor the other escape.
>
> (XXII.199–201)

The death of Hector is a scene played before several audiences. The Trojans watch from the wall. The Greek army watches, kept back by Achilles lest they spoil the scene (XXII.206–7). The gods watch from above, like spectators at the games (XXII.162–66), and argue briefly about whether, after all, the plot must be enacted to the end (XXII.174–85). Athena induces Hector to play his part by impersonating his favorite brother; Hector, deceived by this illusion that his family has come back to him, stands where Achilles can kill him. The whole event is a kind of charade or playing at combat, except that Hector really dies:

> Not for a bull or an ox—
> To win that prize, as men run in a footrace—
> No, they ran for the prize of Hector's life.
>
> (XXII.159–61)

These themes of fantasy, dreaming, games, and theater are appropriate to the death of Hector, for Hector's reality lay in his relations to others. As those relations become negative and isolating, he becomes, in a sense, less real; Hector dies as a kind of shadow of himself. Hector's story leads through false hope, to error, to the paralysis of social solitude; in this story he is progressively deprived of himself. He ceases to be an actor, first by losing his freedom, then his self-respect, and finally his location in the social world. At the end he can do nothing with his fate except know it. Hector dies because there is nothing left for him to do, because for him there no longer exists a world in which he can act.

5

PURIFICATION

Purity is an aspect of things as they are ordered by proprieties and limits. If "dirt is matter out of place," purity has to do with proper places and times, with proportion and distribution, and with the matter proper to a given form.[1] The unclean is often the ambiguous, the anomalous, the interstitial; unclean things escape from categories and blur our comprehension of categories. Thus the body excretions are unclean in that they are neither us nor not us; monsters are unclean because they are neither fish nor fowl.[2] Purity is form; the impure is the formless, the deformed, and that which threatens the forms.

Purity is thus a kind of adherence to essence. Pure water is nothing but water, and pure music is nothing but music. Similarly, pure intentions are unequivocal. The norms of purity in any culture are an application of local concepts of essential form. We purify an object by removing from it accidental accretions and revealing it as it is supposed to be. This is what we mean by "cleaning."

Dirt is one kind of impurity; rot is another. An object may become impure as it starts to turn into something else. But if it actually becomes that other thing, it may again be pure. Transformation thus involves a passage from purity through impurity to purity as one form disappears and another takes its place. Thus the slaughterhouse is a place of impurity, but the kitchen is a place of purity. Digestion is impure, but the healthy organism is pure. Similarly in social life, the transition from one role to another—from boy to man or from man to king—may require a transitional phase of seclusion and debasement. That impurity has in the end been met and overcome marks the reality of the change.[3]

Because purity is not in the matter but in the form, the same object may be pure or impure depending on our concept of it. Thus purification sometimes involves no operation on the object but rather our reclassification or reconceptualization of it. If the object is a hallowed antique, the impurities of the surface are not dirt but patina. Similarly, things impure in ordinary experience—diseased organs or obscene speech—may become pure when they are treated as objects of science. We then no longer perceive them as departures from form but rather as superb examples of what they actually are. The impure is thus made pure by the power of the detached intellect.

160

Art also, insofar as it achieves form, is a purification. In narrative art the form is achieved gradually. Themes are stated, emotions are evoked in us; we are puzzled, stirred, hopeful, and fearful. Then, as the work reaches closure, we come to see that everything is as it should be, that nothing could be added or taken away. The matter of our previous experience—the experience evoked by the work—does not change, but we reconceive that matter within the newly revealed form. Thus the work takes us through impurity to purity; impurity has been met and overcome by the power of formal art.

A work of narrative art thus stands between ceremony and science; it is a process of purification enacted, not actually, but imaginatively, and contrived by the detached, formative understanding of the artist.

Purity in Homer is a purity of surface; no effective distinction is made between aesthetic and ethical categories.[4] Social propriety, technical serviceability, and physical appearance are described in the same language.[5] That a king should entertain the nobles at dinner, for instance, is "seemly, not unseemly" (*aeikes*—IX.70); a worn-out bag is *aeikēs* (xiii.437); so is the destruction of an army (I.341). To mutilate a dead body is to make it *aeikēs* (*aeikizein*). Similarly, one adjective—*aischros*—serves for both "ugly" and "shameful," and a man can be said "to make himself *aischros* (*aischunein*)" with dirt and by tearing his hair (XVIII.24, 27). Dirt disfigures, dishonors, and defiles; a man stained with mire and gore is in no fit state to speak to the gods (VI.266 f.). Those who are dishonorable deserve ugliness and dirt as well; Thersites, who speaks without measure or order (II.212–14), is appropriately ugly, lame, and deformed (II.216–19). Odysseus inflicts upon him an appropriate humiliation by making him bleed and cry (II.265–68). Physical cleaning is itself a kind of ethical purification.[6] The epic does not make a contrast between the physical and the spiritual or between the personal and the social. Rather, it is expected that disorder on one level will be reflected in all and that when things are in order—*en kosmōi*—the order will be pervasive.

Since purity has to do with limits, purity requires protection. Pure honor is a kind of personal integrity. A woman's purity is her chastity; the city walls, so long as they are unbreached, secure a kind of purity to social life.[7] Purity is constantly threatened by incursions; the forms border on the formless. The conflict between the pure and the impure is thus one version of the conflict between culture and nature. Culture, the collective imposition of forms and limits, is the purification of nature—but nature continually threatens culture with impurity. The structure is continually dissolving at the edges. And since the culture is, in Homer, a set of structures so coherently constituted that disorder in any part threatens the disorder of the whole, it follows that each step toward the maintenance of purity, each act of purification, is an act on behalf of the whole complex structure. The Homeric heroes are driven to action by a need to defend their personal honor, the chastity of their women, and the security of their property; by an obligation to maintain the authority of superiors and the subordination of inferiors; and by a commitment to the procedural proprieties of debate, sacrifice, and entertainment. Often their actions bring them into conflict with one another. Yet we can see throughout this ethic a pervasive drive for order, a need to rescue form from the formlessness of the world.

We must add, however, that form is possible to culture only because it is usual in nature. We experience in nature the contrasts between day and night, earth and sky, male and female, need and satiety, growth, maturity, and decay. Culture seizes upon these differentia and forms them further, into a cosmos of elements and species, a hierarchy of diverse beings and cooperative roles, a rhythm of anniversaries and life stages. We turn nature to our use and thus generate a new set of boundaries, many of which are invisible. The human landscape distinguishes town from country, field from forest, public from private, sacred from profane. Cultural time is also newly bounded, numbered, counted, divided. Particular days acquire an identity from human events—as a man may speak, for instance, of the day of his birth or his death.[8] Through memory and anticipation man in culture has created a formed past and future.

Within the fabric of cultural time, ceremonies have a special standing. A ceremony intervenes within the flux of experience and creates an ending and a beginning. Through ceremony, for instance, the solstice can be turned to human use, so that it becomes the beginning of a new year and a new start for those who inhabit the year. Through ceremony the organic events and sequences of life—birth, puberty, mating, maturity, senescence, death—are given a meaning and marked as definite life stages. The mature male, for instance, may be ceremonially classified as an adult; the aging warrior may ceremonially retire from active life and be granted in return a new moral authority. Through ceremony a propriety is conferred on the event and also on what precedes and follows it; the event is certified as having a definite place in an expected sequence.

A ceremony is thus the purification of change. Through ceremony the impure can be made pure as the breakdown of an old form is seen to make way for a new form. Sexual intercourse, for instance, may be considered impure, in that it threatens somatic identity or forms groups and threatens older kinship solidarities; sexual generation, the joint act of two bodies to make a third, involves an anomalous intimacy which may well be thought dangerous. In marriage this strange event is consecrated and reconceived as the source of a social form, a family. In death the somatic identity ceases; the body becomes waste and must be disposed of. Through the funeral this strangest of all events becomes also a transformation.

A ceremony is the enactment of a concept. Through ceremonies persons are classified and placed in categories; their analogical unity with similar persons is asserted. Persons are thus rescued from the flux of nature and purified as they are given a definite standing in the cultural pattern. Thus in a wedding the happy or unhappy couple become for a moment archetypical bride and bridegroom. Their peculiarities are declared irrelevant to the archetype shining through them. The ceremony thus creates an ending and a beginning. Whatever vagrant path brought them to the altar, it is enough, for the moment, that they are getting married and will start life anew as man and wife. In the funeral, similarly, the dead man is welcomed to the ranks of the dead; he becomes one with those who have gone before.

Any given ceremony, therefore, will be efficacious largely to the degree that it is perceived to be a repetition of earlier ceremonies. The same words, the same gestures, the same order of parts, must be valid once again. Ceremony thus implies both the diachronic continuity of the community and its synchronic cohesion.

The coherence of the community gives it the power to classify. Concepts and categories, whatever else they may be, must be communicable and consensual. A purely private concept is a contradiction in terms. The individual's consciousness is thus both an effect and a cause of his solidarity with his community; in the enactment of a ceremony this solidarity is both recognized and celebrated. Thus every ceremony involves an audience—usually actual, occasionally merely evoked.

In ordinary usage, ceremony is practically synonymous with ritual. I distinguish the terms as follows: a ritual is held to act on the world beyond culture, whether that world is thought of as natural or supernatural; ceremony is an event within culture by which the culture defines itself. Ritual is held to have definite effects upon objects; the potency of ceremony is subjective, is limited to the realm of consciousness. Ritual makes something to be so; ceremony is an enacted recognition that it is so. The anointed king of mediaeval Europe received in the course of the ritual certain specific powers, including, for instance, the power to cure specific diseases. An American president is inaugurated in order to mark the fact that powers have been conferred on him. He is permitted to swear or affirm. Swearing, which evokes a supernatural sanction, belongs to the sphere of ritual; within the ceremony of inauguration it is an option which the new president may or may not exercise, a private matter between himself and his God.

Ritual has the power to bless or to curse; ceremony merely praises or blames. Ritual shades into magic, ceremony into manners. Ritual thus approaches a technical process, ceremony a work of art.

The analogies between ceremony and performed art are obvious. Both turn on a complex relation between performers and audience; both create definite occasions within the flow of life, and both offer their audiences formed experience. The relation between a current ceremony and its previous enactments is analogous to the relation between a work of art and its genre. Art may have a place within a ceremonial framework, as at the Attic festivals. Furthermore, performed art and ceremony have a tendency to turn into each other; ceremony becomes art when it is aesthetically appreciated, while art becomes ceremony when an artistic performance, by its assertion or creation of communal solidarity, becomes a mode of social action.

In both cases the transformation occurs through a shift in the relations between performers and audiences. The old man in Saroyan who attended academic convocations in order to appreciate the speakers' rhetoric was treating these occasions as artistic events; he attended as an appreciative stranger rather than a committed participant. Because ceremonies employ aesthetic means, a ceremony can always be appreciated by an outsider as a work of performed art. Such a transformation has in our own time overtaken certain American Indian festivals. On the other hand, performed art becomes ceremony when the audience is made a participant in such a way that the performed event becomes one element in a causal chain of further events within the ordinary social world. Such a transformation is attempted by some contemporary groups, for example by the Living Theater, whose *Paradise Now* ends with the cast leading the audience into the streets, ideally for the commission of acts of revolutionary violence.

Nevertheless, there is a proper and crucial difference between performed art and ceremony, a difference founded on the distinction between the imitated and the actual. That the line between the two is difficult to draw does not make the distinction any less important. Ceremony and art have different functions, and the conflation of the two is likely to injure both. A ceremony constructs an actual path between one of life's stages and the next. Through ceremony we not only see the world differently; we also reach a different world and become different persons. In a wedding the partners actually marry; they come to be differently related, not only to each other but to us. This happens because performers and audience share a conviction about the actuality of the ceremony; this shared conviction, once enacted, makes an actual difference.

Imitative art, on the other hand, is not life; it is about life. Ceremony is founded on belief, art on the suspension of disbelief. To borrow a pair of terms from Geertz: in art the stress is on the symbols themselves and on mood; in ceremony it is on the objects to which the symbols refer and on motivation.[9] The aesthetic appreciation of a ceremony robs it of its power by insulating it from the practical world to which it is intended to contribute. The attempt to inhabit a work of art is, by contrast, literally Quixotic and is a form of madness. Imitated events are always at a certain distance from events; artist and performer, through the conventions of art, warn the audience of this distance. The master of ceremonies gives actual instructions; within his ceremonial domain he is the King. But the poet stands aside from life and looks at it from the outside. He is the spectator of life, its critic, even the Fool. This distance of his—which he shares with us—enables him to create a parallel and secondary order of events.

Yet art, like culture, is form; the work of art is a purification of experience. What it purifies, however, is not actual experience but imaginary experience: the work purifies the experience which the work itself evokes. Since art is a cultural product and, as we saw, presumes culture, art is a further forming of culture; the fictional artist contributes forms to culture by offering his audience a formed representation of themselves. This further forming, however, entails a reduction in content. The mark of this reduction is artistic closure; the meaning of the work gives coherence to material marked off by definite limits, by a standard of relevance laid down by the particular work. These limits are both internal and external; the world of a fictional work is self-contained, and within it only certain facts are relevant to the design. If we respond to *Hamlet* as an artistic unity, we are not left with such unanswered questions as "What book was Hamlet reading?" or "What kind of king did Fortinbras turn out to be?" The work *might*, of course, provide answers to such questions, but it leaves us disinclined to ask them—except insofar as we might want to invent answers in order to express some aspect of our understanding of the work. In this case, as in the Stanislavski method, our further detailing of the work is a further imaginative act of our own, a kind of imitation of the imitation, which will be successful only to the degree that we do not confuse art with actuality.

Art is thus more intelligible than life—at the price of ignoring the actual complexity and continuity of experience. Since art of some kind is an aspect of all cultural systems, it is clear that men everywhere have found this price worth paying. This point, in turn, suggests a further answer to the question implicitly raised in the first chapter of this book: What is the social function of art? Earlier we saw that art can make more intelligible what was already intelligible. Now we add that art in imitating life can make intelligible (at the price of reduction) situations unintelligible in life. The stuff of experience is contradiction; culture, which suggests a resolution of some contradictions, is itself the source of others. Art, particularly narrative art, (unreally) resolves these contradictions by placing them in the artificial environment of artistic closure—subjecting them to a reduced standard of relevance and framing them between a beginning and an ending. The contradictions which can be resolved only at the level of art are the contradictions which cannot be resolved in life. Contradiction in culture makes drama possible; irremediable contradiction makes it necessary.

Art, like culture, consists of form; form is possible in art, as in culture, only because it is usual elsewhere. Art draws on the forms and rhythms of nature, and of culture as well. The poet may give his narrative shape by evoking the alternations of day and night, the sequence of growth and aging; similarly, he may shape his story to the pattern of a technical process, of a journey, of debate and litigation, of planning, achievement, or celebration. Ceremonies, which mark beginnings and endings in life, also make themselves useful in the patterns of narrative art, especially at the end; for while the ceremony gives its participants a new standing and a new beginning, the symbolic content of ceremonies is primarily synthetic and retrospective. The ceremony is a recognition of that which is the case. Thus it is no accident that so many comedies end with a wedding, so many tragedies with a funeral.

The ceremony within a work of art is a real toad in the imaginary garden; the ceremony is a formed performance which now becomes an element in the further form of the work of art. It follows that our analysis of the ceremony must proceed on two levels, the level of culture and the level of art. We have first the question: What does the ceremony mean in itself? and second the question: What did the artist do with it, what did he make it mean? On the first level we think of the work as an imitation or picture of the culture; on the second level we think of it as a construct and a contribution to the culture. Here we ask both questions of the funerals that end the *Iliad*.

FUNERAL AND ANTIFUNERAL

The matter of funerals runs through the *Iliad*, beginning with the pyres kindled to burn those dead of the plague before the action of the poem has properly begun (I.52).[10] The funeral becomes an explicit theme in Hector's challenge to the duel in Book Seven:

> Thus I will state it; Zeus is to be our witness:
> If he should reach me with the sharp-edged bronze,
> Let him strip my arms and take them back to his ships
> But give my body home, so that the fire
> May be my share from Trojans and Trojan wives.
> If I should reach him, and Apollo grants my boast,
> I will strip his armor and take it to Ilium
> And hang it up by the temple of archer Apollo.
> The corpse I will return by the benched ships
> So that the long-haired Achaeans can bury him
> And heap him a marker by the Hellespont.
> Someone will say, even one born much later,
> As he sails his many-oared ship on the broad sea:
> "This is the marker of a man long dead
> Whom once in his pride the shining Hector slew."
> Thus he will say. And my fame will not perish.

(VII.76–91)

The duel between Hector and Ajax which follows is a chivalrous affair, with covert blows ruled out (VII.242–43); declared a tie by the heralds (VII.273–82), it concludes with an exchange of gifts between the combatants (VII.303–5). This reminds us of the exchange of armor between Glaucus and Diomedes in Book Six; and the careful provision, in Hector's challenge, for the funeral of the defeated duelist looks forward to the day of truce and funerals which immediately follows. Before the Plan of Zeus has begun, the Trojan War is still something short of total, still allows some respect for the opponent.

By the time the *Iliad* begins, the war is in its tenth year, and we learn from the poem that at an earlier time the war was less violent and harsh than it has become. We hear that the Greeks have taken and ransomed prisoners,[11] but none is taken in the *Iliad*; and when, in Book Six, Menelaus is about to take a prisoner, Agamemnon stops him:

> Poor fool, Menelaus, why do you care so much
> For men? Or have such fine works been worked in your house

By Trojans? Let not one escape steep death
And our hands, not even the one in his mother's womb,
A boy-child growing. No refuge. Let them all
Perish from Ilium, without any care or trace.

(VI.55–60)

So Menelaus kills his suppliant, having received, the poet tells us, advice that was *aisima*, "proper" or "fitting." The incident looks forward to the harsher war to come, to Diomedes' killing of Dolon and Achilles' of Lycaon.

With the opening of the Great Day of Battle the atmosphere darkens further. A new tone comes into the boasting, as when Odysseus kills Socus:

Socus, son of Hippasus, knowing horseman,
Completed death overtook you, you didn't escape it—
Wretch; no hope that your father and lady mother
Will close your eyes in death, but the flesh-eating birds
Will get you, stretching across you their feathered wings.
But, when I die, the bright Achaeans will mourn me.

(XI.450–55)

From the very beginning of the poem we have heard that birds and dogs eat the dead (I.4–5); to be eaten as carrion has been a fate threatened in a general way to the enemy or to the cowards on one's own side (II.393, IV.237). But here for the first time a warrior promises to feed his victim to the scavengers; the funeral is no longer the common share of the dead but the special privilege of the victor, who boasts that he can withhold it from the vanquished. A little later Hector meets Ajax on the battlefield; they have not met since their chivalrous duel in Book Seven. But there is now no talk of funerals:

Ajax, ranter, braggart, what have you said?
If I could but be child of Zeus of the aegis,
For all my days, and lady Hera bore me—
Honored as are honored Athena, Apollo—
So surely this day brings evil on the Argives,
On all, on you most clearly, if you dare
To wait for my long spear, your lily-white flesh
Bitten. You'll glut the Trojan dogs and birds
With fat and meat, when you fall by Achaean ships.

(XIII.824–32)

When Hector kills Patroclus, he tells him that the birds will eat him (XVI.836); this intention of Hector's provokes the great battle around the corpse of Patroclus. Glaucus wants Patroclus' body so that he can exchange it for Sarpedon's body and armor and save his friend from

168

the dogs (XVII.160–63; cf. XVI.545–46).[12] Hector simply wants to despoil his enemy:

> Hector, once he had taken Patroclus' armor,
> Dragged at him, so he could cut the head from his shoulders
> And drag the corpse to Troy to feed his dogs.
>
> (XVII.125–27)

Achilles is later warned by Iris that Hector intends to fix Patroclus' head on a stake (XVIII.175–77).[13]

This vindictive violence, for which the ugly destruction of the opponent's dead body is the perfection of victory, is another mark of the change which overcomes Hector's character during the Great Day of Battle. The change is echoed and amplified in Achilles. Andromache tells us that when Achilles slew her father, he did not strip him but gave him proper burial with his armor, "for he felt an inhibiting awe in his heart" (VI.417). The Achilles who vanquishes Hector drags his body in the dust, refuses him burial, and threatens to feed him to the dogs. This threat is the leading theme of Books Twenty-two and Twenty-four.

Yet no one is ever fed to the dogs in the *Iliad*.[14] It is as if the poet, having established through general expressions and threats the limiting case of impurity, draws back from that limit. The rising arc of horrors crests in the poem with Lycaon and Asteropaeus in Book Twenty-one—who are fed to the fish[15]—and with Priam's description of man-devouring dogs in the beginning of Book Twenty-two. In the event, the two heroes most threatened with defilement—Patroclus and Hector—are properly mourned and buried. The *Iliad* thus moves from purity through impurity to purity. The question of purity and impurity is dramatized at the end of the *Iliad* as the question of the funeral of Hector—dramatized, that is, through the proprieties owed to the dead and through the willful impropriety of leaving a dead enemy to the dogs. We shall discuss first the meaning of the funeral and then the meaning of the willful defilement, which we shall call the antifuneral. Finally we shall consider the relation between the two. We shall find that this reading of the poem gives us a new sense of the meaning of the hero, whose peculiar role within the community takes him outside the community and sets him on the frontier between culture and nature.

HUMAN NATURE AS CULTURAL CONSTRUCT

Nature is that which continues, whether we would have it so or not; nature endures our makings and unmakings and persists. Nature, thus defined, is that which is common to all men at all times and places;

while cultures vary, nature is invariable. Every culture, further, is, in some special way, a relation to this common nature, and it is this common term which makes it possible to compare the most diverse cultures with one another. The solutions differ, but the problems are, on the deepest level, the same.

It is also true, however, that each culture has its own nature—its own, not as it is, but as it is stated to be. Things may or may not be natural; but names are purely cultural, and they are further culturally patterned into categories, explanations, values. In the pattern of its names a culture implicitly states its picture of nature; and since this must be a functioning picture, the culture states its relation to nature. At the foundation of our study of a culture is a study of its names for natural things.

Man is a natural thing in two senses; he has a nature, and he is a thing in nature. Men form pictures of nature in both senses. Every culture possesses, more or (often) less explicitly, a psychology and a cosmology. Since man is unthinkable without community, the first question, that of the nature of man, is inseparable from the question of community. Since every community must have limits, the second question,. that of the place of man in nature, is inseparable from the question of the defining limits of community—whether those limits are thought of in terms of the community's productive exploitation of nature, the community's relation with other communities, or the community's communion with the sacred. We shall treat these two sets of questions in order, speaking first of the nature of man as it is illuminated by the Homeric funeral and then of man's place in nature as it is illuminated by the antifuneral.

The funeral is unique among the ceremonies of the life-cycle in that the central figure is no longer there. There remains the question: Is he somewhere else? If the dead man survives as a person or potency, we may be obligated to him or may have to deal with him; if he is truly dead, there is nothing to be done for him and nothing to be expected of him. In the first case the funeral may serve to secure the dead a happy afterlife, to protect us from their vengeance, or secure their power on our behalf; in the second case the funeral is a matter for the living and reforms their relations with one another. The funeral thus tends toward ritual or ceremony according to the culture's view of mortality. I would maintain that the Homeric funeral is exclusively a ceremony.[16]

This thesis flouts an obvious fact of Homeric belief: that the *psuchē* of the man continues to exist after his death. The *psuchē*, at least between the man's death and his funeral, can appear to the living in dreams; with the funeral the *psuchē* goes into the house of Hades, where all the dead, in some sense, are, and whence they can be evoked by appropriate rites. The funeral, furthermore, is on behalf of the *psuchē*, which asks that the body be buried (XXIII.70–74, xi.66–78; cf. iii.278–85). However, the facts of belief, like other facts, do not wear their meaning on their faces; we will do well, I believe, to allow our understanding of the *psuchē* to be shaped by a careful interpretation of the Homeric funeral.

When Achilles speaks of Patroclus' funeral, he speaks of it in three parts: "to put Patroclus on the pyre *(pur)*, to dedicate the gravestone *(sēma)*, and to shear the hair" (XXIII.45–46); the funeral thus involves the disposal of the body, the creation of a monument, and certain significant acts by the mourners. The first, I shall suggest, deals with the dead man as an organic being, the second deals with him as a social being; the third states a relation between the dead and the living. Let us take them in order, beginning with the definition of organic life.

Menos AND *Thumos*

When Ajax rouses himself to battle in Book Thirteen, he says:

> So now my unflinching hands around my spear
> Are impelled, and impulse moves me; my two feet
> Rush along below; I feel impelled, though alone,
> Against Hector, who impels his ceaseless battling.
>
> (XIII.77–80)

This awkward translation is intended to bring out the fact that one root (**men-*) is used four times in three lines. Ajax feels impulse, *menos*, within him; he feels it in the firm grip of his hands on the spear, in the quickness of his walking, in his readiness to confront the similar *menos* of Hector. He feels both strong and brave. A single vitality expresses itself in vigor both somatic and psychic—and here we should be clear that we are putting back together something that for Homer is never taken apart. The living man is all one piece; all his processes—metabolic, motoric, affective, and ideational—are aspects of a single functioning. The name of this functioning is *menos*.[17]

Menos is a quality of winds (V.524, v.478, xix.440) and rivers (XII.18, XXI.305, 383). Both winds and rivers in Homer are persons, so that their *menos* is like the *menos* of gods, men, or animals. The transition from the sense "organic vitality" to the sense "material energy" can be seen in the use of *menos* for the power of the sun to corrupt a dead body (XXIII.190) or to make men thirsty (x.160). The *menos* of the sun is its heat. Fire has a *menos*.[18] Or we could better say that *menos* is fire; *menos* is energy, which in organisms is an aspect of their organic functioning.[19]

The life of the animal is slow-burning. In a monster like the chimera the *menos* within is breathed out in fire (VI.182). Less spectacularly, the vigor of a man is also the fire in him (XVII.565). When Agamemnon filled with *menos*, his "eyes were like to shining fire" (I.103–4; cf. XIII.474); at a moment of rage the fire within can actually be seen through the eyes (XIX.365–67). This *menos* must be fed with food and drink (IX.706 = XIX.161); it is organic fire, i.e., the metabolism.[20] *Menos* comes and goes (V.472); it is diminished by pain (XV.60; cf. XV.262 = XX.110). It is absent in those whose bodies are not functioning well; at such times the *menos* is said to be "quenched" (XVI.621; cf. XXII.96).[21] As long as some spark of the metabolic fire persists, however, life continues, as when Odysseus, worn almost to death by his struggles with the sea, lies down in a warm spot in the brush:

> As when one hides a brand in the black ashes,
> Away from the sown land, where there are no neighbors,
> And saves the seed of the fire, that he'll not have to kindle it
>   from elsewhere,
> So Odysseus covered himself with leaves.
>
>   (v.488–91)

Since fire is pure motion and consists of matter in the process of transformation, fire is absolutely insubstantial; it may seem odd that the *menos* of fire should be called *sidēreon*, "made of iron" (XXIII. 177). Fire, however, not only burns; it also tempers, and the hardness of the iron may be thought of as the fire in it. *Menos* also makes the man, like an ax, hard-tempered; as it gives a man the power to move, it also gives him the power to resist change.[22]

Menos as energy is a cause; when nature is perceived as a flux, what stands to be explained is often not motion but stillness. So, often, the warrior's *menos* enables him to stand firm where he is. A *menos* which is *atromon,* "unshaken," comes into the warrior who defends his home (XVII.156–58). He is a man to be reckoned with, not only because he can himself act, but because he is resistant to the acts of others. He is *empedos,* "steady" (V.527, etc.), or the *menos* within him is *empedon*; he does not flinch or tremble (V.251–56).[23] The *menos* of horses makes them run (XXIII.468, etc.), but the *menos* of the charioteer is expressed in the unflinching steadiness of his hands on the reins, a steadiness which makes the horses run straight (V.506; cf. XVII.476). *Menos* thus controls *menos*. *Menos* is often associated with hands, particularly hands that are *aaptoi*, "unflinching" or "not to be turned aside" (VII. 309, XVII.638). Of Achilles, Hector says: "his hands are like fire, his *menos* is like iron" (XX.372); the hardness and the heat, the inner power and the organ through which it acts, strength as energy and strength as hard substance, are here all compressed into one memorable phrase.

Empedos is most often used in connection with the organs and their capacities. A dead body may be called *empedos* because it does not rot (XIX.33, 39). In the living body, to be *empedos* is to be functioning well. Here again, no clear distinction is made between organic and psychic processes.[24] A young man's strength (*biē*) is *empedos* (IV.314, etc.), but in old age it fails him (XXIII.627). Of the aging Priam it is said that he is still *empedos* and not yet *aesiphrōn*, "failing in his wits" (XX.183). In all this the steadiness is that of organic continuity. The organism is in constant flux and yet is self-maintaining and self-repairing; it brings new matter to a continuing form. Its steadiness is like that of the tumbler who leaps from horse to horse and yet can be called *empedos* and *asphalēs*, "secure" or "surefooted" (XV.683–84).

In life, matter is active. The living matter as a whole we call an organism; its parts we call organs. In Homer the *menos* is in the organs, the hands, or the limbs (VI.27). But the *menos* is equally in the consciousness, which is equally an activity of matter, equally organic. Thus *menos* is most frequently linked with *thumos*, as in the formula: *otrune menon kai thumon hekastou*, "he set in motion the *menos* and the *thumos* of each man."

The *thumos* is the seat of the affective life—of passions, wishes, hopes, and inclinations. In my translations in this book *thumos* has generally been translated "heart" because in English the heart is usually the organ singled out as the seat of emotions. But *thumos* is not an organ; rather, it is a substance which fills an organ, namely, the *phrenes*.

The *phrenes* have been (cogently) identified as the lungs, and the *thumos*, therefore, as the breath.[25] Breath must be distinguished from air; air is converted into breath by the organism, which thus (as in digestion) converts a part of the environment into a part of itself. Breath is organic air; it is hot, wet, and in motion. The *menos*, the metabolic fire, is hot; it causes the whole interior of the organism to steam, especially the central thoracic cavity, the *stēthos*. When a god inspires the hero, he breathes into him *menos*. That is, he blows upon the fire, or he breathes confidence into the hero's *thumos*. That is, by blowing on the fire, he increases the density and hotness of the steam.[26] These descriptions of the surge of energy only extend and ascribe to divine intervention the familiar correlation between breathing and energy; breathing slackens in sleep or faintness, quickens in action or anxiety. A man who is preparing to speak or act takes a deep breath and quickens the fire within himself.

Our breathing is that aspect of our organic functioning of which we are most continuously and sensitively aware. Every change in our attitudes and attention is correlated with a change in the pattern of our breathing.[27] The Homeric speaker expresses this fact by saying that he feels or knows something "in his *thumos*" or, alternatively, that his *thumos* feels it. This language may seem alien or even primitive to us, but it is really only an unfamiliar way of describing familiar experiences. We say: "I felt afraid, and my breathing quickened"; the Homeric speaker says: "I felt afraid in my breath." Nor is it really different to say, as the Homeric speaker says: "My breath felt afraid." It is not particularly reasonable to give the feeling, as we do, some extraorganic location and then ascribe the bodily state to our own response to our own feeling, rather than, as the Homeric speaker does, to state the feeling as a specific condition of the body. We say: "I was conscious of my body"; the Homeric speaker says: "My body was conscious." For him, body has never become separate from mind; he therefore does not have to explain how they fit together.

Life is a formed process of matter; consciousness is a further forming of the process of life. Because the creature contains *menos*, he can act and maintain himself; because he contains *thumos*, he can act responsively. *Thumos* is the seat of the whole practical consciousness, from instant rage and pain to planning and deliberation on the basis of lessons laboriously learned. This practical intelligence, in Homer, is presented as a single phenomenon and at the same time with extraordinarily subtle internal differentiation; a careful taxonomy of the whole range of verbal ideas associated with *thumos* would reveal the complexity of the implicit empirical analysis and would illuminate much in the poems. Here it is enough to notice that consciousness, being a further functioning of the body functions, is as mortal as the organism. At death the *menos* is "broken up" (*luthē*);[28] the *thumos* is breathed out and again becomes air.[29] When the continuity of the process is interrupted, the form of the process is dissolved; the parts cease to function as organs and become mere matter.

Psuchē AND *Noos*

Wittgenstein wrote, in *Tractatus Logico-Philosophicus*, "At death the world does not alter; it ceases. Death is not an event of life. No one lives through his death." This very modern formulation recovers the archaic Homeric understanding.[30] Death is not a problem for the Homeric hero; his death concludes his story and completes his fate. The dead hero is a problem for others, for those who must live with the fact of his absence; death is a problem for the hero himself only to the degree that he feels himself one with those others. Thus when Hector speaks to Andromache of his own death, he speaks only of those others, of the fall of the city and his wife's slavery:

> And one will say, who sees your flowing tears:
> "That is Hector's wife; he was best at fighting
> Of the Trojan horsemen who fought before Ilium."
> Thus he will say, and thus renew your pain,
> Widowed of your man who kept you from bondage.
> May the grave mound hide me, dead beneath the earth,
> Before I hear your cry, and you're dragged away.
>
> (VI.459–65)

Hector's wish is to be absent from the events he foresees; he therefore thinks of himself not only as dead but as properly buried. By the funeral, the others who survive the dead man mark the fact of his death and assert his absence. The funeral is the *geras* of the dead (XVI.457 = 675); *geras* is the name for those marks of honor which a man is entitled to claim in virtue of his status or social role. In one sense the *geras* marks the status; in another sense it confers status, so that the loss of *geras* (as in the case of Chryseis or Briseis) threatens a loss of status. The funeral may thus be thought of as a ceremony by which a definite social status is conferred upon the dead. In the funeral the community declares that the dead man is gone and that life continues without him. He has done what he could, and his community declares that it can expect nothing more of him. Since he can no longer be among them, he is entitled to the status of the departed. They thus release him. It is this release for which the *psuchai* pray when, during the interval between death and burial, they speak to the living. The *psuchē*, I shall now suggest, survives death as a consequence of the fact that man dies not only organically but also socially, dies not only to nature but to culture.

Homer is pre-Cartesian and, for that matter, pre-Socratic. He does not make a sharp distinction between body and soul. But he does, in his own way, make a sharp distinction between theory and practice. It is the distinction we must understand if we are to understand the *psuchē*.

The notion of life which centers on the *menos*, *phrenes*, and *thumos* is a notion of life centering on action; the live creature has a source

175

of motion within himself and sets his own direction. There is, however, another notion of life in the poems, by which life is associated with vision.[31] We are reminded that fire has a double meaning; it is both heat and light, the source of both motion and vision.

Associated with vision is *noos*. One is said to *noēsai* with the eyes (see, e.g., XV.422). *Noos* is, however, different from sight; Sarpedon says he cannot *ideein* the Trojans or *noēsai* them either (V.475); he does not see them or notice them anywhere. It is the *noos* which catches a signal, as when Ajax nods to Phoenix, and *noēse . . . Odusseus* (IX.223). The tripods of Hephaestus have a *noos*; they can take instructions (XVIII.419–20). When Eurycleia recognizes the scar, Penelope fails to notice, for "Athena turned aside her *noos*" (xix.479). *Noos* is linked to recognition and responsive understanding: we might say that vision takes in the look of a thing, *noos* its meaning.[32] *Ideein* and *noēsai* are not, therefore, two separate acts; rather, the *noos* further forms perceiving consciousness so that what is perceived is a world of recognized meanings.[33]

Noos is not always linked to perception; one is said to *noēsai* "with the eyes" only in those cases in which the direct experience of the knower is stressed. *Noos* is also connected with words; it is a source of *muthoi*. The unspoken word is concealed in the *noos* (I.363). A *noēma* is a plan or intention.[34] But these uses also are linked to concrete picturings, not in the mode of direct perception, but in the secondary mode of imagination (XVI.80–83).[35] The planner *sees* a future situation and uses words to describe it. *Noos* has to do with plans or intentions because these are themselves a kind of anticipatory vision. Thus it is said that Zeus "does not bring to pass all the *noēmata* of men" (XVIII.328; cf. XXIII.149). Man imagines a future, but it does not come to pass (X.104).

As the recognition of meaning in things perceived or imagined, *noos* is a theoretical faculty. Whereas *thumos* is the consciousness which the organism has of itself in the world, *noos* is consciousness of the world in which the organism is. The objects of recognition are out there: persons, things, and events which are separate from ourselves. *Noos* perceives what is so, what the facts mean, and is in this sense dispassionate.[36] Yet *noos* is a source of passionate excitement. "In all those cases in which the verb *noein* has a direct and concrete object violent emotion is caused by the *noein*."[37] Meaning is *to us*, and the perceived meaning is expressed by the state of the organism. *Noos* is thus, like *thumos*, located in the *stēthos*; *noos* may be thought of as a further forming of *thumos*. "It is not identical in meaning with *thumos* but is rather something in, a defining of, this as e.g. a current in a sense consists of but defines, controls, air or water."[38] Thus even knowledge or vision can be said to be in the *phrenes* or *thumos* when the thing known or seen has some immediate practical or affective relevance (XXI.61, viii.45).

Noos is thus a theoretical faculty which has to do with particulars—particulars in two senses. In the first place, *noos* grasps meaning immediately; the act, *noein*, may follow a period of attention or puzzlement, but the clarity, when it comes, comes with the immediacy of vision. "In Homer *nous* never means 'reason' and *noein* never 'to reason,' whether inductively or deductively."[39] Second, *noos* grasps the meaning which its objects have for the particular knower; thus the *nooi* of different men and of men in different societies differ (i.3).[40] *Noos* does not discover some universal pattern of meaning or eternal truth; rather, it is the faculty by which we discern meaning as we happen to discern it.

The duality of *thumos* and *noos* is thus not based on a distinction between emotion and reason or on a distinction between the particular and the universal. It is based rather on a distinction between the inner and the outer, between the expression of ourselves in the world and the impression the world makes on us. *Noos* is a kind of metaperception. It is a receptivity to meaning and as such is passive;[41] there is no *menos* in *noos*. *Thumos* always involves intention or inclination and thus the active power of the organism to affect its environment; *noos* may involve mere recognition. Thus when Eurypolus is retiring, wounded, from the battle, Patroclus meets him and speaks with him, and "his *noos* at least was still *empedos*" (XI.813). Eurypolus' strength has been subdued by the wound, but he is still conscious and rational; one can talk with him. The connection previously noted between *noos* and language, counsel and planning, helps to explain the fact that, while *thumos* exists also in animals, *noos* is specific to man.[42] It should therefore have some relation to the man-specific soul, the *psuchē*.[43]

The *psuchē* is the eschatological soul; it does nothing except depart from a man when he dies—or is close to death. The *psuchai* of the living are spoken of only as something that is kept in life and lost in death. *Psuchē*, unlike the other souls of which we have been speaking, is not a functioning of the organism or a locus of experience.[44]

It has long been noticed that, in several passages in Homer, when a hero faints, his *psuchē* passes from him, but that when he revives, it is not said to return; rather, his *thumos* returns and "collects itself within him."[45] This, I would suggest, is because unconsciousness, like death, is not an experience. When the man revives, he "comes to himself"; as long as he is unconscious, he exists only for others. The *psuchē*,

I wish to assert, is a self that exists for others, one aspect of the social soul.

Menos, as we saw, is a formed process of matter; *thumos* is a further forming of *menos*, and *noos* of *thumos*. As all of these things are functionings of one another, they are all equally mortal. *Noos*, since it is particular and of particulars, has none of the special standing of the Aristotelian *nous*—which latter is, in a sense, immortal, in that its principle is universal and therefore eternal. In the Homeric picture, rather, some element of the man survives death not because man has *noos* but because he is in life the object of *noos*. The *noos* of others has recognized him and has thus given him a social identity and a proper name.

A proper name is the concept of a particular person; beings with proper names are recognizable, not merely as members of a species but as irreducibly distinct individuals. Proper names are conferred by men on creatures and things—on domestic animals, for instance, and places —insofar as those things are included within the fabric of society. But most creatures and things remain nameless. Human beings, the social creatures par excellence, are the only beings (except possibly gods) to whom a name is of the essence:

> No one is quite nameless among men,
> Neither low nor high, from the moment he is born.
>
> (viii.552–53)

To the proper name—the concept of the individual—corresponds a material fact: his personal appearance. It is by his looks that we recognize him. Because every man has a distinctive appearance, he can be the object of *noos*. As the name is the identity of the man in an ideal sense, his appearance is his identity in a material sense.

At the moment of death the man ceases to function; he is no longer a source of help or harm. But his identity persists. The man is gone, but two new things come into existence—or, we might better say, come to our attention. One is the *sōma* or corpse.[46] The *sōma* is inert matter, organism without *menos*. As it is no longer self-maintaining, its appearance begins to change. The other is the *psuchē*. The *psuchē* is an *eidōlon*, an image; it looks "wonderfully like the man," but "there is no *phrēn* in it at all" (XXIII.103–7). The *psuchē* is immaterial (it cannot be touched) and has no *menos*; it can speak only in dreams or if provided with a quasi *menos* by being fed hot blood. The *psuchē* is the recognizable appearance of the man, his concrete identity. If we remember that we are speaking within the realm of the particular, we shall be correct to say that at the moment of death man is divided into matter and form—particular matter and particular form. Thus we understand why, while the seat of consciousness is the *stēthos*, the *psuchē* is particularly associated with the head and also with the *rhethea*, an old word apparently meaning "face."[47] The head and the face are the most recognizable parts of the person; if his identity is specially located in any part of him, it must be there.

The dead are *amenēna karēna*, "heads without *menos*." Their identity survives, but without power, and they are located somewhere else, in the most distant, dark, unknowable realm. All this objectifies the view of death we noticed earlier: that death is an experience of the living, for whom the dead man survives in the modality of his absence. His face haunts the memory of those who must live without him. The *psuchai* in the house of Hades are precisely the absent ones; the funeral is the ceremony of their departure and the ritual of their release.

The division of the dead person into *psuchē* and *sōma* marks his disintegration into natural and cultural aspects. The Homeric funeral deals with the fact of death in both these aspects.

After Death

A dead body is a puzzle. It is everything the person ever was and yet is nothing like him; in death he is the same and yet opposite to what he was in life. The dead warrior comes into the hands of his women; he who has been so long their protection becomes their task. It is almost impossible to believe that this familiar being is no longer a person; thus Achilles in his farewell to the dead Patroclus puts his hands on the *stēthos* of the corpse, as if by sheer force he could reach the consciousness which is no longer there to hear his words (XVIII. 317 = XXIII.18). The living are reluctant to relinquish their dead; it is the dead Patroclus who is ready to depart.

Yet the dead body begins to rot. Once the *psuchē* is gone, the familiar form begins to turn into something else as it blends into the flux of nature. This is the horror of dead bodies; they are interstitial things, for in death the whole person becomes a kind of excrement, the mere remains of life. To this puzzle there are at least two solutions. One, embalming, was the solution of the Mycenaeans; by this practice the last indignity of death is avoided. The body is preserved, and it may even be held to continue a kind of limited life in its house beneath the ground. Traces of this practice may survive in Homer,[48] but the Homeric solution takes the opposite course. The body is washed, oiled, purified, if wounded, with flour (XVIII.350–53, xxiv.43–45), and shrouded; it is, as it were, cleaned and packaged and thus marked off from nature. It is then burnt. That which had been sustained by the organic *menos* is now handed over to pure *menos* and destroyed. Whereas rotting is unclean, burning is clean; the thing that rots becomes something formless, whereas the thing burnt ceases to exist altogether. To be nothing is an absolute condition and thus is a kind of form; the burnt corpse has been spared decay. The bones persist, because the Homeric fire of wood and suet was not hot enough to burn them; they are in a sense embalmed, as they are folded in layers of fat, placed in a golden vessel, and buried deep, with heavy stones above them, where it is hoped no change of place or state will ever come to them (XXII.238–57, XXIV.792–98).

The fire is one half of the funeral, the half that deals with the dead organism. The other half deals with the departed as a social identity, and from this point of view the funeral is a long farewell. The dead man is thought of as someone going away on a journey; the things and creatures burnt with Patroclus are spoken of as "all that is fitting for the corpse to have in his journey to the misty dark" (XXIII.50–51; cf. 137). The formal laments, the *gooi*, do not speak of the dead man as he was in life; rather they speak of how things are now that he is gone, the difference made by his absence. Mourning is not so much memory of the past as a definition of the new situation; mourning thus looks forward to the situation beyond the funeral and celebrates the departed, not for what he did, but for how much he will be missed. The living person is thus dismissed, and a new social figure, the absent one, is created. At the close of the ceremony this negative figure is immortalized by the *sēma*, which is set up for "men-to-come to inquire about" (xi.76; cf. VII.89–91, iv.584, xxiv.80–84).

The *sēma* is *empedon*; a *sēma* is mentioned in a simile as the typically *empedon* thing (XVII.434–36). The man who is dead to others survives as a name and a history. He will provoke the question: Who is it that is dead?—and to this question men will for a while be able to provide an answer. The *sēma* on earth mirrors the *psuchē* in the house of Hades; both are permanent impotent markers of the identity that is gone.[49] The *psuchai* in Hades survive, in a sense, but they survive in an inert condition. They have no adventures after death. Even in the *Odyssey*, where Odysseus can evoke the *psuchai* by a magical procedure and where the conversations of the dead among themselves are recorded, the world of the *psuchai* is not thought of as a world of experience but of memory.[50] The dead tell each other the events of their lives, and that is all. One recently dead may be thought of as a messenger from the living; otherwise, the dead have no knowledge of events after their own death. They are hungry for news of the living (xi.457–64, 492–540). Anticleia can give Odysseus news of Ithaca only because, having died since his departure, she has been there more recently than he has.[51] In life the *psuchē* is not a locus of experience, and in death it is incapable of experience or change. So the existence of the *psuchē* in Hades is not a continuation of the personal life but rather a kind of monument to the fact that personal life once existed.[52]

The prayer of the *psuchē* before the body's burial is thus not really a prayer for admission to another world; the house of Hades is a world only in a very limited sense. The *psuchē* prays for release from this world, which may be thought of as admission to an antiworld. Hades is lord of one-third of the inheritance of Cronos, but he is "loathed of gods and men," and his realm lies beyond the ocean stream (xi.155–59)—which is to say, outside the world. His world is a nonworld. Similarly, the funeral is a conversion of the person into a nonperson, into the negative of a person. The body is spared decay by being annihilated. The social person is spared social weakness—unfulfilled responsibilities, unrealizable wishes—by being converted from an active person into a remembered and remembering person. In both senses the funeral purifies the dead man by setting a definite period to his existence and converting him into something not subject to change.

For the living, the funeral is a ceremony of parting; the dead depart, and the living take their leave of them. Since, in community, we are one with one another—especially with those to whom we are bound by love or kinship—this parting also tears at the mourner, who, in parting with the dead, parts with a part of himself. This thought leads to an interpretation of the shearing of the hair.[53]

Between death and burning, the dead person is in a liminal condition; he is neither alive nor properly dead. He is decaying, yet he is clung to; his mourners thus enter the liminal realm with him. They share his death and bring on themselves an image of death's befoulment by pouring ashes over themselves, tearing their hair and cheeks, rolling in the dung, and throwing off their clothes.[54] The dead man is going on a journey, and the impulse of the mourners is to go with him; the most perfect mourning would be suicide, and this is treated as a real possibility (XVIII.34). Short of this the mourner may suspend his life, as Achilles abstains from food, sleep, washing, and the act of love (XXIV.129–31). The time of mourning is the last time together for the dead and the living, who share some condition between life and death. This sharing is enacted by the funeral feast of the Myrmi-

181

dons, which is held by the corpse of Patroclus; the mourners eat the meat of the sacrificial animals, while the blood is poured around the corpse in a ceremony of feeding the *psuchē* (XXIII.34).

The shearing of the hair, I suggest, has to do with this common liminality of corpse and mourner. The hair (along with the nails) is unique among body parts in that it grows and yet is inert and can be lost without pain or injury. Furthermore, the hair continues to grow after death. Hair is thus part of us without quite being a part, and has a kind of life of its own; its life is a metonym of our life.[55] When Achilles left Phthia for Troy, Peleus vowed that Achilles would keep his hair uncut and on his return would cut it and dedicate it to the river Spercheius. He thus vowed that, if Achilles brought his (actual) life back to his own soil, his (metaphorical) life would be given to the river; life would be paid for life. At Patroclus' funeral Achilles breaks this vow, cuts his hair, and puts it in Patroclus' hands on the pyre. By sending his life to the fire with the body of his friend (XXIII.144–51), Achilles gives up his hope of returning to Phthia alive; he (metaphorically) dies with Patroclus, just as he later expects (actually) to die at Troy and be buried with Patroclus (XXIII.245–48).

Achilles' act is a more elaborate version of the ordinary ritual of mourning, in which the mourner places a lock of his hair on the body to be burnt (XXIII.134–36). Achilles' explanation of his act can guide us in our understanding of the more ordinary ritual. The mourner, placed between the living and the dead, splits himself in two; he gives a part or a version of his life to the dead man and thus asserts his solidarity with him. The mourner is then free to turn back and reassert his solidarity with the living. As the funeral releases the dead to death, so also it releases the living to life (cf. XXIII.52–53).

The death of a man inflicts a wound on the community. One point on the social network ceases to respond to the gifts and demands of the others. Furthermore, as the body of the dead man begins to rot, the whole social body, of which he had been a part, becomes vulnerable to the processes of nature. The dead man still engages the affections of his mourners, but he is turning into something else. The threat of deformation, formlessness, and impurity, therefore, is not local to the dead man; it affects all bound to him in ties of community.

The funeral pyre cauterizes and heals this wound. At the same time, through mourning and memorial, the social fabric is reconstructed in a new form which takes account of the absence of this member. In the funeral the community acts on its own behalf to reassert its own continuity in spite of the disorderly forces which assail it. By the funeral the community purifies itself.

THE ANTIFUNERAL

So far we have spoken of funerals as an activity of communities. But the heroes of the *Iliad* are warriors, and the theme of the *Iliad* is combat. Combat is not action within communities but between communities. Combat is that kind of social relation which is the negation of community. The warrior's act in battle wounds an alien community. The perfected negation of community, further, inheres not in killing the enemy but in denying him a funeral, for by this means the alien community is not only wounded but is also denied the means of healing itself.

Conflict within community is mediated and measured by agreed-upon procedures. In communal conflict—litigation, ordeal, duelling—there is injury but there is also healing; the impure is held within the forming pattern of the pure. Warriors on the battlefield may also engage in such mediated conflict, to the extent that they share a common code of war. The *Iliad* moves, as we saw, from such mediated conflict in the direction of absolute conflict. So long as the warriors promise each other a funeral—as in the duel between Hector and Ajax—they respect each other's communities and remain in a modified sense in community with each other. The code of the warrior, however, in the absence of a higher authority to which both sides can appeal, cannot be institutionalized and remains somehow arbitrary and insubstantial.

The terror of conflict does not rise from the fact that in conflict men endure injury and death, for injury and death are always and everywhere facts of life. Injury and death, when invested with appropriate meanings, are sufferable things; sometimes, indeed, they may be seen as ennobling and may even be embraced. The terror of conflict lies in the threat of impurity which conflict evokes. Mere conflict, unmediated by cultural forms, lacks conscious content and proves nothing except the existence of preponderant force; force within the cultural sphere is a blind source of formlessness and moral chaos. The emblem of this chaos within the *Iliad* is the antifuneral; the terror of the wrath of Achilles, evoked in the prologue, lies not in the fact that it sent so many *psuchai* of heroes to Hades but that it made them "a prey to dogs and a feast for birds" (I.4–5).[56] The antifuneral, by which the dead are stripped and left to the scavengers, is in the *Iliad* emblematic of the impurity latent in war. As we saw, this ultimate impurity never becomes actual in the poem; yet the threat of this impurity is the quintessential terror of the *Iliad*.

This same terror is expressed mythologically in the *kēres*, weird creatures which are proper to the battlefield and, indeed, are hardly mentioned except in connection with violent death. The *kēres* appear

in the battle scene on the great shield of Achilles, among the allegori-
cal figures which mingle with the warriors:

> There was Strife, there Turmoil, there the cursed Ker,
> Who had one newly wounded, alive, and another unwounded,
> And another, dead, from the fray she dragged by the feet.
> The clothes on her back were smeared with the blood of men.
>
> (XVIII.535–38)

The same lines occur (with one minor variation) in the Hesiodic *Shield
of Heracles,* with the added line: "Looking about terribly, with a roar
of gnashings" (*Aspis* 160). These "gnashings" are explained later in the
same poem:

> Again they fought. And among them
> The black Keres, clashing their white teeth,
> Grim-faced, shaggy, blood-bespattered, dread,
> Kept struggling for the fallen. They all wanted
> To drink black blood. Whom first they caught,
> Lying or fallen newly wounded, around him
> They threw their mighty talons, and the shade to Hades
> Went, in icy Tartarus. Their hearts were glutted
> With human blood; they threw away the corpse
> And back to the tumult and fighting rushed, in new desire.
>
> (*Aspis* 248–57)

The *kēres* in Hesiod eat the wounded; to die—at least in battle—is to
be eaten by a *kēr*. It seems clear that the same idea pervades the *Iliad*,
even though Homer, with quite characteristic tact, never tells us so.[57]
Sarpedon speaks of the "countless winged Keres" (XII.326–27) whom
no one can escape, and the dead Patroclus says: "the *kēr* gaped for
me, the hateful one, alotted to me at my birth" (XXIII.78–79). Each
man has his own *kēr*, who watches him hungrily. The *kēr* has an interest in his death and leads him to it (II.834 = XI.332; VIII.528). The
coward at the moment of danger "thinks of the *kēres*, and his teeth
chatter" (XIII.283).

The *kēres* have teeth; they also have wings and talons. They are
thus a composite of dogs and birds. Unburied bodies may be eaten by
various creatures—maggots, for instance, or fish; but dogs and birds
are the scavengers conventionally mentioned. The *kēres* thus are emblematic of the antifuneral. *Kēres*, however, do not eat the unburied
dead; they eat the dying. The presence of the *kēres* on the battlefield
suggests that the antifuneral is latent in all combat—that the defilement
of the dead by scavengers is an extension of combat and a development
of its inner logic.

Every organic being owes a debt to nature. So long as the metabolic fire burns within him, the animal consumes food and air and converts them into organic substance and the *menos* that moves the organs. At the moment of death the organism is converted from subject to object; flesh becomes meat. The *kēres* devouring the dying are an image of organic death, by which the animal is converted from eater to eaten.

Man, as a cultural creature, has the privilege of a funeral and avoids organic death; his body is embalmed or burnt. By its treatment of the body the community enacts its determination that even *qua* organism a man belongs to the order of culture and not to the realm of nature.

Men enjoy the privileges of culture because they are members of communities. In community men relate to one another as subjects; they perceive in the other a person like themselves whose purposes they in some sense share. Combat, however, is between communities, and in combat we reduce the enemy to an object, an obstacle or threat whom we would cheerfully obliterate in order to secure our own purposes. We thus treat our fellow men as if they were things in nature, forces or elements which it is the task of human virtue and skill to subdue and control. And since this objectification of the enemy is reciprocal, the warrior who goes into combat faces the danger that he also will be treated as a thing of nature. Thus, if the dead warrior is not recovered by his own community, he may well be treated like a dead animal, a mere piece of rubbish for disposal. Even while he is still fighting, the warrior feels that in the eye of the enemy he has become a mere beast or thing, to be overcome by force. Again reciprocally, the opposing forces appear to him like inhuman nature, and he feels that he is threatened, not merely with death, but with being devoured.

This line of thought explains the *kēres* and also explains how the antifuneral is possible, but it does not explain why the antifuneral is used as a threat. In Homer the dead enemy is not simply disregarded and thus left as prey to scavengers; the heroes—Hector and Achilles alike—definitely intend that this fate shall befall their enemies. The terror of combat lies not merely in the withdrawal of the norms of culture but in their reversal: we delight in inflicting on the other what we most fear for ourselves. Impurity is not only endured; it is even celebrated. This reversal of norms occurs, as we shall see, because culture is constructed not only out of nature but also in contrast to nature, so that, as we move in combat from the cultural to the natural, the order of culture is turned inside out. In order to elucidate this dark saying, it will be necessary to take a long step back and reconstruct in general outline the Homeric understanding of man's place in nature. This reconstruction, incidentally, will explain why the anti-funeral conventionally involves precisely this pair: birds and dogs.

The Similes and the Shield of Achilles

The world of the *Iliad* is an inhabited battlefield. This poet, or rather this tradition of poetry, has imagined a world which in this aspect cannot have been drawn from the poets' experience: a world in which warfare has come to be, not an adventure or occasional crisis, but the ordinary business of life. The Trojan War in this poem has a settled, established quality; we know that it had a beginning and will have an end, but neither event is part of the story of the *Iliad*. The men of the *Iliad* have and seem to expect no occupation but combat.

Combat is a purely social activity; in combat men measure themselves against men—and in Homer, against gods—but not against nature. In combat the resources men have gained from nature are deployed and despoiled, but no new resources are generated. With the exception of the Trojan women at their looms, the characters of the *Iliad* engage in no productive activity. The Greeks live by theft, the Trojans by consuming their savings—in effect, from Priam's treasure. The economics of the *Iliad* is an economics of consumption and exchange but not of productivity.

The society of the *Iliad*, therefore, is not self-renewing. We know that the war cannot go on forever and that the society built around it is not a viable or complete society. The world of the *Iliad* is a reduced world; two communities are shown maintaining themselves with dwindling resources under specially restricted conditions. This reduced image of society excludes the full variety of activity proper to a functioning, self-renewing society. In particular, productive nature—the source of life and the fundamental problem of human action—is excluded from the social world of the *Iliad*. These societies, enclosed and encapsulated in the discipline of their struggle with each other, subsist on resources borrowed from a wider, more fully functioning society.

This wider world appears in the minds of the characters, who often speak of a time of peace or of a place at peace. It appears also in the mind of the poet, particularly in the similes. Each simile is a kind of window through which we glimpse a world beyond the battlefield of Troy. Through the device of the simile, the wider world is included in the narrower. Through the similes the battlefield is located within the wider world and, at the same time, resembles all the various aspects of the wider world, so that the part recapitulates the whole.

The rhetorical purpose of the similes is not to describe the world of peace but to make vivid the world of war; that is, the images they convey of the wider world are incidental to their intent. They therefore have some of the quality of dream material. The poet reaches for some memory or image to clarify the scene he has set before us; he takes the image which strikes him as having the greatest potency in its context. Because this process is unreflective, the recurrent themes of the similes can be taken to reflect and express a substratum of the poet's mind or—since probably few similes are his original invention—of the poetic tradition in which he is at home. A catalogue of the recurrent themes in the similes can thus tell us what images were held by this tradition to be particularly striking and meaningful. In the similes, taken as a group, there comes to the surface an inchoate, implicit, collective understanding of what things in the world are of most significance to men.

Against the similes we can set the Shield of Achilles (XVIII.478–608). The Shield is intended as a systematic image of the wider world outside the *Iliad*. The patterns which emerge unreflectively in the similes have here been reflected upon and set into coherence. Yet this very difference makes of the Shield a kind of master simile; the pattern of the Shield can instruct us in our reading of the similes. We shall therefore begin with the Shield and go on to the similes—remembering that our fundamental purpose is to grasp the Homeric understanding of the place of man in nature.

The Shield is laid out in five concentric circles. The poet begins his description at its center and moves outward. The inner circle represents earth, sea, and heaven, the sun and the moon, and the constellations, which are *teirea*—signs or portents (XVIII.485). Thus we are shown nature, in the absence of man, as a realm of order and significance.

The second ring represents the human world per se. Two cities are shown, one at peace and one at war. In the city at peace we see a wedding and a litigation—ceremonies of social solidarity and social conflict. In the city at war we see both a council debating war tactics and an ambush taking place.

The third ring represents the four agricultural seasons: plowing, harvest, vintage, and the fallow time when the cattle are driven into the fields to fertilize them for the plowing to come. In this ring we see man *with* nature and the cycle of man's productive activity.

The fourth ring portrays a round dance; society, in other words, which on the second ring has been portrayed as a structure of cooperation and conflict, here appears as pure *communitas*.[58] And as the fourth ring echoes the second, with a difference, so also the fifth echoes the first; here is the ocean stream, which, as it runs around the whole world, so also runs around this picture of the whole world. The inner two rings portray nature and culture as meaningful structure; the outer two portray culture and nature as pure act or pure process. The Shield moves from nature to culture to productivity, which is the inclusion of nature in culture; it then moves back through culture to nature. The whole is a symmetrical construction, A–B–C–B–A, of the familiar Homeric type.

If we attempt the interpretation of the similes by means of this pattern, no easy correlations leap to the eye. The similes of the *Iliad* are extraordinarily diverse in both their inner content and their application to the poetic context in which they occur, and probably no useful universal statements can be made about them. By noting recurrences, however, some points can be made.

Some few—but very few—of the similes deal with themes from social life and thus link with ring two (and ring four) of the Shield. One thinks, for instance, of the two men disputing over the boundary of a field (XII.421–24), the little girl who cries to be picked up (XVI.7–11), the exiled stranger who arrives unexpectedly (XXIV.480–83). Such similes are relatively rare because social themes are already the themes of the poem proper—just as no simile compares anything to a warrior or a scene of combat.[59] The similes open out the poem; there is no reason for them to contain what the poem already contains.

Broadly speaking, three themes dominate the similes. First, there is the large group devoted to weather: fog, snow, whirlwind, dust storm, flood, etc. To these I would attach similes of forest fires, earthquakes, and thunderbolts, as these are also sent by Zeus. In the great majority of these similes nature is presented as stormy, violent, and dangerous; the weather similes are thus linked to the ocean similes, especially those of the frequent type which refer to waves breaking on the shore or on a crag. Here, then, is the first of our themes: nature as hostile to man. The similes of this theme are linked to the Shield—the ocean and shore similes being linked, obviously, to the outer rim, the weather similes to the center, through the link between stars and weather and through the double role of Zeus as sender of meteorological signs and contriver of the weather.

The second major theme is the technical procedures involved in such human activities as carpentry, weaving, and so forth. Here nature is benign and turned to the purposes of man.[60] Productive activity, excluded from the dramatic world of the *Iliad*, reappears in the similes (which are thus linked to the third ring of the Shield).

A third group of similes (by my classification, the largest single group) involves hunting and herding. Wild animals often appear in these similes—in the hunting similes, obviously, but in the herding similes as well. This group, further—and this group alone—includes similes mentioning dogs.

Finally, we may add a small group of similes representing wild animals among themselves. This group—and this group alone—includes similes mentioning birds.

It is not so easy to discern the basic theme of either group. The similes involving wild animals among themselves have no link to the Shield; an interpretation of them will thus have to wait until we consider their application, as similes, to their context. The hunting and herding similes are linked to the third ring of the Shield through the fallow-time herding scene which appears there. This scene includes two lions who seize a bull and are driven off by men and dogs (XVIII. 579–81). Since herding—and hunting for edible meat—are productive activities, we are at first tempted to include these with the other technical similes, and some few of them do in fact belong in that group (e.g., II.474–76, IV.433–36, XIII.491–95).

In the great majority of hunting and herding similes, however, nature appears not benign and pliant but alien and menacing. These similes thus attach rather to the first group, those involving weather and the sea. The herdsman appears in several similes as an observer to whom nature seems dangerous, or at least distant and alien. Thus the mist "is no friend to the herdsman" (III.11); the goatherd sees the approaching thunderstorm and shivers (IV.275–79); the herdsman far off hears the sound of the two torrents meeting (IV.452–55); he is glad when the heavens clear and reveal the stars (VIII.555–59). Like the sailor (cf. XV.624–29, XIX.375–78), the herdsman is someone who confronts undomesticated nature in a way that most men do not.

Agrou ep' Eschatiēn

The sharpest demarcation in the Homeric landscape, second only to the distinction between land and sea, is the line between tillable lowland and hill or grazing land. On the alluvial plain there are fields, gardens, cities, and houses; the plain is the properly inhabited world of family life and political community. Around the plain runs the mountain wall, and those who climb this wall find themselves in a separate world: the *agrou ep' eschatiēn*, the land beyond the limit of agriculture. Here the herds live (except in the fallow season) with the herdsmen who care for them. The herdsmen do not live in proper houses but in *stathmoi*, lean-tos or sheds, and there are no families;

189

herding is a task for young men (xvii.20–21), before they reach an age
to have a wife, an *oikos*, and a *klēros*—a family, a house, and a tract
of agricultural land (xiv.64). The hill land is included in the description of the Shield in a kind of three-line footnote to the third ring
(XVIII.587–89). This land beyond the limit of the sown is a no-man's-
land between nature and culture; men share it with the wild beasts
who also live there: lions, wolves, jackals, wild boar, and deer.

The *agrou ep' eschatiēn*, then, is a marginal environment, and only
marginally included on the Shield. Yet this environment dominates
the similes. This is because the *agrou ep' eschatiēn* is an image of the
battlefield. In order to understand this point, we must consider the
application of the similes to their context, and specifically to the situation of combat. We begin with the similes of technical activity.

Combat is not a productive activity, but it is technical, involving
planning, skill, and the use of tools. So combat can be compared to
technical activity. But when it is so compared in the *Iliad*, the effect
is nearly always shocking,[61] as when the blood runs down Menelaus'
flesh like the dye carefully traced over ivory (IV.141–47), or when
Achilles' horses trample the corpses like oxen threshing grain (XX.495–
502), or

> As when a man gives the hide of a great ox
> To the folk for stretching, once he's soaked it with oil,
> And they pick it up and, leaning apart, they stretch it
> In a circle; the moisture springs out, the oil soaks in,
> When many tug it; it's all stretched out between—
> So this way and that they tugged in a little space
> At the corpse on both sides.
>
> (XVII.389–95)

What is skill in relation to objects becomes ruthlessness once it is
applied to persons. The technical similes most often remind us that
in combat we treat persons as objects.

The technical simile usually stands in contrast to its context: a peaceful act is unexpectedly compared to the violence of war. The simile
of weather and the sea, on the other hand, most often develops and
reinforces the tone of its context; weather is even more violent than
war. Thus, in Book Eleven, Agamemnon attacks like a forest fire raging
through timber (XI.155–59); Hector counterattacks like a whirlwind
across the sea (XI.297–98) and like a thunderstorm which drives the
foam high up against the shore (XI.305–9). Examples could be multi-
plied into the scores. Combat is an arena of force, and weather appears

in the similes most often as an image of pure force unleashed in the world.

Thus man's war with man is compared to man's struggle with undomesticated nature. Peace, we are reminded, has its violences; man's world is an uncertain achievement, hard won and easily ruined. There is always the threat of the storm which floods the fields (V.87–94) and drowns the children (XXI.281–83). Man's contention with storm can be read as an aspect of man's contention with the gods, particularly with Zeus, who sends the storm (e.g., X.5–8, XII.278–86), perhaps out of his rage with man (XVI.384–93), and who has filled the sky with his portents: thunderbolt, falling star, and rainbow (XIII.242–44, IV.75–77, XII.547–52). There are thus above and below man (as at the center and outer rim of the Shield) horizontal frontiers marking man's relations with forces more powerful than himself: the sky above, from which the weather descends, and the rivers and sea below, which rise in storm and flood to waste his fields and break his ships.[62]

Nature is also menacing in the hunting and herding similes, as we saw; but these similes, although they also compare man's war with man to man's war with nature, do so in a different way. Their recurrent theme is battle between man and a dangerous wild animal, usually a lion or wild boar. Here the struggle is between equals; sometimes the battle inclines toward man, sometimes toward beast. The wild animals have families of their own; the lioness stands to defend her cubs (XVII.133–36) or searches for them (XVIII.318–22); the birds feed their young (IX.323–24); the wasps swarm out to defend their children (XII.167–70, XVI.259–65). The violence of the wild beast is thus dignified, as the violence of the human warrior is dignified, by reference to the weak who depend upon that violence for their protection. In the similes of hunting and herding, man's war with man is compared to man's struggle with the beasts who live around him, who are alien species yet somehow like himself.[63]

The *agrou ep' eschatiēn* is a vertical frontier; it marks both the limit of the community and a no-man's-land between communities.[64] It makes relatively little difference whether the adjoining community is thought of as animal or human. In either case the herdsman's task stations him on the frontier, subject to attack. Most conflicts between communities take the form of border raids for cattle (cf. I.154); the wild animals also attack the cattle. Deer can be thought of as cattle belonging to the wild predators; huntsmen are then raiders of the wild community and will have to contend with its defenders (cf. XV.271–76). In the weather similes the warrior is presented as sheer force; in the technical similes he is reduced to an object; in the similes of hunting and herding we are reminded that the enemy is like ourselves and that conflict arises from this very likeness, as two groups of similar nature contend for the control of scarce resources.

Thus the warrior who is compared to a wild beast is not demeaned; on the contrary, these transformations (in the form of similes) mark moments of high heroic action:

> Achilles across from him rose up like a lion,
> Ravening, whom men have struggled to kill,
> Collecting all the folk. He first ignores them
> And passes, but then some swift young spearman
> Hits him; he crouches, gaping; the foam from his teeth
> **Drips**; the spirit of wrath constrains his heart;
> With his tail the flanks and ribs on his two sides
> He lashes, and he drives himself to battle.
> Eyes gleaming, he springs forward, to slaughter
> Some man, or himself to die in the midst of turmoil.
>
> (XX.164–73)

If we turn to the similes involving wild animals among themselves, we find that nearly all of them represent a predator and its prey. Lions attack deer (XI.113–21, etc.); a dolphin attacks little fish (XXI.22–26); a hawk attacks starlings (XVII.755–59) or a pigeon (XXI.493–96). These similes provide a new image of combat. Whereas the struggle between man and lion presents combat as an equal relation, the struggle between lion and deer presents combat as radically unequal. Both images are needed. Combat, when it comes to conclusions, takes parties previously classified as equals and reclassifies them into victor and vanquished. Every warrior seeks in combat to become the predator and risks becoming the prey. The wild beasts among themselves (since they form no part of the human world) do not appear in the Shield, but they are important in the similes. Predator and prey provide an image of the outcome of combat.

Man the huntsman is also a predator of wild prey, but this point is seldom used in the similes. Where we are shown the hunting of deer, goats, or rabbits, the focus is never on the huntsman but on some predatory animal, either a wild predator, who contests his prey with the huntsman (III.23–27, XV.271–78), or else the hunter's own dogs (VIII.338–42, X.360–64, XV.579–81, XXII.189–93). Prey is defined in relation to predator, and man is not himself a predator but is rather one vicariously, through his dogs. This notion of vicarious predation, is, as we shall see, the key to understanding the role of dogs in the *Iliad*.[65]

Dogs

There are various kinds of dogs in Homer. There is the *trapezeus*, table dog, who is "kept for decoration" (xvii.310).[66] Such dogs are spoken of with contempt (xvii.290–323).

Then there is the *thōs*, the wild dog or jackal. He also is a miserable creature, who attacks wounded game and is frightened off by a lion (XI.474–81).

The proper dog—the dog of the similes—inhabits the *agrou ep' eschatiēn*, the space between the wild and the tame. There he is man's ally in defense of his cattle and in his war with the dangerous beasts. By domesticating the dog, man has taken into his service against the predators a predatory animal. Man has thus, as it were, picked up a piece of his vertical frontier with nature and turned it against itself. Predatory nature has come to be something with a definite place within the human world. But that place is on the frontier; the dog, intermediate between man and beast, properly defends the line between man and beast.

The hunting dog is an instrument; the table dog is an ornament. In either case the dog is an extension of the man. Dogs and men together form a functioning unit. Thus if one warrior is compared to a wild beast, the warrior opposed to him can be compared to a whole group of men and dogs:

> So he spoke, and his heart rose in his breast;
> He went against Idomeneus intent on war.
> Nor did fear seize Idomeneus like a child,
> But he waited, like a mountain boar in its pride
> Which awaits a great troop of men advancing
> In a lonely place, and its back bristles up.
> Its eyes shine with fire; then its teeth
> Are whetted, ready to drive off dogs and men.
> So Idomeneus waited, nor retreated
> From Aeneas coming toward him.
>
> (XIII.468–77)

Elsewhere the huntsman stands for the leading hero, and the dogs for the subordinate troops:

> As when a huntsman sends in the sharp-toothed dogs
> Against a raging wild boar or a lion,
> So against the Achaeans he sent the high-hearted Trojans.
>
> (XI.292–94)

The *plēthus*, the common soldiers, are like dogs because they are mere instruments of war, incapable of maintaining the battle on their own:

So he spoke, and they raised the corpse from the ground,
High, high up. The Trojan folk shouted
On their side, when they saw the corpse raised.
They charged like dogs, who against a wild boar
That's wounded leap ahead before the huntmen;
For a while they rush, and try to tear at it,
But when it twists among them in its pride,
Back they retreat and tremble this way and that.
Thus the Trojans for a while kept up the fray,
Thrusting with swords and with their two-edged spears.
But when the Ajaxes turned about against them
And stood, their color turned; no one of them dared,
Leaping forward, to battle about the corpse.

(XVII.722–34)

The dog is still a jackal at heart; he is a dangerous fighter but lacks stamina and courage. He is unruly and unreliable. When Odysseus is overcome by rage, he calls his heart a dog; it barks at him like a bitch with pups, and he reproves it (xx.10–18). Nothing, he says, "is more doglike than the belly," which demands to be fed, regardless (vii.216–21). A part of the self becomes like a dog when the part is only imperfectly under control.

The dog is thus ornament, instrument, subordinate, or part. The relation between man and dog is metonymic; the dog is a piece of unruly nature next to man or within him.

Yet the relation of man to dog is also metaphoric. A person can be called a dog or addressed as a dog. In the vocative, "dog" is invariably an insult. Sometimes the point of the insult seems to lie merely in the subordinate status of the dog; thus both Diomedes and Achilles call Hector "dog" when Apollo rescues him from battle (XI.362–67 = XX.449–54). Hector could not rescue himself and was saved only because he was Apollo's pet; this suggests the proportion: man is to god as dog is to man.

More often the insult refers to some specific quality of the dog. The dog is thought of as ruled by appetite; thus Hera was "dog-faced" (XVIII.396) when she tried to dispose of her crippled child Hephaestus. She was acting in a self-indulgent, irresponsible way. The goddesses are called dogs when they fail to heed the authority of their betters (VIII.483, XXI.481). The dog is a scavenger (cf. xviii.105); to have a "dog's mind" is also to be "thievish" (Hesiod *Works and Days* 67). Thus Achilles calls Agamemnon a dog (I.159, 225, IX.373) because Agamemnon is *dēmoboros* (I.231), a devourer of public property. The dog's affection can be bought with pleasure; he fawns on the master

194

who brings him sweetmeats (x.216). Thus the adulterous woman is a dog—Helen preeminently, even in her own descriptions of herself (III.180, VI.344, 356, iv.145), but also Clytemnestra (xi.424, 427), Aphrodite (viii.319), and Penelope's faithless serving maids (xix.154).

The serving maids are often called "dogs," but the implication is not always sexual; these women have various vices. Dogs are *hulako-mōroi*, foolish barkers, and Melantho is called a dog when she speaks loudly and improperly (xviii.338). Thus Melanthius calls Eumaeus a dog to disparage Eumaeus' remarks (xvii.248), as if to point out that talk is cheap. More specifically, the serving maids are inhospitable and unkind to the beggar-Odysseus; they fail to entertain the stranger and are therefore dogs (xix.91, 372). Penelope's suitors are the worst possible guests; Odysseus calls them dogs just before he kills them (xxii.35). In all these cases the dog is the emblem of the imperfectly socialized. The dog is the most completely domesticated animal; he is capable even of such human feelings as love and shame. But he is only imperfectly capable; he remains an animal. The dog thus represents man's resistance to acculturation. In Homeric language we would say that the dog lacks *aidōs*. The dog stands for an element within us that is permanently uncivilized. As the dog is a predator within culture, so the dog in us is the predator within us. Thus metonym and metaphor are linked; the man who is called a dog is likened, as it were, to a lower part of himself. He is thus reduced to less than himself. When we are lacking in *aidōs*, in full social humanity, we are liable to become dogs; that is to say, uncontrolled predatory nature within us is liable to take charge.[67]

There is in Homer an instructive contrast between dogs and horses. Both are companions and instruments of man, but they stand to one another rather as Caliban to Ariel. Dogs in Homer are anonymous,[68] but horses have personal names. Horses, like heroes, can have divine parents; they can be immortal; one horse even speaks.[69] Horses thus form a civil series parallel to man; when Hector appeals to his horses, he does so in terms of reciprocity:

> Xanthus and you, Podargus, Aethon, bright Lampon,
> Now pay me back the care in such abundance
> Andromache gave you, daughter of Eëtion.
> She served you first with grain that honeys the heart
> And mixed you wine to drink when you wanted that,
> Even before me, and I am her husband.
> So come on, bestir yourselves.
>
> (VIII.185–91)

There is, as we saw, a parallel between the *agrou ep' eschatiēn* and the battlefield. On the first the herdsman defends his cattle against the predatory beasts; on the second the warrior defends his dependents and property against a predatory enemy. Each defender has also his aggressive version: the herdsman becomes a huntsman, the warrior a raider and sacker of cities. There is, however, this difference. The herdsman has the help of dogs—beasts, like the wild beasts, who can do most of his fighting for him. The warrior has only the help of the peaceful, herbivorous horse. The horse can help him escape from danger, but the warrior must do his own fighting. He must, as it were, be man and dog together—and this, as we have seen, is the usual pattern of the similes. Sometimes he becomes simply a dog:

> Hector went with the foremost, swelling with rage,
> As when a dog with a wild boar or a lion
> Bites at it behind, pursuing with quick feet
> The flanks and rump and watches out for its twistings,
> So Hector drove in on the long-haired Achaeans,
> Always killing the laggard. And they were afraid.
>
> (VIII.337–42)

This is the first of three similes in which a hero is compared to a dog. The second is in Book Ten:

> As when two sharp-toothed dogs, who are skilled in hunting
> Pursue with never a pause a hare or young deer
> Up through the brush, and it struggles to stay ahead,
> So Tydeus' son and city-sacking Odysseus
> Cut off his escape and pursued him with never a pause.
>
> (X.360–64)

The third such simile, which involves Achilles, is in Book Twenty-two and will be quoted later (p. 199). Here we will observe only that Dolon, the "rabbit or young deer" of the Book Ten simile, is no warrior; confronted with warriors, he has no resource except to run. As he becomes mere prey, his pursuers become mere predators.[70]

Combat appears in the similes as a kind of predation, in which the enemy appear alternately as competing predators and as prey. The warrior may become (metaphorically) a predator, or he may mobilize the predator (metonymically) within him—that is, the dog. But the dog as metonym shades into the dog as metaphor; in evoking the dog within himself, he runs the risk of becoming a dog, that is, of becoming something less than himself.

This point can be clarified by a further contrast between the dog and the horse. The dog is carnivorous, the horse herbivorous; man is both. Grain, however—the diet of the horse—is not digestible by man until is has been cooked and made into bread. The line between man and horse is fixed by nature. Meat, by contrast, is digestible when raw; it is eaten cooked as a matter of custom. The line between man and dog is fixed only by culture. On the battlefield, where the rules of culture break down, the warrior may become a raw-meat eater, as it is said of Achilles:

> He is a raw-meat eater, not to be trusted;
> He will show you neither pity nor *aidōs*.
>
> (XXIV.207–8)

The eating of raw meat, since it bypasses a rule of culture, is a kind of impurity; the image of the warrior as raw-meat-eater catches an aspect of the impurity of war. This aspect is developed in a simile describing Achilles' troops:

> Achilles reviewed and armed his Myrmidons
> Through all the camp in armor; they were like wolves,
> Raw-eaters, having at heart quenchless valor.
> They tear apart a great horned stag in the mountains
> And gobble it; their jaws are covered with gore.
> In a pack they come down to the black-watered spring,
> Lapping with narrow tongues the black water's
> Surface, belching bloody gore. The heart
> In each is steadfast, but the bellies groan.
> So the captains and leaders of the Myrmidons
> Around the brave squire of swift-footed Achilles
> Gathered.
>
> (XVI.155–66)

We note that raw-meat-eating, which should be natural to wolves, is shown in the simile as violent and sickening. Hesiod wrote:

> Perses, cast these things into your heart
> And listen to justice; think not of force.
> This law the son of Cronos set out for men,
> But for fish and beasts and winged birds
> To eat each other, since they have no justice.
> To men he gave justice; it is best.
>
> (*Works and Days* 274–79)

The most perfect injustice is cannibalism, since the other is thereby treated as pure object and not only overcome but even digested.[71] The typical situation which puts justice and a man's sense of *aidōs* to the test is the arrival of a stranger. The stranger is helpless, a natural prey, as it were; yet the household is obligated through household ceremonies to convert the stranger from a nonentity to a person with a status. Hostility to the stranger is both natural and monstrous. Polyphemus, that perfectly uncivil monster, did not entertain his guests; he ate them. So Eumaeus' dogs would have eaten stranger-Odysseus if Eumaeus had not restrained them (xiv.29–36). So also: if it were not for the restraints of civility, man would become to man as predator to prey.

But on the battlefield, where all community norms are reversed, the warrior aims to establish exactly this relation with his enemy. As the warrior tends to become a predator, as he mobilizes the dog within him, so also he moves in the direction of eating his enemy. This is a buried theme in the *Iliad*, present in the image of the man-devouring *kēres* and in Hector's characterization of the Greeks as "dogs brought here by the *kēres*" (VIII.527): they have come to eat and be eaten. The theme is present in the simile which describes Menelaus circling Paris

> As a lion delights to come on a great body,
> Finding an antlered stag or a wild goat
> In his hunger. He will eat him, even if
> The swift dogs and young men drive him off—
> So Menelaus delighted to see with his eyes
> Godlike Paris.

> (III.23–28)

The theme is present in the similes in which the dead body fought over by contending armies is compared to the prey which the wild beast tries to seize from the huntsmen and devour (XIII.198–202, XVIII.161–64), and it is present also when Zeus says that Hera wants to "eat the Trojans raw" (IV.35–36) and when Hecuba says of Achilles, "if only I could get the liver from his middle and eat it, rending it with my teeth" (XXIV.212–13). It is present when Achilles says to Hector:

> Hector, cursed, don't talk to me of compacts.
> There are no oaths to be trusted between men and lions,
> Nor do wolves and lambs come to likeness of hearts,
> But ever their wits are fixed on harm to each other;
> So between you and me there is no friendship.

> (XXII.261–65)

Hector has just asked Achilles for an exchange of promises that the victor will grant the loser proper burial; Achilles responds that he will treat his enemy as a wild beast treats its prey.

Finally—and once only in the *Iliad*—the theme of cannibalism comes to the surface: at the moment of greatest terror in the poem, the

moment just before he kills Hector, Achilles rejects his last appeal
and says:

> Do not, dog, make appeals to my knees or your parents.
> If only my *menos* and *thumos* would let me chop you
> Raw, and eat you for meat, such things you have done.
> There is no one who can keep the dogs from your head,
> Not if ten and twenty times your ransom
> They would bring and heap, and promise more yet,
> Not if he told me to weigh your body with gold,
> Dardanian Priam. Not even so will your mother
> Lay you out and weep for you, she who bore you,
> But dogs and birds will share you out in pieces.
>
> (XXII.345–54)

This is the fourth time in the *Iliad* that Hector is addressed as "dog."
Earlier in the same scene, however, Achilles is the dog:

> Behind Hector with constant pursuit followed swift Achilles
> As when a mountain-deer fawn is pursued by a dog;
> It springs from its bed, and away through glens and valleys
> It tries to escape by cowering deep in the brush,
> But he tracks it, running steady, until he finds it—
> So Hector could not escape swift-footed Achilles.
>
> (XXII.188–93)

The duel of Hector and Achilles comes down in the end to dog-eat-
dog; Hector, who had failed to throw Patroclus to the dogs, is thrown
to the dogs himself.

On the battlefield man becomes predator to man. Two different
metaphors are concealed in this phrase. On the one hand, the enemy
may be thought of as an opposing predator, a lion or wild boar. In
this case the enemy retains his dignity, and the warrior thinks of himself as the huntsman who drives on the snarling, cowering dogs. This
metaphor, however, lasts only so long as the adversaries confront each
other as equals. The defeated warrior loses his dignity and generates
a second metaphor; he becomes deer or rabbit, prey. The victorious
warrior comes down with him and becomes his merely predatory self,
that is, a dog. The extreme case of defeat is death; the dead body is
mere inert spoil to the predators, which leap upon it—as in the similes
cited earlier. This second metaphor is enacted in the antifuneral; to
feed one's enemies to the dogs is vicarious cannibalism.[72] The antifuneral is thus an extension of combat by other means; in it the victor
completes his predatory triumph over the vanquished.

THE IMPURITY OF THE HERO

The duality of the antifuneral—expressed in the duality of birds and dogs—is a metaphor of the duality of nature. Birds are wild animals, themselves divided between the predatory species and their prey; unlike the other wild animals, birds have no practical relations with men. They are not (in Homer) hunted by man, nor do they steal his cattle; they appear in the similes only among themselves. Birds therefore stand for nature as it is separate from us, unconnected to culture. Birds, further, inhabit the air; their movements are ominous, and their migrations foretell the seasons. They are a medium for the transmission of divine and cosmic messages. Birds thus form (as Aristophanes saw) a parallel series intermediate between gods and men.[73]

Birds therefore inhabit and are emblematic of man's horizontal frontier with nature. To be eaten by birds is to be consumed by the nature that is beyond our powers to control or conciliate. In the *Odyssey*, with special reference to the seafarer, fish are twice added to birds (xiv.135, xxiv.291); this completes the pattern. Man is threatened by air and water, storm and wave, by the nature above and below him.

Dogs, on the other hand, are specific to man's vertical frontier, to the nature he confronts as an equal and which he has included within himself. The corpse-devouring dog is emblematic of a strand of nature latent within culture, a strand which is imperfectly repressed and which threatens to devour culture from the inside. To be eaten by one's housedogs, as Priam imagines his own fate, is a form of social rot or cancer of the social organism; the proper superordinate-subordinate relation between man and dog is destroyed in the sack of the city, and the structure consumes itself.

What is suppressed in man by his community is mobilized by the same man on the battlefield. The predator in man is allowed—even forced—to run wild. The enemy is objectified, denied the privileges due to persons in community. He becomes mere nature and is left to the birds and fish.

Yet we must add that the enemy, once he has been converted into a thing of nature, can be readmitted to the community in this transformed state. He thus becomes a bit of the nature which culture exploits; he becomes fodder and meat. The warrior *allows* his enemy to be eaten by birds; he *causes* him to be eaten by dogs. The first expresses his carelessness of the vanquished; the second is a form of monstrous caring.

Combat, the negation of community, is (like eating one's guests) both natural and monstrous. Man is essentially a creature of culture, yet sometimes he acts like a creature of nature, like a blind force or appetite. We should not, however, think that the order of culture then drops away from him, revealing a simpler organization beneath. Man cannot escape his essence; if for a time he denies it, this denial must be forced upon him by the enormous pressures which have evicted him from his proper sphere. Man's entry into the sphere of nature can never be spontaneous or relaxed; he appears there as a creature out of place, monstrous and impure.

In the depths of the Great Day of Battle, Menelaus, himself despoiling a corpse, speaks to his enemies:

> Thus will you leave the ships of Danaan horsemen,
> Arrogant Trojans, insatiate of dread turmoil;
> You'll get full measure of every harm and shame,
> As you harmed me. You cowardly bitches, you felt
> No fear of the violent wrath of thundering Zeus,
> The Zeus of guests, who'll yet destroy your city.
> You took my wife, and many possessions with her—
> An easy theft, since she'd received you kindly—
> And now you press your way among the ships
> To hurl dread fire, and kill the warrior Achaeans.
> Yet you'll be held, though Ares push you on.
> Father Zeus, they say you are wise beyond others,
> Men or gods. Yet all this comes from you.
> Look how you favor men in their insolence,
> Trojans, whose force is tireless, nor can they
> Sate themselves with leveling battle and war.
> Of everything comes satiety: sleep and friendship,
> Honey-sweet song and the illustrious dance—
> Yet the longing comes on a man for love of these
> More than of war. But the Trojans are battle-insatiate.
> (XIII.620–39)

The opposite of *menos* is *koros*, satiety. *Menos* exhausts itself in action and is replaced by *koros* (XIX.221). That is the natural rhythm on which the rhythm of culture is based. But the great warrior is *akorētos*, insatiable. He steps outside the rhythm of culture; his *menos* never fails him. He is beyond the human scale—but at a certain cost.

The condition that descends on the warrior in the midst of battle is the *lussa*, a berserk state in which one "respects neither gods nor men" (IX.238–39). *Lussa* in later Greek means "rabies," and the word has this meaning in Homer also.[74] Teucer calls Hector a *kuna lussētēra*, a "rabid dog"; the poet describes Hector on the battlefield:

> He was mad like Ares or the destructive fire
> That goes mad in the mountains, among dense thickets of brush.

The foam came about his mouth, and his two eyes
Gleamed beneath shaggy brows; about him the helmet
Rattled terribly on his temples as he fought.

(XV.605–9)

The *lussa* is the heat of *menos* raised to a pitch of fever. Hector at
another point is "filled with *lussa*, like to a flame" (XIII.53). In the
rage of battle he becomes hot, fiery, foams at the mouth, and shakes
all over. The *lussa* is the highest peak of the warrior's power, yet it is
also a disease. Specifically, it is a disease of dogs.

The dog is thus an emblem of the impurity of battle. The warrior
becomes a mad dog as he enacts the inner contradiction of battle. On
behalf of a human community the warrior is impelled to leave community and act in an inhuman way. He becomes a distorted, impure
being; great in his power, he is at the same time reduced to something
less than himself.

The poet of the *Iliad* does not praise or dispraise war; he describes
it. He shows us the impurity and terror of war and enlists our compassion for those heroes who find themselves obliged to confront that
terror in the enemy—and in themselves. The warrior becomes impure
so that others may remain pure; this contradiction, only latent in the
case of the Greeks, who are so far from home, becomes explicit in the
case of Hector, who appears among his women with the dust and gore
of battle upon him (VI.266–68). The warrior must contend with himself, must contend with the very forces which he mobilizes within
himself. This self-contention gives rise to error. Thus the ethical
reading of Hector's story which we presented in chapter 4 can now be
seen to be grounded in the Homeric psychology. Hector's loss of
heroic balance, his reduction to something less than himself, can be
seen, not as the consequence of a weakness in his character, but as the
consequence of his special place within the action, as the leader of a
hopeless war. Hector is both the vehicle and the focus of enormous
forces, forces necessarily let loose by the impurity of battle.

On only two heroes does the *lussa* ever descend: on Hector and on
Achilles (XXI.542). For Hector the *lussa* is a source of weakness
(IX.304–6); for Achilles it is a source of strength. Thus these two
heroes, driven by fate into a duel, descend together into the pit of
impurity—together, but differently. Hector changes from man to dog
to meat for dogs; Achilles, from man to devourer of men. Achilles becomes something less than man and at the same time something more;
when the fever overtakes him, he becomes a malign demon. Sick himself, he is the bearer of sickness to others. He is both dog and star.
Priam sees him approaching Troy:

All shining like a star he crossed the plain,
The star of harvest, and its rays, far-seen,
Shine among many stars in the milky night.
They call it by the name of "Dog of Orion."
It is the brightest, fixed as an evil sign,
And brings great fevers to unhappy men.
Thus his armor gleamed on his breast as he ran.

(XXII.26–32)

THE PROBLEM OF ENDING THE *Iliad*

The impurity of the *Iliad* infects Achilles as much as Hector—not because the two are the same but because they are bound together in a single enactment. To the passive impurity of Hector—marked by the impure condition of his body and the angry, inconclusive mourning of his family—corresponds the active impurity of Achilles—marked by his inability to find any limit to his act. At no point can Achilles say: he and his have suffered enough; I am satisfied.

Impurity arises in the realm of force and is self-perpetuating through action and reaction. Hector had killed Patroclus and would have despoiled him; Achilles in return kills Hector, despoils and defiles his body, and slaughters prisoners on the pyre of Patroclus. All this Achilles thinks is due to his friend.[75] But the debt is still not paid.

The impurity of murder lies, not in death, but in the fact that death has been inflicted. Killing has always evoked killing; when those we love are murdered, the straight response is to murder the murderers and then to murder them again. To this process there is no limit. Within community, however, a limit can be created; a ceremony can intervene to set an end and a beginning:

Even for his brother's murder
A man takes blood-price, or for a son who is dead,
And the killer stays with his folk, having paid much,
And the other restrains his heart and his raging spirit,
Taking the blood-price.

(IX.632–36)

Hector and Achilles share no such common world.[76]

Combat, which is murder on behalf of others and for the sake of community, takes place between communities. The impurity of combat is thus in a sense beyond the reach of communal ceremony. The community can, by the funeral, purify death, even death in combat; for the man who dies is one of their own. But the community cannot purify the impurity of being killed in combat, for the killer is not one of their own. They can only hope to kill and defile him in return.

Thus, between communities impurity perpetuates itself in an endless chain.

For the poet of the *Iliad* this endless chain poses a problem of artistic closure. This problem he solves twice. The first solution, and the first conclusion of the poem, is the funeral games of Patroclus. Funeral games, according to the interpretation offered here, are a ceremony specifically aimed at purifying the impurity of being killed in combat. Since such purification is in a sense impossible, the ceremonial of the funeral games is to a degree a cultivated illusion. In the enactment of this illusion the action is resolved on the level of culture.

Homer's hero, Achilles, however, has in the course of the action departed from the sphere of culture. When Achilles dedicates himself to revenging Patroclus, he abandons his community and accepts his own death. In abandoning hope, he also abandons illusion; he remains disengaged from the healing illusions of community. Achilles' story must be concluded in another way—in the reconciliation with Priam. This reconciliation, as we shall see, takes place outside the sphere of culture; it is presented as an event possible only in poetry.

FUNERAL GAMES

Homer mentions four funeral games: those of Patroclus, Amaryngeus (XXIII.630), Oedipus (XXIII.679), and Achilles (xxiv.85–94). Hesiod adds one more when he tells us that he competed at the funeral of Amphidamas (*Works and Days* 650–59). The great geometric vases sometimes picture various contests in association with funeral scenes. The funeral games, which by the late archaic period had been replaced by the recurrent civic games familiar in classical times, are one of the relatively few Homeric institutions for which we have evidence independent of Homer. In all cases funeral games seem to have been held for warriors, perhaps always for warriors who died in combat; we shall consider them here as a ceremony designed to purify death in combat.

Games could be held on other occasions; the Phaeacians held games, along with dancing, tumbling, and bardic singing, as part of their entertainment of Odysseus. Tydeus, a messenger and self-invited guest in the house of Eteocles, challenged the Cadmaeans to games and defeated them all (IV.385–90). In these latter games, however, prizes were not awarded. In a simile the poet speaks of horses that run for a prize, "a tripod or a woman, in honor of a man who is dead" (XXII.164). We may conclude that the giving of prizes was specific to funeral games and that every mention of competition for prizes refers to a funeral (e.g., XI.698–702). Such occasions were relatively frequent, and the prizes were of significant value; thus Agamemnon speaks of his twelve horses:

> Stout prize-winners, who win prizes when they run.
> He would not be lacking in spoil, a man who had them,
> Nor lacking in possession of precious gold,
> So many prizes have these hooved horses won me.
>
> (IX.124–27)

Agamemnon, describing to Achilles in the underworld Achilles' own funeral games, says:

> Already you've been to the funeral of many,
> Of men, of heroes, when a king has died;
> The young men gird and ready themselves for prizes.
> But at those, had you seen thém, most would your heart have
> wondered,
> Such marvelous prizes set the goddess around you,
> Bright-shod Thetis. You were dear to the gods.
> So your name did not perish in death, but always
> For all men will your fame [*kleos*] be good,
> Achilles.
>
> (xxiv.87–94)

One common verb for the funeral is *ktereizein*, to use up property. When Andromache believes that Hector's body is lost to her forever, she says:

> There are clothes within your halls,
> Fine and delicate, made by the hands of women.
> I'll burn them all with the devouring fire,
> To you no help, since you will not lie with them,
> But before the Trojan men and women a *kleos*.
>
> (XXII.510–14)

We thus learn that the burning of the dead man's property on the pyre has a double meaning. On the one hand, it provides for the dead the provisions for the journey of which we spoke earlier. On the other hand, the simple destruction of the property is a notable act, which marks the death upon the consciousness of the community. The destruction of property is thus related to the *sēma*; the dead man's possessions are employed in order to perpetuate his name, his negative social existence as the departed one.

In the funeral games one is said *ktereizein aethloisi*, to use up property with prizes (XXIII.646). The prizes include the dead man's most precious possessions—in Patroclus' case, for instance, a Phoenician cup called "the most beautiful in the world" (XXIII.742), which Patroclus had received as a prize for Lycaon, and also the armor which Patroclus had stripped from Sarpedon (XXIII.800). Such objects have both a value and a history, and the man who receives them remembers their source. The prize is won by a memorable act; a victory in the games, like a success in battle or hunting, is an item for a heroic biography. The games thus provide the heroes with an occasion on which they can win fame; they in turn make the occasion famous as they recount their feats. The funeral enters the oral tradition of events retold and elaborated.

The mourners do not compete (XXIII.274–86); they rather offer property—their own and that of the dead man—to others on condition of competing. The games are thus founded on a definite reciprocity between mourners and competitors. The mourners contrive and pay for a historical event; the competitors enact it. The funeral games are thus a kind of *sēma*, constructed, not materially, but within the collective consciousness. Nestor speaks of both reciprocity and memory when he receives his prize from Achilles:

> I'm glad for my part to take it; my spirit is graced.
> You remember me as your friend, nor shall I forget you
> For the fitting honor you've shown me among the Achaeans.
> To you may the gods return grace befitting your spirit.
>
> (XXIII.647–50)

The funeral games are an imitation of combat. There are five canonical events: boxing, wrestling, casting the spear, the foot race, and the chariot race. The first two are forms of dueling; the other three test particular skills of the warrior, who is, characteristically, spearman, horseman, and swift of foot. At the games for Patroclus Achilles adds three more events: a literal warrior's duel in armor, putting the shot, and archery.

The likeness between games and combat shows through in various details. Games, like war, involve horses. The prizes—horses, women, armor, cups, and tripods—are the sorts of things won on the battlefield or in the sack of cities, and in Patroclus' games a number of them are objects actually won in battle. The winning competitors do not wait for prizes to be handed them; their retainers seize them and carry them off (XXIII.511–13, 848–49), much as captured armor or horses are passed to the warrior's retainers on the battlefield. The prize-taking is a kind of ceremony of despoilment.

The gods intervene in the games as on the battlefield, helping some and harming others. Nestor's long speech of advice to Antilochus is very much like Nestor's long speeches of tactical advice. The games of Patroclus even include one *euchē* or formal boast, which has the rhetorical shape of the formal battlefield boastings:

> Let him come quick, who wants the cup with the handles.
> The mule, I assert, no other Achaean will take
> By winning at boxing, since I claim to be the best.
> Is it not enough I'm lacking in battle? One can't
> Become in every act a man who is skilled.
> This much I will say, and it will come to pass:
> I will crush his flesh and break together his bones.
> Let the mourners crowd around him and stand ready
> To carry him off when he's been subdued by my hands.
>
> (XXIII.667–75)

This speech of Epeius is striking for its similarities to a battle speech, and even more for its differences. Epeius is a great boxer but, as he freely admits, no warrior. Furthermore, his threat to kill his opponent, which on the battlefield would be literal, is here mere boxer's hyperbole. Conflict in the games is violent but not dangerous. Games are played by rules, and there is an umpire—at Patroclus' games, Achilles himself. The rule-keeping apparatus is fairly elaborate; Phoenix, for instance, is sent out to monitor the horse race (XXIII. 359–61), and at the end of it Menelaus in effect files a protest with the stewards and receives a hearing. The only really dangerous event is the fight in armor, which the crowd insists be broken off as soon as it appears that one of the duelists is being hurt (XXIII.820–23). In this contest, further, it is stated at the beginning that the prize, Sarpedon's armor, will be shared equally between the duelists (XXIII. 809–10); the winner receives a small dagger in addition. The chief prize, in other words, is for taking part; the small prize, for winning.

In the canonical events, all contestants receive prizes. A certain number of prizes is set out; this number regulates the number of competitors. There is no formal process by which competitors are selected; we must presume, instead, an informal social process by which those most fit to compete know who they are and are so recognized by others. The games, in other words, are not zero sum; all competitors win something, both of honor and of gain.

Just as the audience knows who is supposed to compete, so also they know (but less clearly) who is supposed to win. In two events, the duel and the wrestling, the heroes who compete are evenly matched; both events are allowed to end in a tie, and in both cases it is implied that the audience so prefers it (XXIII.736–37, 822–23). Sometimes accidents disappoint the expectations of the audience and thus create a problem. Eumelus is supposed to win the chariot race; Oelian Ajax, in fact, is sure that, regardless of what anyone says, Eumelus must *be* winning (XXIII.480–81). But Eumelus' chariot breaks; he fails to finish. Achilles suggests, as a sort of compromise between what was supposed to happen and what did happen, that Eumelus be given the second prize. The audience is delighted with this suggestion, and thus the matter would have ended, had not Antilochus protested:

> Achilles, I'll be really enraged if you
> Do what you propose. You're about to take my prize,
> Concerned that his car and horses came to grief
> Although he is good. But he should have made his prayer
> To the gods. Then he wouldn't have finished last.
> If you pity him so, and he is close to your heart,
> You have gold in your hut; you have much bronze
> And cattle; you've got your women and hooved horses.
> Take some and give him even a greater prize.
> You could do it right now, so all the Achaeans will praise you.
> I'll not give this one. Let him try to take it,
> Any man who's ready to feel my fists.
>
> (XXIII.543–54)

This speech, with its delicate mixture of bravado and compliments bestowed in the right places, is successful; Achilles finds a special prize for Eumelus. Antilochus, however, finished second only* by some questionable hard driving, and he still has to resist a challenge from Menelaus. Here Antilochus takes a very different tone; when Menelaus demands that he take an oath of innocence, he instead pleads guilty in a charming speech:

> Let it pass. I am very much younger
> Than you, Menelaus. You are the elder and better.
> You know how a young man's contentiousness turns out;
> His wits are hasty, and his wisdom slight.
> Thus let your heart bear with me. As for the horse,
> Take her, I give her. If you would come to my house
> And ask for a better one, right away I'd give her,
> Rather, Zeus-born, than risk that all my days
> I'd be far from your heart or do wrong in the face of
>   immortals.
>
> (XXIII.587–95)

Antilochus converts the question from one of performance to one of ascription; he yields the prize, on the ground of Menelaus' higher status, and at the same time suggests that, if he himself has done wrong, it is only what should be expected of him. He further shifts the object from a contest of competition to a contest of hospitality and gift-giving. In games the man who takes the prize receives the greater honor, but in gift-giving it is the giver who is most honored. Antilochus thus gives Menelaus a motive for refusing the prize after all. This Menelaus does:

> I give her, though she is mine, so that these may know
> There's nothing rough or savage about my heart.
>
> (XXIII.610–11)

Antilochus manages to keep not only the prize but also the esteem of Achilles, Eumelus, Menelaus, and the audience, and later, after finishing last in the foot race, he receives a special prize in recognition of another of his pretty speeches (XXIII.785–97). Antilochus is having a good games, but his success is as much political as athletic.

In games the audience is involved twice: first, through interest in the outcome, second, as guarantor of rules and witness of victory. The audience, first, participates vicariously in the acts of the contestant and, second, interacts with the competitors as a group. Games thus stimulate vigorous social interaction and the "effervescence" characteristic of occasions rich in rapid social process. In the games for Patroclus this effervescence surfaces repeatedly—particularly in the quarrel between Idomeneus and Oelian Ajax, with its offer of a wager (XXIII.456–87), and in the laughter which rises when Oelian Ajax stands spitting out dung and complaining about Odysseus' special relation with Athena (XXIII.780–84). Laughter rises again at Epeius' cast of the shot (XXIII.839–40).[77]

These games are an arena in which honor can be won, but they are also a stage upon which honor is recognized. The competition is not zero sum, and attention is paid to status as much as to the outcome of the events. The whole occasion thus serves to reconfirm a preexisting order as much as to construct a new one.[78] Prizes are awarded even to those who do not compete. Nestor is too old for any event but receives a prize in virtue of his status; the games would be the less if he were not somehow involved in them. So he is given the unallocated fifth prize from the chariot race:

> Let this be your treasure, old man, to keep
> In memory of Patroclus' burial; him
> You will see no more among the Argives.
>
> (XXIII.618–20)

When Agamemnon and Meriones step forward for the last event, the spear-throwing, Achilles confers the victor's prize on Agamemnon:

Son of Atreus, we know how much you excel us all,
How much in power and with the spear you are best.
Take this prize, and with it to your hollow ships
Return; we will give the spear to hero Meriones,
If you in your heart are willing. Thus I bid you.

(XXIII.890–94)

If the king of kings should be defeated, the result would be a social anomaly. It is best not to put the matter to the test of competition but to confer the prize on him outright, and this solution is acceptable to everyone.

Funeral games thus function as a kind of monument, an event by which the property of the dead man and his mourners is converted into memorials of his death, and as a social occasion through which the community, wounded and disordered by the loss of one of its heroes, reasserts its structure and its vitality. They have a third function as well: by imitating combat, they conceal its real character.

Games and combat are both forms of conflict, but in the games conflict is conditioned by rules, while in combat it is unconditioned. The parties to combat may impose rules and limits on themselves, but such limits are fragile and temporary. Combatants have no mediating community around them.

In combat, as in games, the victor gains honor, but in combat the loser becomes himself the victor's prize, and the honor of one party is secured by the dishonor of the other. Here again the victor may act with restraint, but such limits, being self-imposed, are liable to constant erosion under the strain of continued conflict. The impurity of shaming and mutilation is not an accidental fact in combat but a logical development of its essence.

In funeral games the heroes celebrate the death of a victim of combat by enacting conflicts in which the loser is not a victim. Thus they purify the impurity latent in the status of victim, not by reforming the situation (which is beyond their power), but by denying it. The *Iliad* marks the unreality of the games by setting them against the other half of Achilles' action; all the while that he is purifying his comrade, Achilles continues, to the limit of his powers, to inflict impurity upon the body of Hector. The games purify combat by enacting it within the bounds of community; the defilement of the dead body reminds us of the real nature of conflict between communities.

The Ransoming of Hector

We now turn to the ransoming of Hector and the final purification of the *Iliad*, achieved not by the reconstruction of the human community but by the separation of the hero from the community. The end of the *Iliad* is a ceremonial recognition of the monstrous singularity of Achilles.

At the beginning of Book Twenty-four, we find that for Achilles nothing has changed. These ceremonies are for him inefficacious; they leave him exactly where he was:

> The games were dissolved; the folk went back to their ships
> And scattered. Then they turned their minds to food
> And the fullness of sweet sleep. Achilles alone
> Wept; he remembered his friend, nor ever did sleep
> Come, that subdues us all, but he turned and turned
> In desire for Patroclus' manhood and vivid strength,
> For all he'd traversed with him, the pains they'd suffered
> In wars of men and in crossing the painful waves.
> As he remembered, the tears welled up in him hot;
> On his side he lay for a while, and then for a while
> On his back, then face down. Then he got up
> And twisted grieving, along the shore. Nor did dawn
> Find him unmindful, shining on sea and shore,
> But whenever he had yoked swift horses to their car
> He tied to it Hector for dragging behind the wheels;
> Thrice he would drag him around Patroclus' tomb;
> Then he would rest in the hut and leave him there,
> Stretched face down in the dust. From Hector, Apollo
> Kept off despoilment, in pity for his flesh,
> Dead though he was. He covered him with the aegis
> Of gold, so that the dragging would not tear him.
> Thus Achilles despoiled bright Hector in his raging.
>
> (XXIV.1–22)

In this way the poet sets before us the problem of his final book. Hector and Achilles have descended together into an impure world, a world beyond the reach of ceremonies. For Hector this descent has been into powerlessness, for Achilles into mere power, power without meaning. Achilles enacts and reenacts his conquest of Hector; he cannot even destroy the body, which thus remains an eternal object of his malice. The two heroes are locked together in an everlasting dance of hatred—despoiler and victim, predator and prey.

If this conflict is to be resolved, it must be shifted to a level on which resolution is possible. The war at Troy is a conflict between two human communities, but it is also a conflict within a community, the community of the gods. Within this divine community the conflict can be resolved, and it is, in three swift speeches: statement, counter-statement, and an arbitration by the king:

There spoke among the immortals then Phoebus Apollo:
"You are harsh, gods, malicious; don't you remember
Hector burning the thighs of oxen and goats?
You'll take no step, corpse though he is, to save him,
To where his wife could see him, his mother, his child,
His father Priam, all his folk, who'd quickly
Kindle his pyre and burn his possessions around him.
But destroyer Achilles, gods, has all your help,
Whose heart knows nothing proper, nor is his mind
Responsive within. He thinks like a savage lion
Whose strength is great, who yields to his prideful heart
And springs on the flocks of men, to seize his dinner.
So Achilles destroyed all pity, nor is *aidōs*
His, which surely despoils men and maintains them.
Men can lose those even closer to them—
Even a whole brother, perhaps, or a son—
Yet when they have wept and mourned, they put it from them,
For the Portioners made the heart of man enduring.
But Hector—after he'd taken his spirit from him—
Slung behind horses, around his own friend's tomb
He drags. It is not fine, nor is it proper.
Superior though he is, we might still feel *nemesis*,
For senseless is the earth he despoils in his raging."
     Then in her anger answered white-armed Hera:
"That is the way *you* say it, silver-bow.
Achilles and Hector, perhaps, you'd make equal in honor.
But Hector is mortal, he suckled a woman's breast.
Achilles is born of a goddess, whom I myself
Reared and nursed, and gave to a man as his wife,
To Peleus, who is heart-close to the immortals.
You all came, gods, to the wedding. You were there too,
Playing your lyre at the feast, faithless, untrusted."
     Then to her, answering, spoke cloud-gathering Zeus:
"Hera, do not spoil with rage at the gods.
In honor they won't be the same. But still, this Hector
Was closest to us of mortals who are in Troy,
Especially to me, since he never spared of my gifts,
My altar was never lacking of fitting feasts,
Of wine and fat-steam. That is our proper privilege.
Let's not think of stealing—it can't be done—
By stealth from Achilles, Hector. She's always there,
His mother, who watches beside him night and day.
So let some one of the gods call Thetis to me
That I may tell her my thought, the way Achilles
Will take the gifts of Priam and ransom Hector."

(XXIV.32–76)

The speech of Apollo is godlike in a sense that is uncharacteristic of the *Iliad*. The gods of the *Iliad*, as we have seen, have been drawn into the action, have become persons within an unfolding plot beyond the control even of Zeus. But Apollo here stands back from the action, from the human world, and prescribes for it. This shift of perspective accounts, perhaps, for the oddities of language in the speech, for example the phrase about *aidōs* as maintainer and despoiler and the reference to the "dumb earth." This is the only place in Homer where the Portioners, the *Moirai*, are mentioned in the plural, and it is the only place in the *Iliad* where *moira* is called the source of the way things are in general rather than, narrowly, the source of the finitude of life. Perhaps most significant is the fact that this is the only place in the *Iliad* where *nemesis* is used of the attitude of the gods toward human beings who have broken the moral code.[79] Apollo's moralism is close to Phoenix' moralism in Book Nine; man was meant to be of enduring heart, and Achilles is a transgressor. He, Apollo, is the guarantor of that norm.

This Apollo carries us back to the Apollo of the first book, who sent the plague on those who offended his priest. The appearance of the god in this role—distant from the action rather than part of it—is a sign that the poem is drawing to its conclusion; as the action slackens, the gods disentangle themselves from it. But it is also true that this notion of god as the guarantor of norms is introduced here only to be rejected. Hera protests that Achilles is not human in the ordinary sense; he is a member of the divine community. The gods came to Peleus' wedding; they are joined to Achilles by bonds of kinship and ceremony and cannot simply impose on him the behavior they require.

Zeus agrees with Hera. The notion, circulating a few lines earlier, that Hermes should steal Hector's body, is rejected. Achilles' immortal mother makes such a solution impossible. Rather, Achilles must be drawn into the divine community. Zeus sends for Thetis. As she came to Zeus from her son at the beginning, so he sends her to her son at the end. The social anomaly which was the source of the whole catastrophe becomes the source of the final reconciliation. The action of the poem rounds into completed form.

When Thetis brings Achilles his instructions, he assents in two bare lines:

> So be it. Who brings the ransom will take the corpse,
> If Zeus with thoughtful heart himself instructs me.
>
> (XXIV.139–40)

This compliance should not surprise us; it matches Achilles' compliance to Athena in the first book (I.216–18). Achilles never loses his confidence in the gods, aside from one moment of panic in the river (XXI. 273–83), and on that occasion his angry prayer is promptly answered (XXI.288–97). Achilles' story grows from his marginal standing between two communities, but the disorder thus generated is all between himself and men. In the human community his standing is (ambiguously) high, and he finds himself baffled; in the divine community his standing is unambiguously low, and with his usual clarity he accepts proper instruction.

The dramatic tension of the last book is not in Achilles' consent but in Priam's journey to Achilles. Priam must be introduced into the semihuman, god-inhabited world where Achilles is at home. Iris comes to Priam and promises him Hermes as escort (XXIV.182–83). Hermes in the *Odyssey* is *psuchopompos*, conductor of souls to Hades; here he appears as god of sleep (XXIV.343–44, cf. 445). Priam's journey is a kind of dream voyage or descent into the underworld.[80] Priam declares that he is ready to die with his son (XXIV.224–27, cf. 246); as he goes to him,

> All his dear ones followed,
> Mourning aloud, as if he were going to death.
>
> (XXIV.327–28)

Priam rejects his wife's appeal, reviles his sons, and goes into the dark.

As Priam separates himself from his own world, he is, in a limited but real sense, included in the divine world. He goes as father to son, and to help him, Zeus sends Hermes, "his own son" (XXIV.333); Hermes says to Priam, "I think of you as if you were my own father" (XXIV.371, cf. 398). Father Zeus, that is, sends to father Priam a son to be a son to him. Priam—for the first time in the poem—feels the gods close to him. He says to Hermes:

> Child, it is good and fitting to give gifts to the gods,
> Since never my son—I mean my son that was—
> Forgot in his halls the gods, who hold Olympus;
> So they remembered him, even in death.
>
> (XXIV.425–28)

Before his departure Priam purifies himself with water and pours a libation of wine, praying for an omen, which Zeus sends (XXIV.303–21). He commits himself to the gods. Priam and his herald meet Hermes at the river running between the armies; everything is dark and wrapped in mist (XXIV.349–51). The journey is a rite of departure and crossing-over. Zeus has contrived a ceremony which takes place outside the human world, and therefore at night and by magic.

Priam's gesture of submission to Achilles is itself a kind of impossible act. He says:

> I've endured such as no man ever endured on the earth:
> To raise to my mouth the hand of my son's killer.
>
> (XXIV.505–6)

The poetry of this gesture is complex:

> Great Priam stood by him close;
> His hands took Achilles' knees; he kissed his hands—
> Dread, man-slaying, which killed his many sons—
> As, when the blindness takes a man, and at home
> He's killed a man, and he comes to another's folk,
> To a rich man's house, and awe takes those who see him,
> So Achilles looked in awe upon godlike Priam.
>
> (XXIV.477–83)

By the simile Priam is turned into the slayer and Achilles the rich king—as if, in the eye of the poet, they take on each other's roles for a moment. This likeness is perhaps already there in line 478, which begins with one pair of hands and ends with the other. Achilles' hands are called *androphonos*, man-slaying, both there and when he touches the *stēthos* of the dead Patroclus (XVIII.317 = XXIII.18). In both passages there is a contrast between the killing power of the hands and their gentle gesture. But *androphonos* is properly an epithet of warriors, and this is the epithet specific to Hector (occurring eleven times, including XXIV.509). In kissing Achilles' hands, Priam seems to cross a line, perhaps even to violate a taboo; he caresses the object of his loathing. But the language reminds us that the man-slaying hands slew a manslayer, that Achilles has done nothing to Hector which Hector did not promise Patroclus. This categorical perception of the relation between the parties—by which it is seen that, given different circumstances, each could have been in the place of the other—is the basis of the reconciliation.

Priam speaks to Achilles of Peleus, and Achilles weeps; Priam falls before him, weeping for Hector, and "Achilles wept for his father, and then again for Patroclus" (XXIV.511–12). Priam is like Peleus: both are old men, and fathers, and, as Hector died before his father, so will Achilles die before his. When Achilles weeps for Patroclus, however, he shares Priam's mourning differently; both have lost the persons dearest to them, and their pain is common. Achilles sees himself both in Priam and in Hector. The terrible clarity of Achilles' speech to the embassy is not lost but relocated as the point of view shifts. Achilles' rending sense of his own mortality, which in Book Nine had isolated him from others, even his friends, here becomes a bond with others, even with his enemy. At the moment Achilles feels himself most a mortal man, he stands away from men, as the gods do, and sees himself one with other mortals, "like to the breed of leaves." In their common mourning, Achilles and Priam together experience the limiting finitude of the heroic consciousness. This shift of perspective is the subjective content of the ceremony contrived by Zeus between the worlds.

Achilles states this subjective content in two speeches, one before the release of Hector's body, one after:

> Wretch, your heart has had to bear much evil.
> How did you endure to come to the ships alone,
> Before the eyes of a man who your many and good
> Sons has slaughtered? Iron-hard your spirit.
> Come, sit here, and all this pain of ours
> We shall let rest in the heart, although it hurts us.
> There's no conclusion comes to cruel mourning.
> Thus the gods have spun for wretched men,
> To live in pain. But they themselves are carefree.
> Two are the jars set on the floor of Zeus,
> Full of their gifts of evil, and one full of blessings;
> When he mixes his gifts, Zeus who delights in thunder,
> Sometimes it runs to evil, sometimes to good—
> But when his gifts are sorrow, Zeus marks his victim;
> Evil wasting drives him across the earth;
> He wanders, by gods disowned, by mortal men.
> Thus to Peleus gods gave shining gifts
> From birth. All mankind he excelled
> In happiness and wealth; he was king in Phthia,
> And him, though a mortal, gods gave a goddess-wife.
> But then god gave the evil: he'd not have
> A race of mighty sons born in his house.
> One son he had, short-lived; he'll not even have
> My care in his aging, since so far from home
> I sit in Troy, harming you and your sons.
> You also, old man, once, we hear, were happy.
> All far Lesbos holds, the seat of Makar,
> Wide Phrygia, the trackless Hellespont,
> All that, they say, you excelled in wealth and sons.
> But since they brought this sorrow, the Heavenly Ones,
> Ever about your town are war and dying.
> Bear it. Don't weep forever in your heart.
> You'll not conclude it, grieving a fine son,
> Nor bring him back; you'll just add evil to evil.

(XXIV.518–51)

Your son is ransomed, old man, as you asked;
He lies on the bier. When first light is breaking
You'll see him yours. Now let us think of supper—
For even Niobe remembered to eat,
Although twelve children perished in her house—
Six were daughters, six were full-grown sons.
Apollo killed the boys with his silver bow,
Angry with Niobe; Artemis killed the girls
Because she had likened herself to fair-cheeked Leto:
That Leto's children were two, but she had many.
So those two took her many children from her.
Nine days they lay in gore, nor was anyone there
To bury them; Zeus had turned the folk to stone;
The heavenly gods on the tenth day buried them,
And she remembered to eat, worn out with weeping.
Now in the rocks, on the solitary mountain
In Sipylos, where they say is the lair of nymphs,
Divine girls, who dance by the Achelous,
There, stone though she is, she consumes her sorrow.
But come, we two should also, old man, think
To eat. And later you will mourn your son
When you take him home. He will surely be much wept-for.

(XXIV.599–620)

In these two speeches the hero of the *Iliad* states the concluding synthesis of the poem.[81] The human condition is one of privation; god grants the happiest of men no more than partial happiness. As the gods torment us, they also mock us with their own careless bliss. Man must be modest and enduring or even this partial happiness will be taken from him. Yet just as the gods inflict on man pain and death, so also they have granted man the gift of finitude. Just as happiness is always partial, so also pain must come to some conclusion. The gods destroy, but at the last they bury their victims and there is an ending.

In the ceremonial context of the ransoming, Achilles is able, for the first time, to reflect upon himself and his own fate as one instance of a universal pattern. At this point Achilles, who throughout the poem has been bombarded by the moralisms of others, becomes himself a moralist. His moralism is no different from that already vainly recommended to him by Nestor, Phoenix, Apollo—that men should be *streptoi* and *tlētoi*, flexible and enduring. Their voices could not enter the situation in which Achilles so long was trapped; not even the gods could resolve his dilemma from the outside. But he can resolve it himself in a moment, once the context is no longer one of particular injuries and honors but of universal categories and values.

217

Priam and Achilles are enemies; that is their social relation. When they enter, through ceremony, the divine sphere, that relation disappears. They confront each other as independent beings; they become to each other aesthetic objects:

> Then Dardanian Priam marveled at Achilles,
> His size and quality; he seemed like the gods;
> And at Dardanian Priam wondered Achilles,
> Seeing his excellent face and hearing his voice,
> And so they joyed as they looked upon each other.
>
> (XXIV.629–33)

The ceremony enables Achilles to know his situation and no longer merely experience it. What was baffling in its immediacy becomes lucid at a distance. Achilles surveys and comprehends his world and himself. That is the purification of Achilles.

On the other hand, nothing has changed. Priam is still Achilles' enemy, and their reconciliation is the fragile product of a fabricated ceremonial context. Any outcry from Priam would rend the fabric, and then Achilles would kill him (XXIV.568–70, 582–86). Nor is Achilles reconciled with his own community; his dealings with Priam are explicitly an act to be done in secret, an act which his community does not permit (XXIV.650–55). The purification of Achilles does not heal him. But he does come to repose, to food and sleep.

Throughout the *Iliad*, meals mark the moments of repose and integration. Achilles' refusal to eat after the ceremony of Book Nineteen marks his reconciliation there with Agamemnon as partly illusory. All the resources of culture had been mobilized by Odysseus, that master of procedure: the assembly, the giving of gifts, the taking of an oath. The public order, property, the invocation of divine sanctions—all had proved inefficacious. But at the end of his reconciliation with Priam, Achilles eats. This last ceremony is efficacious, but on another level: culture is overcome.

ART AS THE NEGATION OF CULTURE

Culture confers on life a meaning and at the same time divides men from one another. Men are located and separated by the bonds of kinship and property, by loyalties and obligation, by status, role, and citizenship. Yet mankind remains a unity, most simply and profoundly on the level of organic life. To be human is to be a member of a species and to share with others a specific fate. That fate is to die; this Priam and Achilles recognize in their shared mourning. But the fate of the species is also to live, and this they recognize in their shared meal. In the midst of death we are in life. The reconciliation takes place on the level of nature, outside the human world; it is a ceremony founded on a universal concept of man *qua* man.

Since life takes on meaning only when formed by culture, this ceremony of reconciliation is not a discovery of meaning. It is rather an accurate recognition of meaninglessness. Achilles is not changed; his anger and his isolation remain. He is left, like Niobe, "consuming his sorrows." But the body of Hector is released and the poetic action is concluded.

The end of the *Iliad* echoes its beginning. In the beginning a father is refused the ransoming of his child; at the end a ransoming is permitted. In the beginning Achilles quarrels with a king; at the end he is reconciled with a king. Since the persons are different, however, these echoes are purely formal. The *Iliad* comes to a conclusion, not because the action imitated reaches a resolution, but because the poet has conferred on the event, in the manner of his telling it, a form and an ending.

We must distinguish the form of an action from its resolution. An action is resolved when the needs and demands of the actors are either met or crushed out. Such an outcome is *for the actors* and concludes the action on the ethical level. Form, on the other hand, is *for us*; an action is formed when it reveals a lucid meaning to the contemplative eye of the poet and his audience. The completion of its form concludes the action on the aesthetic level. This shift of levels is the work of imitation, which reduces experience and presents to us the problematic of life in a simplified, comprehensible form. The work of the imitative artist, as it is the invention of form, is also the discovery of meaning; but the meaning which art discovers in life is only theoretical, not practical. Through the work of art we comprehend in some way the order of things, but this comprehension does not necessarily give us a new basis for self-conscious action. Dramatic art rises from the dilemmas and contradictions of life, but it makes no promise to resolve these dilemmas; on the contrary, tragic art may well reach its highest formal perfection at the moment when it reveals to us these dilemmas as universal, pervasive, and necessary.

In Homeric language we would say that poetry is the work of *noos*, not *thumos*. The poet is detached; he recognizes. He stands apart from action and discerns its form. Contradiction, which baffles action and appears to the actor as formlessness, becomes (for the poet) itself a kind of form. The lucidity of a situation is often revealed at the moment we see it as held together by the tension of self-contradictory oppositions. In this sense the poet will discern form at the moment he ceases to see the situation as unresolved and comes to see it as unresolvable.

Thus, as culture is the purification of nature, so art is the purification of culture. That which baffles ethical forming, when further formed through imitative art, becomes itself a source of aesthetic form. As the forming of art is a further forming of forms already present in nature and culture, so it follows that artistic form is inclusive of culture and nature. Art may achieve form at the moment it recovers nature in relation to culture, recovers a comprehension of the intractability of nature to cultural form. In this sense art is the opposite of culture and at the same time completes culture. Poetry is about life and at the same time is a release from life. Through poetry man sees himself from a distance; poetry offers him not gratification but intelligibility. In tragic art, the pains and terrors of life are transformed from experiences to objects of knowledge; tragic art attains to form when it makes a lucid theoretical statement of the practical opacities of the human condition. In this sense tragic form is a "purification of these experiences."

It is a peculiarity of the epic that its heroes can, at certain moments, share the perspective of poet and audience and look down upon themselves. We observe such a shift of perspective in the occasions when the characters speak of their fate, that is, speak of their place in the story as a whole. In this respect, as in others, Achilles tests the limits of the heroic; when he commits himself to the killing of Hector, he sees his own death also before him and accepts it. He is thus an actor who both acts and knows his own actions as part of an unfolding pattern. He can do this because he is between man and god.

Specific to Homeric epic—and its descendant, Attic tragedy—are the Olympian gods, who, as we saw, are both part of the action and detached from it. They thus mediate between the actors and the audience. The gods' knowledge of fate is partial; otherwise they could not participate in the action. Their knowledge of fate is greater than men's; that is the mark of their greater detachment. They can intervene in the action on behalf of their favorites and to punish their enemies, but that intervention is, as we saw in the cases of Sarpedon and Hector, limited by the overriding necessities of the plot. The gods must allow the action to occur.

But then, after an action is completed, they can intervene to conclude it. This is intervention in quite a different sense. The gods have a concern for purity, that is, for the proper endings of things, a concern represented in their concern for funerals. They contrive the funeral of Sarpedon, protect the body of Patroclus, protect the body and contrive the funeral of Hector. Here the intervention is, as it were, from outside the action. The gods, who are outside any human community, can intervene to confer that purity which is beyond the power of human community; they can impose a limit on the impurity of combat. But this limitation, since it is from the outside, has an arbitrary element; it is less like the purity which rises from the orderings of culture and more like the purity imposed by the forming power of art.

Achilles, the hero who is closest to the gods, is at the end of the *Iliad* privileged to stand aside from his world and describe it. The ransoming of Hector is imposed upon him by Zeus; he accepts it because he shares to a degree the understanding of Zeus. He can look upon man as an ephemeral thing in nature and recognize him as unworthy of his hatred. Or, we must add, of his love.

The ransoming of Hector, by this reading, dissolves the distinction between victor and vanquished. Both are seen as sharing a common nature and a common fate. This is not to resolve the contradiction of combat but to erase it; for if the vanquished is no different from the victor, combat is meaningless. And if combat is meaningless, then community, for the sake of which combat is waged, is also meaningless.[82]

Such a conclusion is not tolerable in life, for life must be lived in and for communities. That Achilles retains—with one part of his divided self—a place in the human world is marked by the anger which, he knows, at any moment might recover its power over him, which is only for a moment set aside by his contemplation of himself. In this contemplation Achilles—the only character in the *Iliad* who is himself a poet—shares the understanding of the poet. We thus leave him in a strange divided state, tensely poised between life and art. It is a strange paradox that conclusions which in life lead only to paralysis and despair in art are ennobling and sublime. That is the paradox of the tragic consciousness.

The ransoming of Hector is in contrast to the funeral games of Patroclus; the two stand to each other as drama to ceremony. In the games the reality of combat is concealed and denied; combat is transferred to a sphere in which it can be seen as unreal. This is an imitation which moves from reality to unreality.

In the ransoming of Hector the parties to conflict are also transferred —not to a different cultural sphere, but to a location outside culture. The distant inclusive perspective of the Olympian gods (which was at the first an invention of poets) becomes an Archimedean point where the poet, his audience, and even his hero can stand aside from the human world and judge it. The ransoming of Hector is a ceremony contrived by the god on behalf of the poet to complete and purify the poetic action. The ceremony of Book Twenty-four takes place outside the human world because the contradictions which it reveals cannot be resolved within the human world. The vision of man revealed in Achilles' two speeches is not a vision tolerable in practice. It is possible only in theory, in the moments when men like Glaucus, Sarpedon, and Achilles stand aside from the heroic role and see it. At such moments the hero is his own poet; the vision which he captures is proper to art. At these moments he abandons much of life—its particularities, affections, hopes—but something is gained. Art is an imitation which moves from reality to another reality—reduced, less rich in matter, but more coherent in form.

The action of the *Iliad* is an enactment of the contradictions of the warrior's role. The warrior on behalf of culture must leave culture and enter nature. In asserting the order of culture, he must deny himself a place in that order. That others may be pure, he must become impure.

Achilles and Hector experience the resulting tension differently. Hector's responsibilities outrun his powers. As he turns himself over to the sphere of nature, he loses reflective control and becomes subject to error. Error shames him before his community and separates him; he is the victim of the contradictory demands his community makes on him. The social order retains its meaning for him, but he can no longer find his place in it. And thus he dies.

Achilles retains his power but loses the social context which gave power responsible meaning. Achilles also is a victim of error—not primarily his own, but Agamemnon's. Wrong is done to him, and he is baffled. He feels his community shamed in relation to himself; the Greeks in their acquiescence to Agamemnon's injustice have become *outidanoi,* "mere nothings" (I.231), and he himself would become *outidanos* if he were to consent (I.293). Whereas Hector, in service to his community, loses his sense of identity and dissolves into fantasy and panic, Achilles, in order to save his identity, is forced to withdraw from his community—even in his return to action. Whereas Hector can do nothing but die, Achilles can do nothing but kill—kill, and despoil, torment others and himself. At the end of the poem he is tied to this fate still, and he knows it will lead to the destruction of Troy and to his own futile death.

The inner unity of the *Iliad* thus lies in the mirror opposition of the two heroes. In the concluding ceremony they are revealed to us— and to the surviving hero—as contrasting emblems of a single pattern. Achilles and Hector represent the two aspects of war, aggressive and defensive, something suffered and something done. What is necessary and yet unjustifiable in fact justifies itself, at the end, as an object of poetic knowledge. What is incomprehensible in experience becomes patterned and even beautiful in the imitation of experience. And since poetic imitation, which claims to stand outside experience, is itself a human achievement, poetry claims for itself a place both outside and within the human world as it recovers for man a tragic meaning in the experience of meaninglessness.

> Zeus sent this evil portion, so that later,
> For men to come, we should be themes for song.
>
> (VI.357–58)

NOTES

PREFACE

1. There is an extended discussion of Hector in Scott 1921. Of the more recent literary appreciators of Homer only Schadewaldt (1944) has devoted much space to Hector. He treats the two great scenes—Hector and Andromache, the Death of Hector—from the point of view of the poet's technique and his delineation of character; he has little to say about the *story* of Hector. Whitman (1958) sketches Hector's story in eight or ten pages and treats it as a subsystem of the story of Achilles. Bespaloff (1943) has a character sketch of Hector, similarly brief.

2. I would associate myself with Kirk, in both his argument and his conclusion:

> From the aesthetic point of view the *effect* of unity in the *Iliad* . . . is what really matters. . . . Yet the problem of composition is not irrelevant; for it is only by understanding how and why the poems were composed that one can hope to penetrate their real meaning and effect for a contemporary Greek audience. The kind of unity they possess is certainly not that of a modern work of literature. . . . On the other hand it is in no way incompatible with the hypothesis . . . that each poem reflects the creative endeavour of a great singer, using many traditional elements and providing much of his own. [Kirk 1962, p. 267.]

3. See Lord 1953. Dodds (1968) comments: "The present writer is tempted to agree with Page (*Antiquity* 36 [1962]: 308 ff.) that the picture of Homer dictating, like a modern Jugoslav bard to a 'Collector,' 'will one day take its place among the curiosities of Homeric scholarship' " (p. 42, n. 13). But in the history of the Homeric Question more than one notion has been rescued from the curiosity shop or even the rubbish heap and restored to a place of honor. For a fuller statement of my views see Redfield 1967.

4. Thus we find that Simone Weil's eloquent and suggestive essay (1955) comes to an extraordinary conclusion: "L'Evangile est la dernière et merveilleuse expression du génie grec, comme l'*Iliade* en est la première" (p. 38). We may suspect that this conclusion was made possible to her by her attributing to Homer an idea of the *soul* which neither appears in the poet nor was possible within his system of thought.

225

INTRODUCTION

1. The speech is the third-longest in the entire poem, exceeded only by Phoenix' speech, immediately following it, and by Nestor's speech in Book Eleven (ll. 656–803), both of which are old men's speeches, with lengthy inserted narrative.

2. Bowra 1930, p. 19.

3. Ibid., pp. 20–22.

4. Parry 1956, pp. 5 f.

5. Whitman 1958, p. 191.

6. Ibid., p. 193.

7. Ibid., p. 197.

8. Ibid., p. 203.

9. Ibid., p. 218.

10. Ibid., p. 199.

11. Ibid., p. 213.

12. Cf. Zarker 1965.

13. As Diomedes points out (IX.32–33). Contrast Diomedes' submissiveness to the king on the battlefield (IV.401–18) and the cautious self-qualification with which he breaks into an informal council between Agamemnon and Odysseus (XIV.110 ff.). The heroes are permitted a special freedom of speech in formal meetings of the *agorē*; that is one of the things such assemblies are for.

14. Cf. Whitman 1958, p. 190.

15. Note the (stative) perfect *hestēkei* (XI.600).

16. This, I believe, is the solution to the famous puzzle: that Achilles, who has refused the gifts in Book Nine, still seems to be expecting them in Book Sixteen. He says there that the tide of battle would turn if Agamemnon would "show me a gentle mind" (XVI.71–73) and warns Patroclus not to go too far; the Greeks would still be in need of Achilles, so that they "would take the beautiful girl away from him [this I take to be the force of *hoi*] and provide lovely gifts in addition" (XVI.85–86). Achilles has the same picture in his mind as before: an Agamemnon humbled and deprived of Briseis by the collectivity of the Greeks. Furthermore, he thinks of the collectivity, not the king, as the agents of reconciliation. Achilles is now able to be somewhat clearer about all this (although still far from clear) because his mood has changed; he is now able to think about gifts and reconciliation because the gifts would have some meaning for him.

17. Cf. Whitman 1958, p. 191.

18. These resonances are already struck in the prologue in the words *mēnis* and *iphthimos*; both have connotations of the divine realm. On the latter term see Warden 1969.

19. The summary which follows is drawn from "Der homerische Mensch" in Fränkel 1962, pp. 83–94.

20. Fränkel 1962, p. 92.

21. Fränkel says (ibid., pp. 93 f.):

Die Helden der Ilias führen ein öffentliches Leben, und die Rücksicht auf das Urteil der Um- und Nach-welt bestimmt ihre Handlungsweise (*Il.* 6.441–43, 9.459–61). Die öffentliche Meinung spricht auf ungehöriges Verhalten vernehmlich an (*nemessaō*), und kein Zweifel wird rege, dass etwa dieses Instrument falsch und ungerecht arbeiten könne. Man hat in der Ilias keine verborgenen Motive und dunklen Untergründe; man ist so, wie man wirkt.

22. Fränkel (ibid., p. 87, n. 11) cites XI.403–11, where Odysseus, "perplexed" (*ochthēsas*; on this word cf. Adkins 1969b), speaks to his *thumos*—his "spirit" or "heart." Once he has rejected his own momentary notion, however, the same notion becomes something his *thumos* said to him; in being rejected, it is exteriorized, made into something not belonging to the inner self. The poet summarizes: "thus he stirred up, within, his *thumos* and *phrēn*." The process of deciding what to do is felt as a process of finding those thoughts that are properly one's own. Cf. Böhme 1929 pp. 79 f.

This internal dialogue (for which the Homeric verb is *mermērizein*) whereby a man alone with himself seeks to discover himself is itself the internalization of a social process; the man "comes to himself" to the degree that he recognizes what society expects of him. See Speier 1952, p. 44:

When a man of honor is faced with a difficult decision he is in danger of losing his honor as long as he is uncertain whether he should follow its demands of him. Since he is divided into two parts, he represents two persons: as the man whose personal honor demands that he do *this*, he is to himself the image of the right life; as he whose convenience, or safety, or comfort, suggests that he do *that*, even though it violate his honor, he is a potential apostate from that image. His moral monologue is in reality a dialogue, which corresponds to the relation existing in public honor between the observers and the bearers [of honor], where the two are different persons.

23. Cf. Böhme 1929, p. 76:

Den eigentlichen Begriff "Charakter" kennt Homer nicht. Die Begriffe *thumos* und *noos* gehen ja nicht auf den ganzen Menschen, sondern immer nur auf eine Seite seines Wesens, eben die, auf die es in der betreffenden Situation ankommt. Das Wesen eines Menschen wird erfasst in seiner Bewährung in der einzelnen Tat.

24. For these terms see Dahrendorf 1973. Dahrendorf speaks of *Homo sociologicus*, of the man defined by his positions and roles, as a "glass man," an artificial construct including only some features of the real man. *Homo sociologicus* is such a glass man, and so is the autonomous individual of the romantics.

25. For further qualifications see Seel 1953 and Schwabl 1954. The controversy up to now has largely turned on the interpretation of the divine interventions: the moments when a god implants in a hero a thought or impulse. Schwabl points out that the gods are characters in the plot, not forces exterior to it; the relations between men and gods are not qualitatively different from the relations between men and men (cf. also Latte 1920–21, pp. 256 f.). Schwabl says (p. 56): "Die Darstellung des Göttereinflusses nach dem Bild der Beeinflussung von Mensch zu Mensch vorgestellt ist." Schwabl does not go on to draw what seems to me the appropriate conclusion: that Homeric men also can "intervene" in the lives of their fellow men and implant in them a thought or an impulse—as Agamemnon implants the *cholos* in Achilles. Here, as elsewhere, the gods are greater in power but not different in kind.

The obvious differences from the *Iliad* displayed by the treatment of characters in the *Odyssey* may well represent not some change or development within the culture but simply the different themes and artistic requirements of the later poem; cf. Schwabl 1954, p. 62, n. 23.

26. Whitman 1958, p. 188.

27. The learning story, which turns on the passage of the hero from ignorance to knowledge or from folly to wisdom—the most frequent cliché plot of modern fiction—seems to me not a Greek kind of plot. The only clear case of such a hero, it seems to me, in Greek narrative before Plato is Strepsiades in the *Clouds*—and that is, after all, a play about education. Telemachus in the *Odyssey* certainly matures in the course of the poem; but while the process of his tutelage is carefully treated, the process of his learning is left undramatized. We see his education from the outside; we see how it is done, and we see him change in his behavior, but at no point does he say: "Now I see . . ." or "How foolish I was then to. . . ." Odysseus in the same poem is presented as a man of mature wisdom who has learned much—and in a hard school; but again the process of his learning is not dramatized. In tragedy the frequent event is not learning but discovery; the hero does not learn a lesson but finds out a secret.

28. Jones 1962, p. 37.

29. Ibid., p. 17.

30. Ibid., p. 43.

31. Ibid., p. 33.

32. Ibid., p. 52.

33. Ibid., p. 276.

34. Ibid., p. 33. Here also I am close to Jones, and in the next chapter I shall review the conceptions of poetry from Homer to Aristotle, sketch the developments, and observe the continuities.

35. Fränkel 1962, p. 88.

36. This point was seen by Pagliaro (1963, pp. 4 f.):

Uno stato d'animo può essere assunto e definito come argomento di canto epico solo a condizione che si possa dare di ciò motivazione; vale a dire, che di esso risulti subito il rilievo causale nel quadro di circostanze particolari e, sopratutto, in riferimento agli effetti, in modo che se ne possa avvertire sino dall'inizio l'importanza; è ovvio che la narrazione epica non può scegliersi un punto di partenza, e di raccordo al tempo stesso, così tipico, se no in vista della validità causale di esso rispetto al corso degli eventi. Difatti, questa *mēnis* di Achille si qualifica subito, a partire dal secondo verso, per le gravi sciagure che essa apporterà agli Achei.

37. Hector, a figure less intensely drawn, is in fact more widely present in the *Iliad* than Achilles. "Hector has the distinction of being the only person who is named in every one of the twenty-four books of the *Iliad*" (Scott 1921, p. 218).

CHAPTER ONE

1. Pagliaro 1961, pp. 14–15.
2. He is said to *exarchein*, to "initiate" (ibid., pp. 27–34).
3. Ibid., pp. 19–27.
4. Ibid., p. 26.
5. Pagliaro (ibid., pp. 15–17) points out that the Muse is usually asked not *aeidein*, "to sing," but *enepein*, "to say"; this is because epic is not thought of as primarily song (as a lyric is) but as primarily story.
6. Compare the account of the place of training in an oral tradition in Lord 1960, ch. 2.
7. Other such stories are alluded to in speeches, for example the stories of Hephaestus' fall from heaven (I.586–94) and of Zeus's expulsion of Ate (XIX.91–133).
8. Compare the following:

> Like the majority of American Indians, the Winnebago distinguish sharply between what might be called myths and realistic tales. Under "myth" is included everything regarded as having taken place in a distant past; under "tale" everything that has occurred within comparatively recent times. The word for myth means "sacred"; that for tale, "what is told"; i.e., what is considered as a real happening. It matters not how completely mythical the content of a story may be; as long as it is thought of as portraying an actual occurrence it is a tale. Stylistically a very interesting difference exists between the two, the former always having a happy, the latter . . . an unhappy ending. The Winnebago themselves appear to be well aware of this trait of their myths as the following personal experience indicates.
>
> While engaged in translating a text I must have unconsciously given my interpreter the impression of being worried about the

fate of the hero of the particular story. He had been cut up into pieces and was being slowly boiled in a cauldron at the particular moment that my face apparently attracted the interpreter's attention, for he stopped short and said to me very kindly, "Don't worry. He isn't dead. They never die." Whether the Winnebago are equally conscious of the tragic ending of their realistic tales I had no means of determining; that, consciously or not, a definite selection of subject-matter has taken place is quite evident, for otherwise the invariable tragic dénouement would be inexplicable. The impression conveyed is that they regarded life, the contact and pitting of man against man, of peoples against peoples, as leading inevitably to tragedy, an inference perhaps not so strange in a civilization where the highest ambition of man was to die on the warpath, and where the most insistent pursuit of life was prestige. [Radin 1927, pp. 172–73.]

But see Detienne 1967, pp. 16–20, for an explanation of the two types of song in terms of a hypothetical Mycenaean distinction between priest's song and warrior's song. Such reference to early "tripartite organization" appears to me both dubious and unnecessary.

9. Schmitt 1967, ch. 2, presents the argument which identifies this phrase as a reflex of a Proto-Indo-European syntagm.

10. See Parry 1972 for an interpretation of these passages.

11. See Fränkel 1962, p. 88, n. 14.

12. "Si le *kudos* vient des dieux, le *kleos* monte jusqu'à eux" (Detienne 1967, p. 20).

13. See Speier 1952, pp. 41, 47:

Fame does not establish distinctions of rank. In contrast to honor it is not bestowed and observed, but only spread. Fame grows with the number of those who are conscious of it. Someone may be more famous than another who excells him in honor. . . .

Honor is socially the less effective the more frequently it is bestowed. The discriminating force of honor grows with the exclusiveness of its bearers. The smaller the circle of the honored, the greater the distinction to belong to it. Accordingly, inflations of honor may occur.

It is also true that a high degree of *timē*—the status of king, for instance—confers *kudos* or evokes it from Zeus (I.279). This is the familiar phenomenon called by Max Weber "routinized charisma."

14. See p. 180.

15. Sometimes this association between gravestone and *kleos* seems purely conventional; Menelaus, for example, dedicates a cenotaph to Agamemnon "so that the *kleos* will be unquenchable" (iv.584), even though the spot is almost literally at the ends of the earth, and no one who knew Agamemnon will ever be likely to see it. Similarly, Elpenor asks for a grave on Circe's island *"essomenoisi puthesthai"* (xi.76).

16. See Carpenter 1946, pp. 27–31.

17. See Harriott 1969, pp. 18–20; Detienne 1967, pp. 7–27.

18. For a defense of this statement see Redfield 1973.

19. "The appeal to the Muses . . . is . . . a way of expressing the certainty and inner conviction which the 'inspired' poet feels. The Muses know all things, past, present and future, and he, sharing their knowledge, will say what is precisely right, and deserves to be heard" (Harriott 1969, p. 51). See also Detienne 1967, p. 15.

20. For Calliope as the chief of the Muses see Harriott 1969, pp. 16–17. The assignment of particular arts to the various Muses is post-classical, although Socrates in the *Phaedrus* (259c–d) makes a (playful) start, associating Calliope and Ourania with philosophy. Originally the names of the Muses, as given in Hesiod *Theogony* 77–79, were no doubt a list of names like those of the Nereids in *Iliad* XVIII.38–49 and of the Phaeacians in *Odyssey* viii.111–19: names formed on roots suggestive of the general ambience in which they functioned. Thus the names of the Nereids suggest sea, wave, and seashore; the names of the Phaeacians suggest ships and seafaring; and the names of the Muses suggest types of song, singers, and occasions for song. Cf. Detienne 1967, pp. 12 f.

21. See Plato *Gorgias* 456c–d.

22. "The concentration on the processes of composition may reduce the poet to the level of artisan, one who merely glues things together or hammers in nails. Again the attitude which regards poetry as a commodity like any other diminishes the mystique with which a Cinesias would have liked to surround it" (Harriott 1969, p. 97).

23. For more on this theme, including citations of other discussions, see Pohlenz 1956.

24. See Harriott 1969, pp. 106–7.

25. Harriott remarks (ibid., pp. 82–83):

While Plato seems to have given a new and exalted conception of the poet, we should not be blind to what he has taken away. He has disposed of the belief that the poet transmitted knowledge, the gift of the Muses with whom he had a personal relationship, that he was in control of his material, that he was concerned to communicate with an audience. The matter-of-fact acceptance of poetry conspicuous previously has vanished. . . . Plato's message is almost entirely new . . . it is made acceptable by being dressed in language and imagery familiar from tradition.

26. Socrates' best statement on literary criticism is probably *Phaedrus* 229d–230a, although formally what is dismissed there is not criticism of literature but criticism of myth. He says: "I am not able (in the Delphic phrase) to know myself; I find it obviously ridiculous, when I am ignorant of *that*, to investigate irrelevancies [*ta allotria*]." This

position is parallel to the position taken toward science in *Phaedo* 98c–100a.

27. Socrates is perhaps making precisely this argument at the end of the *Symposium*, where we get a glimpse of him forcing Agathon and Aristophanes to agree that "it belongs to the same man to know how to compose comedies and tragedies" (*Symposium* 223d). In the *Ion* the fact that particular poets are successful only in particular genres is taken as proof that the poets are inspired, "since if they knew by art how to speak well in one, they would also in all" (*Ion* 534c). Socrates seems in the *Symposium* to have reversed this argument and to be suggesting to Agathon and Aristophanes the consequences of a claim that their poetic powers are founded on knowledge. In *Philebus* 48–50 Socrates offers an explanation of comedy and tragedy as based on the mixture of pleasure and pain resulting from a recognition of good and evil in others. Poetry would thus be based on knowledge of these things and would become a proper art of the philosopher.

28. Cf. Grene 1950, p. 123:

> For Plato the theater would have been the natural expression of his philosophic genius, which was to see always the relations of thought and the composite of will and action which mark the boundaries of a human character. . . . The dialogues of the middle period are true animations of situations, intellectual and emotional, and it is as such, as the dramatic statement of relation, that we must see them, not as doctrinal expositions of an author's thesis.

29. Homer is mentioned at the beginning of the discussion of imitation as the "teacher and leader of all these fine tragedians" (595c) and, at the end, as "most poetic and first of tragic poets" (607a); in between he is mentioned a score of times.

30. See Else 1958.

31. Cf. Verdenius 1949, pp. 16–17:

> Plato's doctrine of imitation is closely related to his hierarchical conception of reality. In fact "the idea of imitation is at the centre of his philosophy." Our thoughts and arguments are imitations of reality (*Timaeus* 47b–c, *Critias* 107b–c), words are imitations of things (*Cratylus* 423e–424b), sounds are imitations of divine harmony (*Timaeus* 80b), time imitates eternity (*Timaeus* 38a), laws imitate truth (*Politicus* 300c), human governments are imitations of true government (*Politicus* 293e, 297c), devout men try to imitate their gods (*Phaedrus* 252c–d, 253b, *Laws* 713e), visible figures are imitations of eternal ones (*Timaeus* 50c), etc.

32. The analogy between poetry and figurative painting is at least as old as Simonides; see Harriott 1969, p. 143.

33. Socrates' use here of the phrase *allotriou . . . pathous* is probably an intended reference to Gorgias *Helen* 9: *ep' allotriōn te prag-*

matōn . . . idion ti pathēma. This reference may well be carried forward in *Republic* 606b.

34. This conflation of epistemology and ethics is quite characteristic of the Socratic arguments. Just as rational inquiry requires the criticism of the less-real in the light of the more-real, so rational action requires the control of the less-real (the appetites) by the more-real (the reason). The passions and appetite, being relatively formless, are more suitable objects of poetic imitation (*Republic* 604e). Thus we can understand why Socrates says that objections to imitation, put already in Book Three, are "clearer . . . now that the parts of the soul have been distinguished" (595a). Socrates uses the passage on imitation to put together the picture of the practical soul drawn in Book Four with the Simile of Light in Books Six and Seven.

35. The first cause is that *mimēsis* is *sumphuton.* But what is the second? Either the second cause is that it is *sumphuton* to take pleasure in imitation—in which case Aristotle is making a distinction between the enactment or performance of imitation and the contemplation of an imitative work—or the second cause is that *harmonia* and *rhuthmos* are, like *mimēsis, kata phusin*—in which case Aristotle is making a distinction between the imitative content of performed art and its musical form. The commentators are divided (Else 1957, p. 127). It does not make much difference how we come down on this point, since we require *both* distinctions, that between performer and audience and that between imitative content and musical form.

36. Lévi-Strauss 1962, p. 34. The whole section (pp. 33–44) deserves comparison with the *Poetics.* Both authors approach art primarily through its imitative content, since for both it is as imitator that the artist makes an important contribution to the human world. With Aristotle's rather offhand mention of the pleasure produced by "workmanship or color" we may compare Lévi-Strauss's characterization of nonfigurative painting: "C'est une école de peinture académique, où chaque artiste s'évertue à représenter la manière dont il exécuterait ses tableaux, si d'aventure il en peignait" (p. 43 n.).

37. Ibid. p. 37:

> Toujours à mi-chemin entre le schème et l'anecdote, la génie du peintre consiste à unir une connaissance interne et externe, un être et un devenir; à produire, avec son pinceau, un objet qui n'existe pas comme objet et qu'il sait pourtant créer sur sa toile: synthèse exactement équilibrée d'une ou de plusieurs structures artificielles et naturelles, et d'un ou plusieurs événements, naturels et sociaux. L'émotion esthétique provient de cette union instituée au sein d'une chose créée par l'homme, donc aussi virtuellement par le spectateur qui en découvre la possibilité à travers l'oeuvre d'art, entre l'ordre de la structure et l'ordre de l'événement.

38. Ibid., pp. 35–36:

Pour connaître l'objet réel dans sa totalité, nous avons toujours tendance à opérer depuis ses parties. La résistance qu'il nous oppose est surmontée en la divisant . . . A l'inverse . . . dans le modèle réduit *la connaissance du tout précède celle des parties.* Et même si c'est là une illusion, la raison du procédé est de créer ou d'entretenir cette illusion, qui gratifie l'intelligence et la sensibilité d'un plaisir qui, sur cette seule base, peut déjà être appelé esthétique . . .

La science eût, en effet, travaillé à l'échelle réelle, mais par le moyen de l'invention d'un métier, tandis que l'art travaille à l'échelle réduite, avec pour fin une image homologue de l'objet. La première démarche est de l'ordre de la métonymie, elle remplace un être par un autre être, un effet par sa cause, tandis que la seconde est de l'ordre de la métaphore. [Italics in original.]

39. This expression may appear paradoxical, and it is clear that Aristotelian language is here pulled out of shape. We need some way, however, of distinguishing two kinds of imitations of the particular. Elder Olson writes (1965, p. xiii, n. 3):

That either particulars or universals may be imitated is clear from these considerations: (1) man is not the only imitative animal, but the *most* imitative; if other animals imitate, they must imitate particulars since they have no grasp of universals (*Metaphysics* iii.1 980b25 ff.); imitation is therefore possible of the particular; (2) it is also possible of the universal, since in fact comedy shifted from imitation of the particular to that of the universal (*Poetics* 4:1449b8–9) . . . . Imitation of the particular is, of course, *copying*.

But while the animal may copy, the comic poet does not. Both imitate particulars, but differently. The imitative animal does not (so far as we can tell) intend his imitation to be recognized by another; he imitates in responsive enactment or indwelling with others he perceives. Such imitation may be the fundamental source of all imitation, but when imitation has become a form of communication, as in comic poetry, it becomes something else. A caricature is nothing like a copy of a face; it is an attempt to reveal to us the most recognizable elements of the face, so that we can see it as it actually is in its most perfectly individualized particularity.

40. Aristotle himself has no term except *poiēsis,* "poetry," which meant for his audience, as poetry does to us, compositions in meter. We can see him groping for another term at the places where he asserts that meter is not an important defining characteristic, as at 1447b13–20 and 1451b2–4.

41. In Plato there are still traces of a view of the heroic stories as quasi history; Socrates says that one kind of permissible lying is that

which takes place "in the storytelling we were just speaking of; because we do not know how things truly were in the ancient times, we liken the falsehood to the truth as much as we can and thus make it useful" (*Republic* 382c–d).

42. Thus Socrates in the *Phaedrus* says that standard rhetorical textbooks prescribed a sequence: narration—testimony—evidence—probabilities (266e). Discussion of arguments from probability can be traced all the way back to the beginnings of rhetorical theory in Corax (Aristotle *Rhetoric* 1402a18).

43. The *locus classicus* for this sort of argument in Greek is Antiphon's *First Tetralogy*, esp. 1.4–8 and 2.3–9.

44. The poem is an imitation of a *praxis*, but mere incidents do not constitute a *praxis*; in a sense there is no *praxis* for the poet to imitate until he has conceived the events as an internally coherent plot. Thus the poet in effect constructs the thing he imitates. This may appear paradoxical, but the case is no different with any sort of imitation which rises above the mere recording of particulars. In order to set before us a form, the imitator must discover (or invent) the form which he imitates.

45. Aristotle himself had a taste for realism in the ordinary sense; while he saw that imitation lies in the intermediate causes, he also preferred that the premises should be such as we might encounter in ordinary experience. However, given a choice between the intermediate causes and the premises, he knew how to choose; that is why he says, "Impossibilities which are probable are to be selected ahead of possibilities which are unpersuasive" (*Poetics* 1460a26–27). A possibility is unpersuasive not because we do not believe that it could be so but because we have not seen why it should be so; that is, the poet has not shown us the intermediate causes. The probable or necessary consequence of an impossible premise, on the other hand, is a probable impossibility.

46. Owen, in his excellent book on the *Iliad* (1966), approaches the poem almost entirely from this point of view. He says, for example (p. 36):

> The poet's whole interest seems concentrated on the incident he is reciting, and consequently the hearer's or reader's interest is so concentrated too. We need not look beyond it nor think beyond it. . . . Homer roams freely, no doubt, in search of topics of interest, but he never loses his grip on the essential movement of the poem. The incident may be logically unnecessary, but in its effect on the feelings it turns out to be an event in the emotional plot that is building in the hearer's mind. And that is the fundamental test of artistry. . . . In estimating the purpose of any particular incident, the critic should consider not

so much its effect on the happenings of the story as its effect on the feelings of the reader.

Note that the term "plot" is used here entirely differently from the way in which I use it; the test of plot here is the subjective coherence of the audience's experience, not the objective coherence of the incidents.

47. It is a premise of the story of the *Odyssey* that Odysseus, kept from his home for a period of years, is so resourceful and enduring that, although he suffers much, he is able at last to return. Therefore he has to have adventures. Nothing in the logic of the story, however, requires him to have those particular adventures; the poet of the *Odyssey* has apparently taken the best stories he knew and worked them together into a patterned sequence.

48. See above, n. 38.

49. Cf. Snell 1928, pp. 10–12.

50. Thus Aristotle's sentence "The *telos* is a *praxis*" is ambiguous. He may mean either that the *telos* of the poet is to show us a *praxis* (and not some incomplete, unbounded behavior) or that action is unintelligible to the actor unless its *telos* is conceived of as a *praxis*. He may mean both. Cf. Fyfe 1910, pp. 233 f.

51. See above, n. 37.

52. For a discussion of "die tragische Erschütterung" as "Begriffe von schwer ausschöpfbarer Bedeutung" see Schadewaldt 1955, pp. 169–70. For Schadewaldt the tragic terror is evoked in us by an unexpected insight into reality.

53. Schadewaldt distinguishes eight separate meanings which have been offered for *katharsis* in the *Poetics*, and adds: "So viele Köpfe, so viele Meinungen, von denen kaum eine unwidersprochen geblieben ist und jede auch wirklich ihre speziellen Schwierigkeiten mit sich führt" (ibid., p. 150).

54. I attempt no review of the enormous literature on Aristotle's use of *katharsis*. It will be clear that I stand with those who hold that he "conceived of catharsis as an intellectual climax to the artistic process" (Golden 1962, p. 60). Through imitation, events are reduced to form; and thus, however impure in themselves, the events portrayed are purified—clarified—into intelligibility. The recognition of an intelligible pattern is the proper pleasure of tragedy and, indeed, of art in general, insofar as it appeals to a "free and educated audience." One may even wonder if, after all, the alternative reading in *Poetics* 1449b27—*mathēmatōn* for *pathēmatōn*—might be correct; it is certainly the *lectio difficilior* there. The antecedent would still be "pity and fear," but Aristotle's implication would be that those *pathēmata* are capable of purification precisely because, when we experience them in an imitative work, they are modes of learning rather than raw experi-

ence. (This notion was suggested to me many years ago by Seth Benardete.)

The passage from the *Politics* cannot, however, be ignored; the cross-reference to the *Poetics* is explicit, even if the promise of a full discussion of *katharsis* is not kept in the later work. I suggest that the two passages are consistent, although different; they approach the same question from distinct points of view.

Aristotle's point in the *Politics* is that the healing effects of music, which are obvious in the case of "enthusiastic" music, work also within the more cultivated sphere of "practical" music, although the effect is not so obvious since the "free and educated" audience does not experience emotion in such an exaggerated form:

> The experience [*pathos*] which comes over some souls powerfully is really found in all; the difference is a matter of less and more, so that it is [felt as] pity and fear, or goes as far as enthusiasm. Some people become possessed by this latter perturbation, and we see that they are affected by the sacred melodies . . . in such a way that they obtain healing and purification. But this must be the experience of those who feel pity and fear and the emotions in general . . . that they all come to some purification and relief accompanied by pleasure. Thus it is in the same way that practical music provides a noninjurious pleasure for human beings. [*Politics* 1342a4–16]

As the musical healer soothes the hysteric, so also the poet, in a less spectacular fashion, soothes his audience by the power of his music. It might be objected that, in contrast to the healer, the poet himself stimulates the emotions which he lays to rest; but since the poem is imitative, there is always some evocation and recollection of emotions felt in ordinary life, and a well-made work, properly experienced, does have some steadying effect on our disorderly spirits. So far we can see what Aristotle is talking about. It is also clear that the use of *katharsis* in this passage is "therapeutic," while in the *Poetics* (if the interpretation of our school is correct) the use is "intellectual."

The two uses of the term, however, merely stress different aspects of a single phenomenon. The apprehension of a universal, on which the *Poetics* lays the emphasis, is not something which occurs independently of the experience of the work, as though we could abstract some sort of message and say, "Now I can tell you what the poet meant to say." The poet meant what he said, and he said it in music.

A performed work is apprehended in two different ways: it is experienced through time, and it is known as a whole instantaneously. When I attend a performance of *Macbeth*, I become absorbed in the play of the scenes, the alternation of vocal rhythms, rapid and somber, assertive and despairing. At the same time, I am aware of the play as whole, as the imitation of an action, that is, the discovery and communication of some pattern within human experience. Both apprehensions are (in a successful performance) "pure": first, because the emotions and expectations evoked by the play are dealt with by its linear (in a broad sense, its musical) order; second, because through the power of his art Shakespeare converts treason and murder from objects of terror to objects of knowledge. Nor are these two kinds of purity distinct from each other; the play makes possible the detached and clarified contemplation of the events which it imitates precisely because it shapes them into a formed experience. The *Poetics* lays stress on the meaning, the *Politics* on the immediate experience; the former speaks of poetry as it shapes the intellectual virtues, the latter as it shapes the ethical virtues. But Aristotle always understood that these two kinds of virtues are aspects of a single personality and are separable only in analysis.

CHAPTER TWO

1. Aristotle associates thought with speech because only through speech is thought known to us. The actor's character is visible in his act: he is such-and-such a man in that he does such-and-such things. He does them for reasons, but his reasons cannot be deduced from his acts; they are known to us only as he states them. Thus for Aristotle the element of thought in a narrative is not in everything the actors say (a deceitful persuasive speech, for instance, is itself an act, and a speech of mourning may simply express a state of mind, a *pathos*) but only in those speeches or elements of speeches in which a character gives some explanation of his actions.

2. It is of course possible for someone—the author of *Tristes Tropiques* for example—to make of the very idea that values are culturally conditioned a life-orientation and thus (in effect) an unconditioned source of values.

3. The actor may say: "This is the code of my people; others may have other codes, valid for them, but I must live by mine." But this assertion is founded on the value of loyalty to one's own code. He may say: "Irrespective of the norms of the culture in which I live, I must be faithful to that which, in the process of my reasoning, has come to seem best to me." But this assertion is founded on the value of reasoning. Both values can be, and have been, contested; both are adhered to only under specific cultural conditions.

4. It can of course be a premise of fiction that history is remediable: that one can go back and start over or that what has mattered can be made not to matter.

5. It may appear odd to speak of a magic ring as a constraint. But a man who has been given such a ring cannot make it be that he has

not been given it. The ring presents him with a problem to which he must respond somehow—even if by doing nothing.

6. Finley 1954, p. 43.

7. Kirk 1962, p. 181.

8. Cf. Vidal-Naquet 1965, pp. 114–18.

9. For a statement of this view, and a criticism of it, see Schwabl 1954, p. 48.

10. So in his own speech Lycaon attributes his misfortune to a *moir' oloē* (XXI.83) and a *daimon* (XXI.93); both are practically synonymous, in this usage, with *theos*. Cf. Dietrich 1965, p. 199.

11. Shakespeare, of course, wrote for his own audience, not Romans; his Rome was a kind of heroic world, a system of premises within which an action relevant to Jacobean England could be set at a distance. In order to discuss Shakespeare's communication with his audience we should have to discuss their shared assumptions about the Roman setting.

12. For the history of this word see Tromp de Ruiter 1932. The word is first applied to gods—to Prometheus and Hermes—and is not used of men before Xenophon. Xenophon and others also apply the word to thoroughly domesticated animals. Thus, initially, *philanthrōpos* is exactly analogous to *philathēnaios*: the latter would not be applied to an Athenian or the former to a human being. Later the word is extended to human beings who (as if they were favorable gods) make a free gift of good things; Socrates says that he taught everyone *hupo philanthrōpias*; he "just couldn't say no" (Plato *Euthyphro* 3d). The use of the word is much developed in the fourth century B.C. and later. Tromp de Ruiter quotes a late definition:

> Of *philanthrōpia* there are three kinds. One occurs in forms of address, for example if a man greets everyone he meets and gives them his hand and says hello. Another kind is when one is helpful to everyone in distress. Another kind of *philanthrōpia* is when people enjoy going to dinner parties. [Diogenes Laertius 3.98]

The *philanthrōpos* is thus a person openhearted, generous, and companionable. The word, says Tromp de Ruiter, often has further connotations of pity, sympathy, and good will (*eleos, suggnōme, eunoia*).

For a different interpretation of *philanthrōpos* as used in the *Poetics*, and a review of earlier opinion on the matter, see Else 1957, pp. 368 ff. Cf. also Schadewaldt 1955, p. 135.

13. Tragedy thus presupposes a "results culture" (for which term see Adkins 1970, p. 29), for only in such a culture can a good man be held to have acted badly, and this paradox is the central problematic (in Aristotle's view) of a tragedy. Notice that the "acting badly" cannot *simply* consist (as Adkins seems to imply) in failure or

in an undesirable outcome; a man who knowingly took a necessary risk and lost would not be (in Aristotle's view) a tragic figure. The "acting badly" must arise from some incapacity in the figure himself, but this incapacity may consist in something as (from our point of view) morally irrelevant as the failure, through no fault of his own, to possess certain crucial information.

Nor should we, I think, underrate the extent to which we still live in a "results culture." A man who shot his son under the illusion that he was a burglar threatening his life—even if we suppose that the mistake was unavoidable, that he had taken all proper care under the circumstances, and so forth—would feel very different from a man whose son, through no fault of his own, was struck by a passing car. The first man would even, I think, be guilty of something in the eyes of the courts; although if the mistake were completely unavoidable, there might well be a discretionary decision not to prosecute. We do judge others and (more important) ourselves by our acts and their consequences and not only by our intentions (although we may not do it quite as the Homeric Greeks did it; cf. Adkins 1971, p. 8).

14. Finley 1954, p. 112.

15. Cf. Idomeneus' almost instinctive choice of Agamemnon to be *istōr*, to hold the stakes in a bet (XXIII.486).

16. Cf. Lacey 1966, p. 51: "The law in Homeric society is based on recognized usage, it is true, but this is made effective only by deeds which assert its validity."

17. For the link between *atē* and *hamartia* see Dawe 1967.

18. In presenting Agamemnon's action both as his own and as the effect on him of an overwhelming exterior force, Homer is not different from a modern kind of scientific analyst. Compare, for example, the passage in Trotsky's *History of the Russian Revolution* on the likeness between Louis XVI and Czar Nicholas, where Trotsky speaks of

> those traits of character which have been grafted, or more or less directly imposed, on a person by the mighty force of conditions, and which throw a sharp light on the interrelation of personality and the objective forces of history. . . .
>
> They both go toward the abyss "with the crown pushed down over their eyes." But would it after all be easier to go to an abyss, which you cannot escape anyway, with your eyes open? What difference would it have made? . . .
>
> Similar (of course far from identical) irritations in similar conditions call out similar reflexes; the more powerful the irritation, the sooner it overcomes personal peculiarities. To a tickle, people react differently, but to a red-hot iron, alike. [L. Trotsky, *The History of the Russian Revolution*, trans. Max Eastman (London: Gollancz, 1965), pp. 113–14.]

The red-hot iron, in Homeric language, is felt as *atē*; the word names the experience one has in crisis situations of being a helpless victim, so that one continues to act, yet does not act for oneself.

CHAPTER THREE

1. Murray (1924) understood and stated eloquently the fact that the Homeric poems can be understood only against a background of extreme social instability and tight small-group loyalty. Murray drew this point, not from his reconstruction of the historical background, but from the poems themselves; whatever one thinks of his historical reconstructions, his literary intelligence remains unexcelled. Murray understood that the Greek world had been constructed on a layer of rubble and that many elements in Greek religion, social life, and political institutions can be understood only by presupposing a sharp break with the past. This break, furthermore, must precede the composition of the epics as we have them. See also Vernant 1969.

2. Cf. Adkins 1960, pp. 35 ff., and the development (partly through controversy) of the views there expressed in Adkins 1963, Long 1970, and Adkins 1971.

3. This statement requires some qualification, at least for the *Odyssey*, where *hērōs* is used very widely, being applied even to the blind bard Demodocus (viii.483), who is neither warrior nor aristocrat. There can be little question, however, that the society presented in the Homeric poems is a society divided into two distinct classes divided by a "deep horizontal cleavage" (Finley 1954, p. 49). Members of the upper class are leading warriors and monopolize political initiative; the collectivity of the subordinate class plays a supporting role in both war and peace. The *locus classicus* for the distinction is *Iliad* II.188–206. I have called the members of the upper class "heroes" rather than *aristoi* or by some other of the Homeric terms for them because I wished to call attention to a literary consequence of this class differentiation. The leading warriors in the *Iliad* have proper names; the folk are an anonymous mass (see XI.299–309, where Hector kills nine *hēgemones* or leaders, each of whom is carefully named [even though the names were probably invented for this passage] and also kills an indeterminate number of the anonymous *plēthus*, "multitude"). It follows that only the leading warriors can be heroes in *our* sense, that is, central figures in a fictional narrative; they alone have known personal stories. Aristotle (*Problems* 922b) assumes that this same class differentiation gave rise to the distinction between actors and chorus in tragedy; in heroic times, he says, only the *hēgemones* were *hērōes*; the masses were simply *anthrōpoi*, "human beings." The *anthrōpoi* found voice in the tragic chorus but remained, as they always were, anonymous. For a modern restatement of this last notion, see Vernant 1973, pp. 24 ff.

4. This passage, which was already famous in early antiquity (cf. Simonides fr. 8 [West]), sets an insoluble problem to the English translator. *Geneē*, the word I have here translated "breed" and "breeding," means both "lineage" and "generation"; that is, it means "birth" from the point of view of both kinship and time of birth. Everyone who is born is thereby placed in a line of predecessors and possible descendants and is also placed temporally in relation to his elders, contemporaries, and juniors. *Geneē* refers to both aspects. When, therefore, Glaucus refers to the *geneē* of leaves, he alludes to both the familiar analogy between a tree and a lineage (cf. Latin *stirps*) and the analogy between the succession of the seasons and the succession of the generations. A lineage puts forth men as a tree puts forth leaves; in the passage of time, men are born and die as the leaves fall from the tree and grow again. In both respects human kinship is seen as analogous to natural process.

5. Bowra (1930, pp. 22 ff.) notes the likeness between Achilles and Coriolanus.

6. Whitman, 1958, pp. 202 f.

7. Ibid., p. 206. One can, however, overstate Achilles' detachment from the ceremony of reconciliation; he does take back Briseis, and he does spontaneously utter the little prayer which closes the ceremonies (XIX.270–75). Homer was a close student of the efficacy of ceremonial and knew, I suspect, that they often work even on those who resist them or feel themselves uninvolved. Friedrich, in his unpublished manuscript (1973), has analyzed the ceremony of reconciliation in Book Nineteen and has shown its efficacy.

8. Cf. Campbell 1966, pp. 148 f.:

> Between the age of twenty-three . . . and the time of his marriage . . . a young man belongs to the *pallikari* age group. . . . The *pallikari* is the hero-warrior with physical strength and assertive courage who is prepared to die, if necessary, for the honour of his family. For him physical perfection is an important ideal attribute and any kind of physical deformity is fatal to his reputation. These, indeed, are the years of perfected manliness when a young shepherd is still free from the responsibilities of family leadership and the need for caution, compromise, and lies, which it inevitably imposes.
>
> The critical moment in the development of the young shepherd's reputation is his first quarrel. Quarrels are necessarily public. . . . It is the critical nature of these first important tests of his manliness that makes the self-regard (*egoismos*) of the young shepherd so extremely sensitive. It is not only the reality of an obvious insult which provokes him to action, but even the finest of allusions on which it is possible to place some unflattering construction.

When a man has assumed the status of head of family he becomes more cautious. He resorts to violence only when he must. For now he has to consider what will happen to his family. . . . Cleverness is the quality he must cultivate. It implies quickness of mind and a degree of foresight; also the skill to plot with guile, and to lie with effect. In some respects this period of leadership is perhaps more testing for a man than his years in the *pallikari* age group. Expediency must be balanced against honour in ways that do not endanger reputation; this is not always easy. Only after his retirement when his reputation is definitely established does a man at last enter a period of life which is free from competitive strain.

9. No one has ever put this point more eloquently, or seen its implications better, than Sir Henry Maine, who writes:

Contrasted with the organisation of a modern state, the commonwealths of primitive times may be fairly described as consisting of a number of little despotic governments, each perfectly distinct from the rest, each absolutely controlled by the prerogative of a single monarch. But though the Patriarch, for we must not yet call him the Pater-familias, had rights thus extensive, it is impossible to doubt that he lay under an equal amplitude of obligations. If he governed the family, it was for its behoof. If he was lord of its possessions, he held them as trustee for his children and kindred. He had no privilege or position distinct from that conferred on him by the petty commonwealth which he governed. The Family, in fact, was a Corporation; and he was its representative or, we might almost say, its Public Officer. [Maine 1920, p. 197.]

10. Gates, 1971, p. 5.

11. Finley 1954, pp. 90 ff.

12. The situation in Troy is complicated by the fact that Priam's household is polygamous. Probably the poet found this polygamous household in his poetic tradition; Homer himself was probably somewhat unclear as to how it was supposed to work.

13. Cf. Scott 1921, p. 229.

14. Strictly speaking, *aidōs* is (sometimes) a form of *deos*, as in XXIV. 435, where the disguised Hermes joins the two in speaking of his feelings toward Achilles, his superior. But in other contexts the two terms appear contrasted, as in XV.657–58, where the Achaeans hold their places, "for *aidōs* and *deos* held them." Here the poet seems to mean that they stood firm, first because they thought they ought to, second because they were terrified of the consequences of defeat. In VII.93 we have the two emotions working in opposite directions; challenged to a duel, the Achaeans "felt *aidōs* to refuse, and *deos* to accept."

15. On *aidōs* see Murray 1924, pp. 80–90; von Erffa 1937, pp. 4–43; Verdenius 1945; and Cheyns 1967.

16. The translation here is somewhat free. Thetis refers to her *ache' akrita*, which I take to mean "unresolved sorrows"; Cunliffe, *Lexicon of the Homeric Dialect*, s.v., translates *akrita* in this phrase as "endless, never-ending," but this translation is not consistent with the meaning of *akrita* in other contexts. The only other occurrence of the phrase is in Helen's speech, III.412; Helen there, like Thetis here, seems to be saying that she has feelings she has not yet come to terms with. Cf. Amory 1966, pp. 17 f., n. 22.

17. Cheyns (1967, p. 11), citing XXIV.44–45, 53–54, and XV.115–18, 128–29, says, "Le verbe *nemesaō* désigne une réaction de la société dirigée contre celui qui ne possède pas l'*aidōs*."

18. Dodds 1951, pp. 17 f.

19. Athena, however, does not accept Ares' emotional outburst; she prevents him from going forward, telling him that he has lost both *noos* and *aidōs*; that is, his behavior is neither sensible nor proper (XV.128–41).

20. Cf. von Erffa 1937, p. 36.

21. Sexuality: *aidōs*: vi.66, 221, viii.324 (cf. the use for "private parts," XXII.75); *nemesis*: III.410, XIV.336, vi.286. Hospitality: *aidōs*: IX. 640, viii.544, ix.266–71, xv.373, xix.243, 316; *nemesis*: i.119, xvii. 481. Battle: *aidōs*: V.529–32 = XV.561–64, XV.561 = 661 (cf. the "battle cry" use, below); *nemesis*: IV.507, XVII.91ff., XVII.254; both together: XIII.95–124. For the structural interrelations and analogies between woman, guest, and enemy see Pitt-Rivers 1970.

22. Hector says: "My *thumos* does not instruct me [to shrink from battle] because *mathon* [I learned] to be *esthlos* [good]." In other words, he feels no impulse or desire to be a shirker because he has made himself into the sort of man who does not shirk. The verb *mathon* implies that he had once been different (even if only as a child) and that he would be different now if he had made different choices. Thus it is said of a beggar in the *Odyssey* that he has given up work since *erga kak' emmathen*, "he has learned evil acts" (xvii.226)—or, as we would say, since he has "picked up bad habits."

Snell comments on Hector's speech (1924, p. 73): "Sich geistig etwas zu eigen machen, das eine bestimmte Wirkung gewinnt. Äussert sich diese Wirkung in Praktischen, so erhalten wir die Bedeutung, 'sich gewöhnen' . . . Und für eine Zeit, die eine geistige Bildung noch nicht kannte, war jedes Lernen auch eher ein Sich-Üben und Gewöhnen." The qualities thus acquired through practice become a second nature; a man does not feel them driving him in some direction counter to his fundamental impulses. To this degree the comment of Verdenius is correct (1945, p. 56): "[Die] Möglichkeit des Zweifels kommt für Hektor nicht einmal in Frage. Seine Ehre treibt ihn nicht mit einem mahnenden 'Du Sollst' zum Kampfe, sondern sie geht unmittelbar und von selbst in die Tat über."

On the other hand, the most significant fact about Hector's speech is that he makes it about himself. He perceives his own acts as conditioned by his history and thus does not say, "I love what I do," or "I do what must be done," but "I do what I, being what I have become, must do." In describing himself, he lets us know that he is aware that others are different and that he could have been different.

Snell says elsewhere (1928, pp. 82 f.): "Hektor nimmt die Weltordnung, so wie sie ist, und stellt keine Frage nach Recht oder Unrecht. . . . Sein 'Ich' bezeichnet er nur als Objekt für die Weisungen des *thymos*. Er hat nie in einem Konflikt gestanden. Die Erwägung, feige zu sein, ist niemals in seinem *thymos* gedrungen, so dass der ihn von seinem Wege hätte abbringen wollen." Snell concludes: "Seine Lage ist traurig und rührend, seine Haltung ist edel, aber tragisch soll man sie nicht nennen."

If the first were entirely true, the second would be true also; a Hector without doubt or conflict would be a mere victim, not a tragic hero. As we examine the story of Hector in detail, however, we shall see that it is by no means lacking in conflict and doubt. It may be true that Hector does not question the order of things—does not question that the world is as it is; neither does Hector question the ethical norm —he does not question whether the norm is as it ought to be. But he does ask questions about the content of the norm, and he finds no clear answers. Hector does not reject his society, but he finds that his society gives him conflicting instructions; he is not in conflict with the value system, but he experiences conflict within it. It is this experience, and his self-consciousness of it, which gives him tragic status.

Hector's awareness of his own virtues as conditioned rather than natural or spontaneous is the foundation of his self-consciousness. Therefore, the ethical content of his tragedy is already latent in his speech to his wife.

23. Gates 1971, p. 8.

24. In the *Odyssey* the threat of slavery hangs over grown men; Odysseus, in his accounts of his imaginary adventures in Egypt, says that the Egyptians enslaved his men (xiv.272 = xvii.441) and that he himself was intended to be sold as a slave in Libya (xiv.297). A Greek, in other words, could be a slave among a foreign people; the foreigner, like the child and the woman, is a structural inferior and can be kept in an inferior position. At one point a suitor says that Telemachus should sell his guests *eis Sikelous*, "to the Sicilians"—meaning the barbarian population in Sicily, not the Greeks there. It is at any rate notable that no one suggests making the strangers slaves right there in Ithaca—presumably not out of any delicacy of feeling but because it would be impractical. (Cf. Melanthus' vague threat to sell

the stranger "far from Ithaca" [xvii.250]). In one version of his Egyptian adventures Odysseus says that he was given as a guest gift to a visiting king of Cyprus, whence, by some means unexplained, he has arrived in Ithaca. Presumably he had simply escaped; and this simple point no doubt explains why grown Greek males were not made slaves by Greeks: it was too easy for them to disappear into the surrounding territories.

Those who were sent to Echetos were sent, not for slavery, but for the sadistic pleasures of that monstrous monarch (xviii.84–87).

25. Wilamowitz 1916, p. 303.

26. Owen 1966, p. 65.

27. Ibid., p. 72.: "Hector the *warrior* the baby has never seen, but Hector he knows well. A little touch that goes straight home to the heart, and, more than that, plays an integral part in shaping the eternal significance of the farewell scene."

CHAPTER FOUR

1. Pitt-Rivers 1966, p. 22.

2. Cf. Adkins 1969a, p. 33: "It was incumbent on the Homeric hero to proclaim his existence, his value, and his claims upon those whose help he needed." Thus boasting is a kind of obligation and is continuous with prayer.

3. On the distinction between the gods as seen by the characters and the gods as seen by the poet cf. Jörgensen 1904.

4. Cf. Grene 1960, pp. 371, 374:

> The gods are personal in the *Iliad*, yet not so personal as the men, perhaps because they lack the sobering necessity of facing death. They are somewhat lightweight interventionists, whimsical and rather theatrical in character, but in fact we do not believe in their existence nearly so completely as in that of Achilles and Odysseus, Hector, Helen and Paris. They are mere figures of particular passions and less complete people. . . .
>
> The total impression of the *Iliad* is that men and women live without certainty, belief, or faith in any universal sanction for morality, without, that is, believing that the just or righteous man has any special reason to anticipate good fortune in this world or the next, and draw all their deepest ethical sentiments from their human solidarity.

5. Or rather: anything which happens may be spoken of as fated. A reference to *moira* or to some related term usually carries two implications: the event is looked upon as significant and as unavoidable. The unavoidability is attached to the particular event, not to any general deterministic system; for in such a system particular events would lose their significance. "Homeric man knows nothing of a 'clockwork' universe or an omnipotent god" (Adkins 1960, p. 21); Homeric

determinism is not a determinism of mechanism but of plot. We are shown, not the pervasive operation of general laws, but the special interconnections of particular significant events.

6. As Aristotle says: "The most wonderful of chance events are those which appear to have happened on purpose, as when Mityas' statue in Argos killed the man responsible for Mityas' death—it fell on him while he was looking at it. It seems such things do not happen at random" (*Poetics* 1452a6–10). In life such events are fascinating because they seem to reveal an authorial hand behind apparent chance. In literature, however (Aristotle here means to say), such events are *less* impressive precisely *because* they reveal the authorial hand; poetic justice is startling in life, but we know that in poetry we can have it whenever we want. Therefore life excites wonder when it looks like poetry, and poetry, when it looks like life, when the events happen *di' allēla*—which Butcher correctly translates "as cause and effect."

7. Cf. Whitman 1958, p. 243: "What Zeus states is not the law of the world but the law of the poem. It is not by theology, but by a telescopic view of existence, that the gods mingle with and transcend the world of men."

8. Cf. Adkins 1960, p. 21.

9. On the Plan of Zeus, *Dios boulē*, cf. Pagliaro 1963, pp. 13–18. The Zeus of ordinary belief is a figure parallel to fate; what is attributed to Zeus by the characters is a chain of events perceived as a plot, a story revealing an authorial hand; the events thus classified are perceived as significant and unavoidable. Thus Achilles ascribes the quarrel to Zeus, who "must have wished many Achaeans to die" (XIX.274). Like an appeal to fate, this appeal can be made only *post facto*; once the result has occurred, it is evident that Zeus wished this result.

The poet, however, in contriving his plot, can ascribe it to Zeus *ab initio*. He will then state the will or plan of Zeus according to the plot he has to tell. Thus in the *Cypria* the poet explained that the Trojan War was in fulfillment of the plan of Zeus to reduce the population of the world (T. W. Allen, ed., *Homeri Opera*, 5:118); at the end of the *Cypria* the same poet, now looking forward to a subplot within the Trojan story, explained that the quarrel between Agamemnon and Achilles was in fulfillment of a plan of Zeus to give the Trojans some respite (idem, p. 105).

In the *Iliad*, however, the Plan of Zeus, the *Dios boulē*, is not the cause of the quarrel but rather a consequence of it. The Plan does not originate with Zeus but with Thetis (as Aristophanes and Aristarchus noticed; see Pagliaro 1963, p. 15, n. 9). Zeus thus appears not as the high god, source of plot, but as an actor within the plot—an actor who does not even initiate events but responds to the response of another. It is in this narrow sense that I use the term "Plan of Zeus" in these pages.

We should, however, notice that according to the *Odyssey* Apollo had given Agamemnon an oracle that the *pēmatos archē*, the beginning of catastrophe for Troy, would be marked by a quarrel between the "best of the Achaeans" (viii.75–82). Troy would then begin to move toward its fall "through the plans of Zeus (*Dios megalou dia boulas*)." Zeus here appears as the high god whose plan, in a wide sense, is brought to fulfillment through the quarrel and his responsive plan, in the narrow sense. This oracle is not mentioned in the *Iliad* but was probably known to its audience. There is thus an ambiguity in the phrase "Plan of Zeus" in the proem (I.5). In the narrow sense the reference is to Zeus's intervention as an actor within the plot; in the wider sense the reference is to the plot of the *Iliad* itself, with its central reversal: the moment of Greek weakness and Trojan success is the moment when the Trojans first become vulnerable and Greek success becomes inevitable. The Plan of Zeus in the narrow sense included this reversal: Zeus granted Hector a victory in order to bring Achilles back to the battle. This reversal, on a larger scale, is part of the pre-ordained and prefigured Plan of Zeus in the wider sense; the fall of Troy would come about only after a moment of weakness in the Greek army and the resulting Trojan success. Thus Pagliaro explains the reference to the *Dios boulē* in I.5 (which he connects syntactically with *ex hou* in the next line; i.e., the Plan of Zeus was being fulfilled from the moment the quarrel broke out):

> In verità, il poeta deve dare una spiegazione del perché la sua *oimē* ha inizio a quel punto, in cui si dichiara l'ira di Achille. A questo iniziare egli dà come fondamento il fatto che la volontà [in the wider sense] di Zeus ha incominciato a manifestarsi solo dal momento in cui scoppiò il dissidio fra Achille e Agamennone. Prima la guerra si era trascinata per lunghi anni in alterne vicende e con la diversa e opposta partecipazione degli dèi. Solo con l'ira di Achille si entra nella fase definitiva, poiché interviene la volontà [in the narrow sense] di Zeus ad imprimere un nuovo ritmo al corso degli eventi. [Pagliaro 1963, pp. 16 f.]

10. Wade-Gery (1952, p. 16) points out that in a full performance of the *Iliad*, spread over three days, the Great Day of Battle would exactly occupy the middle day of performance.

11. This number is conventional and adds another touch of formality to the scene. Twice before, Patroclus has slain a group of nine: XVI. 415–18 and 692–97 (cf. Hector's slaying: XI.299–309). So also nine chiefs collect in VIII.253–67; Teucer, "who arrived as the ninth," kills eight on the Trojan side and points out that Hector would make the ninth (VIII.297–99). Nine chiefs meet in council in X.194–97; Poseidon, having stirred to battle the two Ajaxes, stirs seven more warriors to help them (XIII.89–93); and in XVI.306–49 there are nine single combats in a row.

12. Nilsson (1923–24, p. 365, n. 1) points out that the Trojans in the *Iliad* take very little booty. Hector's despoilment of Patroclus is thereby so much the more significant.

13. Thus Glaucus in his protest to Hector (XVII.147–48) echoes the exact words of Achilles' protest against Agamemnon (IX.316–17).

14. Hecuba's formula—*aideo kai m' eleēson* (XXII.82)—is that of a captive appealing for mercy on the battlefield.

15. *Aidōs* might prevent the best man from being chosen (X.234–39) or prevent Telemachus' informants from being frank with him (iii.96 = iv.326).

16. Cf. Aristotle, *Nicomachean Ethics* 1108a30–35.

17. Cf. xvii.578 and iii.14–18.

CHAPTER FIVE

1. Cf. Douglas 1970, p. 48: "Where there is dirt there is system. Dirt is the by-product of a systematic ordering and classification of matter, in so far as ordering involves rejecting inappropriate elements."

2. Cf. Leach 1964.

3. Cf. Turner 1969, pp. 169 f.:
In the Tsonga boys' circumcision rites . . . the boys are . . . subjected to cold; . . . they are absolutely forbidden to drink a drop of water during the whole initiation; they must eat insipid or unsavory food which "nauseates them at first" to the point of vomiting; they are severely punished. . . . These trials are not only . . . to teach the boys endurance, obedience, and manliness. Manifold evidence from other societies suggests that they have the social significance of rendering them down into some kind of human *prima materia*, divested of specific form and reduced to a condition that, although it is still social, is without or beneath all accepted forms of status.

4. Cf. Moulinier 1952, p. 29:
Il est très important de noter cette laideur, car, dès lors, et plus encore pour un Grec que pour nous, c'est à la fois du moral et du social qui est exprimé: c'est sous le regard de quelqu'un qu'on est laid et il y a là une infériorité morale. Bien entendu, il ne s'agit ici que de la morale sociale et non point du tout de la morale personnelle. Aussi enlaidir un homme, vivant ou mort, comme nous l'avons dit plus haut, c'est l'outrager: d'où, chez l'être ainsi avili, la honte.

5. Cf. the definition in Eberling, *Lexicon Homericum*, s.v. *aeikēs*: "indecorus, indignus, turpis, foedus, improbus, tenuis, vilis."

6. Cf. Moulinier 1952, p. 33:
La seule vrai souillure, la seule dont on se purifie dans l'*Iliade* et dans l'*Odyssée* . . . c'est la saleté . . . Conception bien peu morale de l'impureté religieuse, peut-on penser. Et certes aucune

disposition spirituelle n'est requise pour l'exécution des rites. Or l'adhésion intime du sujet apparaît aux modernes comme le facteur constitutif de la valeur morale. Mais pour ma part je me demande si un fidèle qui obéit à ses dieux, n'est pas, ipso facto, de quelque façon, moral. Plus encore, la pureté d'Homère est bien matérielle, certes, c'est une propreté. Mais je crains que nous ne puissions jamais comprendre ce qu'était la pureté pour un Grec, si nous n'admettons pas, fût-ce un moment, que la propreté physique a, par elle-même, une valeur morale et religieuse.

7. For a discussion of the Homeric analogy between the chastity of women and the security of cities—a discussion centering on the ambiguity of *krēdemnon*, "a woman's veil" or "a city wall"—see Nagler 1967.

8. Cf. Fränkel 1960, pp. 4–6.

9. Geertz 1966.

10. For a thorough review of the themes of mutilation and burial see Segal 1971.

11. More exactly: we hear that *Achilles* has taken prisoners: VI. 425–27, XI.104–6, XXI.34–43.

12. On the latter passage, Segal (1971) comments: "Here the verb *aeikizein* (to despoil or treat impurely) appears for the first time in the *Iliad*. It is to recur frequently in the coming books" (p. 18).

13. For the theme of decapitation see ibid., pp. 20 f.

14. See Pagliaro 1963, pp. 31–33.

15. On Lycaon and Asteropaeus see Segal 1971, pp. 30–32. Segal writes (p. 31): "The battle in the river brings the corpse theme to a new pitch of horror in two ways. First, not just dogs and vultures devour the corpses, as is so often threatened in the *Iliad*, but eels and fish, and the mutilation is actually a fact, not just a remote threat." This way of putting it presumes that eels and fish are more horrific than dogs and vultures, but the opposite is surely the case. Lycaon and Asteropaeus are eaten by wild creatures, but under water, out of human sight; the impurity is literally washed away by the purifying streams of river and ocean. (Compare the *lumata*—bearers of impurity—which are cast into the purifying sea: I.314). Priam, on the other hand, foretells that he will be eaten by his own dogs in his courtyard, disgraced and exposed among his own people. The two scenes are parallel; in the river scene a mutilation one step short of the worst is enacted; in Priam's speech the very worst is described but not enacted.

The combat between Achilles and Asteropaeus is represented as a combat between two natural spheres; in his boast over the fallen Asteropaeus, Achilles says that his enemy was descended from a river, while he himself is descended from Zeus, "who is greater than any river" (XXI.190); even the ocean stream fears the thunders of great

Zeus. We are reminded of the ocean stream around the rim of the shield of Achilles and the sky at the center; there is possibly a scheme latent here distinguishing a superordinate sky world of form and meanful signs from a subordinate water world of pure process. To these two correspond the two chief purifying elements: fire and water (cf. Friedrich 1973). When Achilles chokes the Scamander with bodies, he taxes the purifying power of the stream beyond its limits, and the stream protests against his "outrageous acts" (XXI.214). In return, Scamander threatens Achilles with defilement: he will cover him with mud and prevent his proper burial (XXI.314–21). As always in the *Iliad*, defilement brings about further defilement in a reciprocal process. The intervention of Hephaestus—the higher purifying element —restores purity and burns the corpses (XXI.343, 348–49).

16. There is no evidence in Homer for anything approaching a cult of the dead, although such a cult probably existed before, and certainly existed soon after, the composition of the *Iliad*. The Homeric view of death seems to be specific to the literary tradition of the epic; cf. Dietrich 1965, ch. 2. For a thorough review of the Homeric evidence and secondary literature relating to the afterlife and to funerals see Schnaufer 1970. Schnaufer follows the tradition firmly established by Rohde and sees much of Homeric practice as explicable only in terms of survivals of rituals connected with an earlier, pre-Homeric belief in the continued potency of the dead body. Interest in survivals and primitive, pre-Homeric beliefs has bedeviled inquiry in this field since the nineteenth century, not because such survivals are nonexistent— Homeric belief, like the Homeric language, is evidently some sort of amalgam of contemporary, archaic, and artificial elements—but because the explanation of a custom as a survival tends to substitute for an explanation of the function or meaning of the custom within the Homeric context. In cultural, as in linguistic, studies, diachronic analysis cannot substitute for synchronic study of the system as it comes before us. Even if, as I think, the system does not reflect the ordinary beliefs of *any* historical period but is specific to the epic tradition, it remains true that the meaning the elements have in the epic is the meaning conferred on them by the understanding the poet and his audience have as to their place in that context.

17. *Menos* is the most general Homeric word for vitality or energy. *Menos* shows itself in the warrior's *alkē*, "valor" (VI.265, etc.; xxii.226), or *tharsos*, "daring" (V.2; cf. XIX.37, i.321). Most commonly, *menos* is aggressive energy, but it is also *menos* which enables a man to run away (XX.93, XXII.204). *Menos* is not used of mortal women in the *Iliad*, but Eurycleia in the *Odyssey* has *menos* (xix.493–94). *Menos* fills horses in a race (XXIII.468, 524) but also enables the domestic mule to pull a cart (vii.2). *Menos* is characteristic of dangerous wild animals (XVII.20–22), especially lions (V.136, XX.172), but it is also the life

taken from sacrificed cattle (iii.450) or lambs (III.294). *Menos,* in other words, is vitality in general; the term appears most often in contexts of aggression, because the vitality of the creature is most clearly expressed in his aggressive acts.

18. In Homer, *menos* is only of the fire of the funeral pyre: XXIII. 177; XXIII.238 = XXIV.792.

19. Böhme (1929, pp. 13 ff.) notes that *menos* usually means some kind of striving toward a purpose; he therefore denies that *menos* means "physical strength" or anything of that sort; *menos,* he says, is not *Kraft* but *Wille:* "als das wesentliche Merkmal von *menos* ergibt sich . . . eine starke Aktivität, ein Drängen nach einem Ziel." I think that Böhme is here troubled by a false distinction; the fluctuating energies of the animal come and go as his resources are or are not concentrated on the achievement of some aim, and all organic activity, whether growth, appetitive activity, or rational choice, is teleological and aims at some goal. Mere energy—restlessness—is felt by the animal not as strength but as weakness.

On the other hand, Böhme is clearly right when he denies that *menos* means "muscular energy" or "impetus, momentum" (although at one point *menos* seems to mean the momentum imparted to an inanimate object when a man has put it in motion: XVII.529). *Menos* is not force or energy, as something exterior to us or at our service; it is primarily energy as experienced by us in our own actions:

> Denn viel näher als irgendwelche mechanischen Bewegungen steht dem Menschen sein eigenes Tun, sein Streben nach einem Ziel, sein Anlaufen gegen den Feind. Aus solchen Erfahrungen, die nicht nur den "inneren" Menschen angehen und nicht nur den Mechanismus seines Körpers, müssen wir die Bildung von Worten wie *memaa* und *menos* verstehen. [Idem, p. 18.]

20. Thus wood is *menoeikea,* "fit for the *menos*" of the funeral pyre (XXIII.139); wood feeds fire as food (the stuff most commonly called *menoeikea*) feeds man.

21. Elsewhere (XVII.111–12) the *ētor* is said to be frozen (*pachnoutai*); cf. Hesiod *Works and Days* 360.

22. So Demeter kept the child each night "in the *menos* of the fire, like a torch" and thus might have made him immortal (*Hymn to Demeter* 238–42).

23. Similarly, Eurycleia's *menos,* "like stone or iron," enables her to keep a secret (xix.493–94); her strength is expressed in her self-control. And it is Achilles' *menos* that enables him to refuse the gifts in Book Nine (IX.679).

24. A man's limbs may be *empeda* (XIII.512, XXIII.627) or his heart (X.93–94); his wits (*phrenes*) may be *empedoi* (VI.352), or his mind (*noos*; XI.813).

25. The *phrenes* were identified as the lungs by Justesen (1928); the suggestion has perhaps received too little attention because of its author's other extravagances. Böhme (1929), for example, flatly rejected it, but it has been convincingly revived, with careful analysis of Homer's detailed anatomical descriptions, by Onians (1951, pp. 23 ff.).

26. Because *thumos* implies *menos*, *thumos* like *menos* is increased by food and drink and diminished by hunger; so Odysseus' companions after their long journey are *askelees kai athumoi* (x.463). Cf. Böhme 1929, p. 31 (Böhme notes: "*askelees* verstehe ich nicht"; but see now Harrison 1954).

When Hector makes his brief visit to Troy, Hecuba offers him wine, "for wine much increases the *menos* of a man when he is tired" (VI. 261); Hector refuses, "lest you strip my limbs of *menos* and I forget my valor" (VI.265). This flat contradiction is based (like so much else in Homer) on exact observation of the physiological facts: alcohol is first an excitant, then a depressant, so that both statements are true.

Possibly this double nature of alcohol accounts for the use of wine to quench the funeral pyre (XXIII.250 = XXIV.791); wine, which leads first to uproarious activity and then to sleep, is a kind of "mediator" between life and death; it has a *menos* in it, felt in the flush of heat it brings us, but it also quenches *menos*.

27. Onians 1951, p. 50:

> To *pant* with eagerness, to *gasp* or *whistle* with astonishment, to *snort* with indignation, to *sob* with grief, to *yawn* with weariness, to *laugh* with mirth, to *sigh* with sadness or relief are some of the more marked variations of breathing with feeling that have found distinct expression in everyday speech. The *"breast heaving with emotion"* is a commonplace. We *"catch our breath"* at a sudden sound, *"hold our breath"* in suspense, *"breathe more freely,"* and so the list might be continued.

28. Cf. Böhme 1929, p. 13, n. 2.

29. When Sarpedon faints (V.696–98), the North Wind "takes his *thumos* prisoner (*zōgrei*)"—that is, keeps it intact for him. Therefore he does not die; and when the *thumos* has come back into him, he revives.

30. It is really not fair to equate the modern understanding with the Homeric; the Homeric view of death, like that of all preurban peoples, is enacted in ceremonies, whereas the modern view tends toward an abandonment of ceremonies. I could better have said that the Homeric is as close to the modern as it can be without losing its archaic ceremonial character.

This point can be put another way. In much of what follows, my line of analysis will be perceived to be close to that of Robert Hertz (1928). Hertz (to oversimplify) has two basic principles: first, that the funeral is a rite of initiation; second, that every death implies a resurrection. For Homer I would assert the first and deny the second. For this point of view the Homeric funeral represents a limiting case within the general type of ceremony investigated by Hertz.

31. To be alive is to be "casting glances across the earth" (I.88). In one Homeric formula, death comes on a man and *ton de skotos osse kalupse*, "darkness covered his eyes," or *amphi de osse kelaine nux ekalupse*, "dark night covered his eyes." The newborn child is "brought into the light and sees the light of the sun" (XVI.188). To be alive is to see the sunlight (V.120, XVIII.61 = 442, XXIV.558), and to die is to leave the sunlight (XVIII.11).

32 "So stehen *noein* und *idein* nebeneinander, das eine um die einfache Wahrnehmung, das andere um das Erkennen resp. Wiedererkennen, das Durchdringen durch die Oberfläche in die Tiefe der Erscheinung zu bezeichnen" (Böhme 1929, p. 24).

33. For a more extensive discussion see Olmsted 1974, pp. 16–25.

34. Cf. Webster 1957, p. 149:

> *Noos* . . . is a verbal abstract and verbal abstracts in Greek mean not only a process but also the agent or the result of the process; as a process, it means "appreciating the situation" in the military sense in which appreciate involves also making a plan; as an agent it means "the appreciating mind"; as a result it means "the plan or thought" which results from the appreciation.

See also Bona 1959, pp. 6 f.:

> *Noein* indica in primo luogo l'intuizione che il singolo ha di una determinata realtà. . . . Il modo con cui l'uomo intuisce una determinata situazione determina necessariamente il suo comportimento, il piano della sua condotta.

35. So it is the bard's *noos*—his vision or concept of his *oimē*, his theme—which draws him into composition of *aoidē* or song (cf. i.347).

36. Cf. Böhme 1929, pp. 52 f.:

> Affekte als solchen haben mit *noos* nichts zu tun. Die wenigen Stellen, die diesem Satz zu widersprechen scheinen, bestätigen ihn bei genauer Prüfung. Agamemnon "freut" sich über den Streit zwischen Odysseus und Achill (*chaire noōi*, viii.78). Man muss sich dieser Freude wundern, denn der unmittelbare Eindruck des Streites musste doch unerfreulich sein. Aber—der Dichter gibt die Erklärung—Agamemnon "wusste," dass ohne diesen Streit der endliche Sieg nicht möglich war. . . .
>
> Auch als Träger von Willensregungen kann der *noos* angesehen werden; aber alle durch den *noos* erstrebten Ziele sind vernünftig, unvernünftiges Begehren kann sich nur im Gegensatz zum *noos* durchsetzen.

37. Von Fritz 1943, p. 84.

38. Onians 1951, p. 83.

39. Von Fritz 1943, p. 90.

40. In XXIII.484 it is said of Oelian Ajax that his *noos* is *apēnēs*, his "mind is harsh." Here *noos* means "his whole way of thinking." This extended sense is much developed in the *Odyssey*; see Bona 1959.

41. The passivity of *noos* should not cause us to conclude that it is an inert or inactive faculty; *noos* is passive only in the sense that it recognizes what is so rather than determines what should be so. *Noos* is associated with planning because it is associated with insight, that is, with a recognition of appropriate means. Insight often involves active attention, as in the recurrent phrase *oxu noēse*. Furthermore, the *noos* can be active imaginatively, as it allows one picture after another to come before the mind. See the simile:

As darts the mind of a man, who has traveled much
Over the earth, and imagines it in his wits:
"Here could I be, or here" and the impulse moves him. . . .
(XV.80–82)

42. *Noein* is used of the dog Argos at the moment he recognizes Odysseus (xvii.301). This is no exception; the dog in effect performs a human mental act. Cf. Böhme 1929, p. 25.

43. At xiv.426 the *psuchē* leaves a sacrificed animal; I find this unique ascription of *psuchē* to an animal completely baffling. "Einige Anomalien wird man Homer wohl lassen müssen," says Herter (1957, p. 210, n. 29), and I can do no better. Equally anomalous is VII.131, where the *thumos* goes to Hades.

44. Rohde 1894, pp. 2–4.

45. Bickel 1926, pp. 52 ff.; cf. Schnaufer 1970, pp. 191–201.

46. *Sōma* has been associated with the root of *sinein*, "to despoil"; cf. *pōma pinein*, "drink" (Koller 1958, p. 280). This etymology could be wrong and still, as a folk etymology, affect the semantics of the words. *Sōma* is used of a living body only when it is the prey of animals. At the moment of death, as we shall see, the warrior is transformed from predator to prey; this transformation is marked by reference to his *sōma*. It is misleading to say: "the presence or absence of life is irrelevant to the word's meaning" (Harrison 1960, p. 64); the *sōma* is something liable to be despoiled or devoured, and this is the *meaning* of death in the Homeric view.

47. Onians 1951, pp. 95 ff., where a quite different explanation of the association is offered.

48. Traces of embalming perhaps survive in the use of the verb *tarchuein* (which should mean "embalm" or "preserve"; cf. the later word for "salt fish": *tarichos*) for the funeral rites in general (e.g., XVI. 456) and in the inclusion of honey among the substances burnt on the pyre (XXIII.170, xxiv.68); honey is used in many cultures for embalming (see Murray 1924, pp. 161 f.). But neither trace is incontestable.

Murray accepts an etymology for *tarchuein* which is by no means certain (cf. Frisk, *Griechisches Etymologisches Wörterbuch*, s.v.), and there can be other reasons for the inclusion of honey in the funeral rite. Honey is the livelihood of the bee stored against the winter; furthermore, unlike most organic things, it does not rot (that, in fact, is why it is employed in embalming). Therefore honey (like evergreen trees) is associated with the persistence of organic substance and is the appropriate food of the dead; since it does not change (rot), honey is the food of those who do not change (digest).

Schmid (1916, pp. 1414 ff.) suggested that the verb *meilissemen*, generally translated "soothe" or "assuage" and associated with the dead (one is said to "*meilissemen* the dead with fire": VII.410) should be derived from *meli*, "honey," and translated "embalm." This etymology was attacked by Kretschmer (1919, p. 242), nor was it accepted by Chantraine (1937, pp. 169 ff.), who, however, suggests that the two words may well have been associated in Homeric Greek through folk etymology. Compare the adjective used of sleep and wine: *meliphrōn*: "what soothes (honeys) the heart." Similarly, the dead may have been soothed or honeyed by the funeral. But there is no need to bring in embalming; the folk etymology could equally well reinforce the symbolic, rather than technical, association of honey with the dead. For another view see Schnaufer 1970, pp. 169–71.

We should, I think, be struck by the sharp contrast between Homeric and Mycenaean practice in this as in other respects; the epic, while formally historical, seems to be founded on a certain active resistance to the authentic historical tradition. Cf. Hesiod *Theogony* 83–84.

49. This association of the soul or spirit with the actual tombstone is made more explicit in some cultures; for the association of the life-force with (to name only the headings relevant to Homer) specific organic substances, the look of the man (as in a picture of him), his appearance in dreams, his shadow, and his tombstone see Nilsson 1949, pp. 87–88.

50. There are some significant differences in the pictures of the afterlife presented in the *Iliad* as against the *Odyssey*, as there are differences within the *Odyssey* between books eleven and twenty-four, and even within book eleven. We may have here signs of multiple authorship or interpolation, or we may have a single poet who draws on a complex and unrationalized range of belief for the version suited to his poetic purposes at any given moment. "Immer muss man bei den Vorstellungen von dem Wesen der Toten auf widersprechende Züge gefasst sein, . . . weil die Menschen zu allen Zeiten, also auch heute, dem ewigen Rätsel gleich hilflos gegenüberstehen und je nach Stimmung und Gefühl, Glauben und Zweifel das Verschiedenste nebeneinander gelten lassen" (Wilamowitz 1927, p. 193).

Homer himself dramatizes this complex of belief and doubt in Achilles' surprised cry on awaking from the dream of Patroclus: "There is in Hades a *psuchē* and an *eidōlon*, but no *phrenes* in it at all" (XXIII.103–4)—as if he were to say: "People (and bards) have always told me these things, but now I know they are true."

51. Anticleia does speak of Laertes' retirement to the country (xi.187 ff.); Eumaeus later in the poem seems to imply that Laertes retired only after his wife's death (xv.355–57). But this is not clear, and in any case there are other difficulties about Anticleia's speech; for instance, the interview between her and Odysseus takes place before Odysseus' long stay with Calypso and therefore at a time when Telemachus is still a child—yet he is spoken of as a grown man (xi.185–86). Probably none of these points should be pushed too hard; the poet seems somewhat careless of his own chronology.

52. Cf. Rahn 1953–54, pp. 443 f., 450 f.:

Suchen wir . . . diese "homerische Logik" . . . . Zugrunde liegt . . . die Voraussetzung, dass es "anschaubar" sei, wenn es denn etwas Wirkliches sein solle; es muss "als etwas" anschaubar, also dasein, und zwar als etwas irgendwie dasein, also "bestimmt" dasein. . . .

So kann z.B. der *anthrōpos* als *autos* nach dem Tode zwar nicht mehr so dasein, wie er lebend war, aber er muss als irgendetwas dasein, kann kein "Nichts" geworden sein. Und er ist irgendwie da als *psuchē* oder *nekros*—und selbst die Zerstörung der Anschaubarkeit des *nekros* kann nicht verhindern, dass er irgendwie da ist, und zwar anschaulich bestimmt durch die Sprachwirklichkeit als *psuchē* . . . .

Die *psuchai* sind bei Homer soweit dem "Nichts" genähert, wie er den Menschen überhaupt dem Nichts anschaulich nähern kann; sie haben kaum noch triebhafte Kraft, kaum noch Gestalt, sind Schattengebilde (*eidōla*), haben kaum noch Stimme (sie piepsen), keine Besinnungskraft (*phrenes*), kein Blut mehr—kurz, sie sind so negiert, wie es anschaulich möglich ist. Aber sie sind da, sie existieren immer weiter und habe ihre eigene Ordnung. . . .

Im homerischen Epos . . . ist die *psuchē* . . . Negation des lebenden Menschen, anschauliches Beinah-Nichts . . . das anschaubare, wesenlose Nichts des Lebens.

53. The interpretation given is close to neither of the two offered by Schnaufer (1970, pp. 163 f., with references to earlier discussions), although it agrees with the first that the hair is a gift offered to the dead in exchange for the mourner himself, and with the second that hair is offered because it is a special locus of vitality. There is no need to found the first notion on an assertion that at one time mourners did indeed sacrifice themselves, or the second on an assertion that at one time men thought they were actually conferring vitality on the

dead. Discussions of this point, as of so many points connected with Homeric cult, have been distorted by the constant attempt to see in Homeric practice faint echoes of earlier belief rather than a system functioning in its own right.

54. Some have held ("die gewöhnliche Erklärung"—Schnaufer 1970, p. 162) that the mourners make themselves bleed in order to feed the dead with their blood or that self-mutilation in the Homeric funeral is a "survival" of such a practice. This explanation takes no account of the other gestures which go with tearing the skin: rolling in the dust, etc. To be bloody is to be dirty (VI.266–68); it seems clear that the mourners bloody themselves as an act of "homeopathic self-pollution" (Friedrich 1973, pp. 15 f.).

55. For a review of material relevant to this notion and to the related association of the hair with (specifically genital) libido see Leach 1958.

56. Cf. Pagliaro 1963, pp. 31–33:

> Nell'Iliade appare spesso il motivo del cadavere del nemico straziato dai cani e dagli uccelli, ma non è più che un motivo, poiché ricorre solo nelle minacce che il guerriero rivolge al suo avversario. . . . Il proemio . . . [fa] di esso un dato della realtà effettiva, un fatto da rappresentare: in altre parole, in esso i cadaveri abbandonati ai cani e agli avvoltoi sono un fatto reale, qualcosa che, dopo tale dichiarazione preliminare, ci aspetteremmo di vedere narrativamente rappresentato nel poema. Quello che nel corso di questo, nononstante le occasioni possibili, si mantiene sul piano del dato formale ed è, si potrebbe dire, un modulo della retorica eroica, qui nel proemio appare come risultato effettivo.

The horror to which Homer has pinned his tragedy is not the horror of the mutilated corpse but the horror that men are willing to inflict such mutilation. Actual mutilation would distract us from the poet's ethical theme. On the other hand, the terror of the work would be much diminished if we thought that the threat of mutilation was a mere threat, that man or god would always intervene to prevent the actuality of mutilation. The proem thus sets before us the actuality of mutilation as a leading theme of the poem and lays a foundation for the ethical theme developed in the body of the poem.

Similarly, in the *Odyssey* Nestor says that, had Menelaus returned in time to kill Aegistheus, he would have fed him to the dogs (iii.256–61); in fact Orestes gave Aegistheus and Clytemnestra a proper burial (iii. 306–10). Thus Menelaus' anger is dramatized, but at the same time the story of the house of Atreus is (in this brief version of it) brought to closure with a proper ceremonial ending.

57. Dietrich (1965, p. 242) reviews the extra-Homeric evidence for *kēres* and calls them "a primitive, yet vivid concept of defilement or impurity imagined as ever present and against which certain apotro-

paeic measures have to be taken." This meaning he finds also in Homer, although in the majority of cases the term *kēr* has been generalized to mean simply "death" or "the fate that leads to death."

58. This term is borrowed from Turner (1969), as is "liminal," used above.

59. The warrior may be compared to Ares, god of war: VII.208–10, XIII.298–300. Also, there are similes which refer to war as seen or heard from afar: XVIII.207–13, 219–20, XXI.522–24.

60. There are similes of women coloring ivory (IV.141–47), weighing wool (XII.433–36), or weaving (XXIII.760–63), of men irrigating (XXI. 257–64), winnowing (V.499–505, XIII.588–92), reaping (XI.67–71), shearing (XII.451–53), cutting wood (IX.482–89, XVI.633–35), carpentering (XV.410–13), building (XVI.212–14, XXIII.711–13), butchering (XVII. 520–23), tanning (XVII.389–95), and fishing (XVI.406–9, XXIV.80–82). Domestic animals at work also appear in these similes: mules drag timber (XVII.742–46), and oxen plow (XIII.703–8) or turn a mill (XX. 495–99).

61. Thus Patroclus' speech, which compares the dying warrior to the diver (XVI.745–50), is said in harsh mockery (*epikertomeōn*).

62. The association of gods with weather and with the horizontal frontiers of the human world grants to the gods a *numen* and places them apart from man within the cosmic order. It seems to me probable that the gods of the similes are far closer to the gods of cult and of the ordinary belief of Homer's audience than are the gods of the epic narration. In this respect, as in others, the similes reach out beyond the epic conventions to the world of daily life.

63. So Rahn (1953–54, pp. 289 f.) draws attention to the similarities between Odysseus' encounter with the stag on Circe's island and an encounter between two warriors on the battlefield: "so wird er nicht einfach 'Jagdbeute,' sondern die Jagd wird im Sinne der Ilias-Kämpfe stilisiert als Kampf-Begegnung."

64. For the continuation of these notions in later Greek see Robert 1949 and Vidal-Naquet 1968.

65. For a general review of Homeric evidence regarding dogs in the context of the contrast between "Tierfrass" and "Leichenverbrennung" see Faust 1970.

66. Perhaps such dogs made themselves useful as watchdogs; we are told this of the golden dogs of Alcinous, yet even they are primarily decorative works of art (vii.91–94). Telemachus appears with dogs at his heels (ii.11, xvii.62 = xx.145), and this picture is almost as formulaic as that of a woman accompanied by her maids (III.143 = i.331 = xviii. 207) or a warrior accompanied by his *therapōn* (XXIV.573). The house dog, like the servant, ornaments his master simply by being servile.

67. The dog is an interstitial creature, between man and animal, and thus is impure, just as monsters are impure. Cf. Rahn 1953–54, p. 469:

Dass sich beim Schimpfen die Tiermetapher auch im Homer findet, (vor allem "Hund, Hundsgesicht, Hundefliege") ziegt, dass im Tier etwas Hässliches gesehen wird. . . . Das Hässlichere . . . ist in den Mischgestalten der Kentauren, Skylla oder Chimaira zum Bilde gräulicher tierisch-göttlicher Hässlichkeit gesteigert.

68. Except for Odysseus' Argos, whose name is merely a particular use of the formulaic epithet for dogs, *argoi*. This epithet means "bright": it is a descriptive name for a hunting dog, who must be seen as he flashes through the undergrowth. Homeric names for dogs, if they all followed this pattern, would form a metaphoric, syntagmatic series (like names of French cattle; cf. Lévi-Strauss 1962, pp. 272 f.). The names recommended by Xenophon for dogs were all of this kind (*Kynegetikus* vii.5); Greek descriptive names for dogs place the dog (to follow Lévi-Strauss's suggestion) firmly within the technico-economic order, as instrument rather than companion

69. When Achilles' horses mourn for the dead Patroclus, Zeus pities them; they are immortal and should share the detachment of the gods, yet they allow themselves affection for humankind (XVII.443–47). That a horse can be immortal actually places the horse, in one respect, closer to god than to man. The parallelism between man and horse appears in the Catalogue, where the poet asks: "Who was the best man who came to Troy, and who were the best horses?" (II.761–62).

70. Later in the same scene Diomedes asks himself what "most dog-like thing he can do" before returning to his own lines (X.503). This is the only place in Homer where this adjective, elsewhere pejorative, is used in a positive sense. And this reversal is appropriate to Book Ten—the Doloneia—which takes place at night and in which Diomedes and Odysseus execute a secret raid on the enemy, stealing their horses and killing men in their sleep. Diomedes looks about for some possible act of malicious damage he can execute before creeping back to his own lines. This sort of raid, while it requires exceptional courage and skill on the part of the warrior, is in a certain sense a transformation of combat; it is combat executed under special restrictive conditions. It is appropriate that the warrior appears here as a dog, that is, as a reduced form of himself.

71. Cf. Schnaufer 1970, p. 142.

72. Cf. Rahn 1953–54, p. 471:

Dass sie Fleisch fressen, ist nichts Besonderes, aber dass sie die menschlichen Leichen bedrohen, gibt ihnen bei ihrer Unterlegenheit gegenüber dem menschlichen Selbstbewusstsein zugleich etwas dem Menschen Ungreifbar-Überlegenes, das in einem im Menschen dumpf schlummernden kannibalischen Vernichtungstrieb einen kaum bewussten Widerhall findet.

73. Cf. Lévi-Strauss 1962, p. 271.

74. If not technically "rabies," the word does at least mean a frenzy which overtakes dogs—as Priam imagines it will overtake his dogs when they lick his blood (XXII.70).

75. In his promise to Patroclus (XVIII.334–37) Achilles puts together his intention to kill and despoil Hector (despoilment is the implication of *kephalēn*) and to kill the twelve prisoners.

76. According to Bassett (1933, pp. 51 f.):

> Homer has used all the means that were possible to make it clear that Hector intended to throw the body of Patroclus to the dogs —by the words of Hector to Patroclus, by the poet's statement in the narrative, by the thought of Zeus, and by the words of the two Greek leaders—and he has taken pains to show that Achilles was aware of this intention. It therefore seems an exaggeration of sentimentality, a refusal to let Homer interpret Homer, and the inability to think in terms of the Heroic Age of Greece, which have led so many modern scholars to think the worse of Achilles for refusing Hector's plea not to throw his body to the dogs. The evidence which we have presented from Homer would, we think, acquit Achilles, before any intelligent jury, of the charge of conduct unbecoming a knight of the Greek Heroic Age.

Bassett was clearly right to stress this point of likeness between the two heroes; the *Iliad* does not tell of a conflict between two ethical systems but rather shows us a conflict between two heroes who, with different personal capacities, social circumstances, and ultimate fates, share a common ethic. On the other hand, it does not follow that Achilles' acts are "becoming"; rather, I would assert that Achilles, like Hector, moves in the direction of acts which, to the poet and his audience, are terrifying, repulsive, and impure. The poet's aim, however, is not to "acquit" either hero—or to prosecute either one—but to explore the implications of the ethic itself and its transformation under the contradictory social conditions of warfare. From this point of view, Book Twenty-four can be seen, not as an unmotivated appendix in which Achilles is oddly transformed and gentle virtues, hitherto disregarded, are for the first time praised, but rather as a logical outcome and completion of the dramatized ethical dilemma set before us in the first twenty-three books.

77. Laughter is otherwise rare in the *Iliad*. There are tears and laughter together in Hector and Andromache's common love of their child (VI.471, 484); a similar intimate laughter rises in Zeus as he comforts the wounded goddess (XXI.508). Athena laughs at her own success in battle (XXI.408); so, once, does Paris (XI.378). Hera is provoked to angry laughter (XV.101). Then there is the laughter which rises at the table of the gods when Hephaestus distracts them from

their quarrel by serving the wine (I.559) and the laughter which rises in the host when Odysseus beats the laughable Thersites (II.270; cf. 215). On all these occasions, as in the games, laughter is the mark of the release of social tension.

78. Funeral games are thus midway between games and ritual; they are both *disjunctive* (generating a distinction between winners and losers) and *conjunctive* (constructing an organic unity among the players, between players and audience, and between the living, on the one hand, and, on the other hand, the dead warrior in whose honor honor is bestowed on the living). Cf. Lévi-Strauss 1962, pp. 46 f.

79. Once also of Zeus Xenius in the *Odyssey* (xiv.284). The statement in Liddell-Scott-Jones, *Greek-English Lexicon*, s.v. *nemesis*, "not used of the gods in Homer," disregards these passages—which, however, involve the verb, not the noun.

80. Whitman 1958, pp. 217 f.

81. It should be clear that I state here not the *message* of the *Iliad*, but an aspect of its *meaning*; we are left not with an ethical truth, proper to all times and situations, but with an ethical synthesis proper to the premises and formed action of this particular poetic construct. Achilles' two speeches, one should note, state as the outcome and ending of the *Iliad* an ethical position which is by contrast a premise of the *Odyssey*—and there not the end of action but its beginning. The mature and sympathetic figures of the *Odyssey* are sharply aware of man's insignificance and his plasticity to circumstance—as in Nausicaa's speech to Odysseus (vi.188–90) and, most expressively, in Odysseus' speech to Amphinomus (xviii.125–50). These characters, in this very differently organized poem, act with an acceptance of finitude which confers on them a certain humility; they act for the sake of the meanings which they themselves confer on the persons and institutions they value. It is consistent with this very different ethical premise that the Odysseus of the *Odyssey* is, not occasionally but throughout the poem, his own poet, acting and at the same time observing his own act. For a fuller treatment see Redfield 1973.

82. Cf. Vacca 1973, p. 124:

> There is no more poignant moment in the *Iliad* than when Achilles looks at Priam and sees—not his Enemy with the eyes of Hekabe but—Peleus. Yet the two old men are one only through their shared relation to a doomed and nihilistic world. All else divides them and breeds hatred, envy, and fear. There is compassion, then, but there is nothing to *do*.

REFERENCES

Adkins, A. W. H. 1960. *Merit and Responsibility: A Study in Greek Values.* Oxford: Clarendon Press.

———. 1963. " 'Friendship' and 'Self-Sufficiency' in Homer and Aristotle." *Classical Quarterly* n.s. 12:30–45.

———. 1969a. *"Euchomai, Euchōlē,* and *Euchos* in Homer." *Classical Quarterly* n.s. 19:20–33.

———.1969b. "Threatening, Abusing, and Feeling Angry in the Homeric Poems." *Journal of Hellenic Studies* 89:7–21.

———. 1970. *From the Many to the One.* Ithaca: Cornell University Press.

———. 1971. "Homeric Values and Homeric Society." *Journal of Hellenic Studies* 91:1–14.

Amory, A. 1966. "The Gates of Horn and Ivory." *Yale Classical Studies* 20:3–51.

Bassett, S. E. 1933. "Achilles' Treatment of Hector's Body." *Transactions and Proceedings of the American Philological Association* 64:41–65.

Bespaloff, R. 1943. *De l'Iliade.* New York: Brentano's. English translation, *On the "Iliad."* Trans. M. McCarthy. Princeton: Princeton University Press, 1947.

Bickel, E. 1926. *Homerischer Seelenglaube.* Berlin: Deutsche Verlagsgesellschaft für Politik und Geschichte.

Böhme, J. 1929. *Die Seele und das Ich im Homerischen Epos.* Leipzig and Berlin: B. G. Teubner.

Bona, G. 1959. "Il 'Noos' e i 'Nooi' nell'*Odissea.*" *Università di Torino Pubblicazioni della Facoltà di Lettere e Filosofia* 11, fasc. 1.

Bowra, C. M. 1930. *Tradition and Design in the Iliad.* Oxford: Clarendon Press.

Campbell, J. K. 1966. "Honour and the Devil." In *Honour and Shame,* ed. J. G. Peristiany, pp. 139–70. Chicago: University of Chicago Press.

Carpenter, R. 1946. *Folk Tale, Fiction and Saga in the Homeric Epics.* Berkeley and Los Angeles: University of California Press.

Chantraine, P. 1937. "Grec *meilichos.*" In *Mélanges Emile Boisacq.* Vol. 1. *Annuaire de l'Institut de Philologie et d'Histoire Orientales et Slaves de l'Université libre de Bruxelles* 5:169–74.

Cheyns, A. 1967. "Sens et valeurs du mot *aidōs* dans les contextes homériques." *Recherches de Philologies et de Linguistique* (Louvain) 1:3–33.

Dahrendorf, R. 1973. *Homo Sociologicus.* London: Routledge & Kegan Paul. Title essay originally published in *Kölner Zeitschrift für Soziologie* 10, nos. 2–3 (1958).

Dawe, R. D. 1967. "Some Reflections on *atē* and *hamartia.*" *Harvard Studies in Classical Philology* 72:89–123.

Detienne, M. 1967. *Les Maîtres de vérité dans le grèce archaïque.* Paris: François Maspero.

Dietrich, B. C. 1965. *Death, Fate and the Gods.* London: University of London, Athlone Press.

Dodds, E. R. 1951. *The Greeks and the Irrational.* Berkeley and Los Angeles: University of California Press.

———. 1968. "Homer: i–iii." In *Fifty Years (and Twelve) of Classical Scholarship,* ed. M. Platnauer. Oxford: Basil Blackwell.

Douglas, M. 1970. *Purity and Danger: An Analysis of Concepts of Pollution and Taboo.* London: Pelican Books. 1st ed., New York: Praeger, 1966.

Else, G. 1957. *Aristotle's "Poetics": The Argument.* Cambridge, Mass.: Harvard University Press.

———. 1958. "Imitation in the Fifth Century." *Classical Philology* 53: 73–90.

von Erffa, C. E. F. 1937. "Aidōs und verwandte Begriffe in ihrer Entwicklung von Homer bis Demokrit." *Philologus,* supp. vol. 30, fasc. 2.

Faust, M. 1970. "Die künstlerische Verwendung von *kuōn* 'Hund' in den homerischen Epen." *Glotta* 48:8–31.

Finley, M. I. 1954. *The World of Odysseus.* New York: Viking Press.

Fränkel, H. 1960. "Die Zeitauffassung in der archäischen griechischen Literatur." In *Wege und Formen frühgriechischen Denkens.* Munich: C. H. Beck. First published in *Beilagenheft zur Zeitschrift für Ästhetik und allgemeine Kunstwissenschaft* 25 (1931):97–118.

———. 1962. *Dichtung und Philosophie des frühen Griechentums.* 2d ed. Munich: C. H. Beck. 1st ed., 1950. English translation, *Early Greek Poetry and Philosophy.* Trans. M. Hadas and J. Willis. Oxford: Blackwell, forthcoming.

Friedrich, P. 1973. "Defilement and Honor in the *Iliad.*" Mimeographed. Abstract in *Journal of Indo-European Studies* 1:119–26.

von Fritz, K. 1943. "*Noos* and *noein* in the Homeric poems." *Classical Philology* 38:79–93.

Fyfe, W. H. 1910. "Seven Passages in Aristotle's *Poetics.*" *Classical Review* 24:233–35.

Gates, H. P. 1971. *The Kinship Terminology of Homeric Greek.* Indiana University Publications in Anthropology and Linguistics, mem. 27. Supplement to *International Journal of American Linguistics* 37, no. 4, pt. II.

Geertz, C. 1966. "Religion as a Cultural System." In *Anthropological Approaches to the Study of Religion*, ed. M. Banton, pp. 1–46. London: Tavistock.

Golden, L. 1962. "Catharsis." *Transactions and Proceedings of the American Philological Association* 93:51–60.

Grene, D. 1950. *Man in His Pride*. Chicago: University of Chicago Press. Reissued as *Greek Political Theory*. Chicago: University of Chicago Press, 1965.

———. 1960. "Man's Day of Fate." In *City Invincible*, ed. C. H. Kraeling and R. M. Adams, pp. 367–89. Chicago: University of Chicago Press.

Harriott, R. 1969. *Poetry and Criticism before Plato*. London: Methuen.

Harrison, E. L. 1954. " 'Last Legs' in Homer." *Classical Review* n.s. 4: 189–92.

———. 1960. "Notes on Homeric Psychology." *Phoenix* 14:63–80.

Herter, H. 1957. "*Sōma* bei Homer." In *Charites*, ed. K. Schauenberg, pp. 206–17. Bonn: Athenäum.

Hertz, R. 1928. "Contribution à une étude sur la représentation collective de la mort." In *Mélanges de sociologie religieuse et folklore*. Paris: Alcan. Originally published in *Année sociologique* 10 (1907): 48–137. English translation, "A Contribution to the Study of the Collective Representation of Death." Trans. R. Needham and C. Needham. In R. Hertz, *Death and the Right Hand*. Glencoe, Ill.: Free Press, 1960.

Jones, J. 1962. *On Aristotle and Greek Tragedy*. New York: Oxford University Press.

Jörgensen, O. 1904. "Das Auftreten der Götter in den Büchern ix–xii der *Odyssee*." *Hermes* 3:357–82.

Justesen, P. Th. 1928. *Les Principes psychologiques d'Homère*. Copenhagen: Chr. Justesen.

Kirk, G. S. 1962. *The Songs of Homer*. Cambridge, Eng.: At the University Press.

Koller, H. 1958. "*Sōma* bei Homer." *Glotta* 37:276–81.

Kretschmer, P. 1919. "Literarbericht für das Jahr 1916." *Glotta* 10: 213–45.

Lacey, W. K. 1966. "Homeric *hedna* and Penelope's *kurios*." *Journal of Hellenic Studies* 86:55–68.

Latte, K. 1920–21. "Schuld und Sünde in der griechischen Religion." *Archiv für Religionswissenschaft* 20:254–98.

Leach, E. R. 1958. "Magical Hair." *Journal of the Royal Anthropological Institute* 88:147–64.

———. 1964. "Animal Categories and Verbal Abuse." In *New Directions in the Study of Language*, ed. E. H. Lenneberg, pp. 23–63. Cambridge, Mass.: Massachusetts Institute of Technology Press.

Lévi-Strauss, C. 1962. *La Pensée sauvage.* Paris: Plon. English translation, *The Savage Mind.* Chicago: University of Chicago Press, 1966.

Long, A. A. 1970. "Morals and Values in Homer." *Journal of Hellenic Studies* 90:121–39.

Lord, A. B. 1953. "Homer's Originality: Oral Dictated Texts." *Transactions and Proceedings of the American Philological Association* 84:124–34.

———. 1960. *The Singer of Tales.* Cambridge, Mass.: Harvard University Press.

Maine, H. S. 1920. *Ancient Law.* With introduction and notes by F. Pollock. London: J. Murray. 1st ed., 1861.

Moulinier, L. 1952. *Le Pur et l'impur dans la pensée des Grecs d'Homère à Aristote.* Paris: C. Klincksieck.

Murray, G. 1924. *The Rise of the Greek Epic.* 3d ed. Oxford: Clarendon Press. 1st ed., 1907.

Nagler, M. N. 1967. "Toward a Generative View of the Oral Formula." *Transactions and Proceedings of the American Philological Association* 98:269–311.

Nilsson, M. P. 1923–24. "Götter und Psychologie bei Homer." *Archiv für Religionswissenschaft* 22:363–90.

———. 1949. "A Letter to Professor Nock." *Harvard Theological Review* 42:71–107.

Olmsted, W. 1974. "An Examination of the Relations between Thought and Perception with Reference to Homer, the Pythagoreans, Heraclitus, Plato, and Aristotle." Ph.D. dissertation, University of Chicago.

Olson, E. 1965. Editor's Introduction to *Aristotle's "Poetics" and English Literature.* Chicago: University of Chicago Press.

Onians, R. B. 1951. *The Origins of European Thought about the Body, the Mind, the Soul, the World, Time, and Fate.* Cambridge, Eng.: At the University Press.

Owen, E. T. 1966. *The Story of the Iliad.* Ann Arbor: University of Michigan Press, Ann Arbor Paperbacks. 1st ed., New York: Oxford University Press, 1947.

Pagliaro, A. 1961. "Aedi e Rapsodi." Chap. 1 in *Saggi di Critica Semantica.* 2d ed. Messina and Florence: G. d'Anna. 1st ed., 1953.

———. 1963. "Il Proemio dell' *Iliade.*" Chap. 1 in *Nuovi Saggi di Critica Semantica.* 2d ed. Messina and Florence: G. d'Anna. First published in *Rendiconti della Classe di Scienze morali, storiche e filologiche dell' Accademia dei Lincei,* 8th ser. 10 (1955): 369–96.

Parry, A. 1956. "The Language of Achilles." *Transactions and Proceedings of the American Philological Association* 87:1–7.

———. 1972. "Language and Characterization in Homer." *Harvard Studies in Classical Philology* 76:1–22.

References

Pitt-Rivers, J. 1966. "Honour and Social Status." In *Honour and Shame,* ed. J. G. Peristiany, pp. 21–77. Chicago: University of Chicago Press.

———. 1970. "Women and Sanctuary in the Mediterranean." In *Echanges et communications: Mélanges offerts à Lévi-Strauss,* 2: 862–75. Studies in General Anthropology, no. 5. Paris and The Hague: Mouton.

Pohlenz, M. 1956. "Furcht und Mitleid? Ein Nachwort." *Hermes* 84: 49–74.

Radin, P. 1956. *Primitive Man as Philosopher.* Reprint. New York: Dover. 1st ed., 1927.

Rahn, H. 1953–54. "Tier und Mensch in der Homerischen Auffassung der Wirklichkeit." *Paideuma* 5:227–97, 431–80.

Redfield, J. M. 1973. "The Making of the *Odyssey.*" In *Parnassus Revisited,* ed. A. C. Yu, pp. 141–54. Chicago: American Library Association. First published in *Essays in Western Civilization in Honor of Christian W. Mackauer,* ed. L. Botstein and E. Karnovsky, pp. 1–17. Chicago: The College of The University of Chicago, 1967.

Robert, L. 1949. "Epitaphe d'un berger à Thasos." Chap. 16 in *Hellenica,* vol. 7. Paris: Adrien-Maisonneuve.

Rohde, E. 1894. *Psyche.* Freiburg and Leipzig: J. C. B. Mohr. English translation, *Psyche.* Trans. W. B. Hillis. New York: Harcourt, Brace, 1925.

Schadewaldt, W. 1944. *Von Homers Welt und Werk.* Leipzig: Koehler & Amelang.

———. 1955. "Furcht und Mitleid?" *Hermes* 83:129–71.

Schmid, W. 1916. "*Meilissō.*" *Berliner Philologische Wochenschrift* 36: 1414–15.

Schmitt, R. 1967. *Dichtung und Dichtersprache in Indogermanischer Zeit.* Wiesbaden: Otto Harrassowitz.

Schnaufer, A. 1970. *Frühgriechischer Totenglaube.* Hildesheim and New York: Georg Olms.

Schwabl, H. 1954. "Zur Selbständigkeit des Menschen bei Homer." *Wiener Studien* 67:46–64.

Scott, J. A. 1921. *The Unity of Homer.* Berkeley: University of California Press.

Seel, O. 1953. "Zur Vorgeschichte des Gewissensbedenke im altgriechischen Denken." In *Festchrift Franz Dornseiff,* ed. H. Kusch. Leipzig: VEB Bibliographisches Institut.

Segal, C. 1971. "The Theme of the Mutilation of the Corpse in the Iliad." *Mnemosyne,* supp. 17.

Snell, B. 1924. "Die Ausdrücke für den Begriff des Wissens in der vorplatonischen Philosophie." *Philologische Untersuchungen,* vol. 29. Berlin. Weidmann.

————. 1928. "Aischylos und das Handeln im Drama." *Philologus,* supp. vol. 20, fasc. 1.

Speier, H. 1952. "Honor and Social Structure." Chap. 4 in *Social Order and the Risks of War.* New York: George W. Stewart. First published in *Social Research* 2 (1935):74–97.

Tromp de Ruiter, S. 1932. "De vocis quae est *philanthrōpia* significatione atque usu." *Mnemosyne* n.s. 59:271–306.

Turner, V. 1969. *The Ritual Process.* Chicago: Aldine.

Vacca, R. A. 1973. "The Development of Sophrosyne in Homer and Aeschylus." Ph.D. dissertation, University of Chicago.

Verdenius, W. J. 1945. "*Aidōs* bei Homer." *Mnemosyne* 3d ser. 12: 47–60.

————. 1949. *Mimesis.* Leiden: E. J. Brill.

Vernant, J.-P. 1969. *Les Origines de la pensée grecque.* 2d ed. Paris: Presses Universitaires de France. 1st ed., 1962.

————. 1973. "Tensions et ambiguïtés dans le tragédie grecque." Chap. 2 in J.-P. Vernant and P. Vidal-Naquet, *Mythe et tragédie en Grèce ancienne.* Paris: Maspero. Earlier, English version, "Tensions and Ambiguities in Greek Tragedy." In *Interpretation: Theory and Practice,* pp. 105–21. Baltimore: Johns Hopkins University Press, 1969.

Vidal-Naquet, P. 1965. "Economie et société dans la Grèce ancienne: l'oeuvre de Moses I. Finley." *Archives européennes de sociologie* 6:111–48.

————. 1968. "Le Chausseur noir et l'origine de l'ephébie athénienne." *Annales: Economies—sociétés—civilisations* 23:947–64. Published earlier in English, "The Black Hunter and the Origin of the Athenian Ephebeia." Trans. Mrs. J. Lloyd. *Proceedings of the Cambridge Philological Society* n.s. 14:49–64.

Wade-Gery, H. T. 1952. *The Poet of the "Iliad."* Cambridge, Eng.: At the University Press.

Warden, J. 1969. "*Iphthimos*: A Semantic Analysis." *Phoenix* 23:143–58.

Webster, T. B. L. 1957. "Some Psychological Terms in Greek Tragedy." *Journal of Hellenic Studies* 77:149–54.

Weil, S. 1953. "L'*Iliade* ou le poème de la force." Chap. 1 in *La Source grecque.* Paris: Gallimard. First published in *Cahiers du Sud,* December 1940–January 1941, under the pseudonym Emile Novis. English translation, "The Iliad: Poem of Might." In *Intimations of Christianity among the Ancient Greeks,* pp. 24–59. Ed. and trans. E. C. Geissbuhler. London: Routledge & Kegan Paul, 1957.

Whitman, C. H. 1958. *Homer and the Homeric Tradition.* Cambridge, Mass.: Harvard University Press.

von Wilamowitz-Möllendorf, U. 1916. *Die Ilias und Homer.* Berlin: Weidmann.

————. 1927. "*Thumos, Psuchē, Phrēn, Kradiē.*" Appendix to *Die Heimkehr des Odysseus*, pp. 189–201. Berlin: Weidmann.

Zarker, J. W. 1965. "King Eëtion and Thebe as Symbols in the *Iliad.*" *Classical Journal* 61:110–14.

INDEX OF GREEK WORDS

271

dēmoboros, devourer of public property, of Agamemnon, 194

dēmou phēmis, the voice of the folk, 116

deos, fear, contrasted with aidōs, 115, 243 n.14

di' allēla, the inner logic of events, 67; cause and effect (Butcher), 247 n.6

Dios boulē, the Plan of Zeus, 247–48 n.9

dmōes, servitors, 111

duskleia, negative kleos or fame, 33. See also kleos

eeldōr, a claim to recompense, 136, 137; desire, 141

eidōlon (pl. eidōla), an image, 178, 257 n.50, n.52

eikos, probable, 57

eleeinon, pitiable, 89. See also eleos

eleos, pity, 89, 118, 239 n.12. See also eleeinon

empedos (neut. empedon), steady, 172; in connection with organs and their vital capacities, 173, 177, 180, 252 n.24

en kosmōi, in order, 161

enepein, to say, 229 n.5

energeia, functioning, 61. See also ergon

ergon, function, 61. See also argon, energeia

essomenoisi puthesthai, "for men-to-come to inquire about," v; of gravestones, 34, 230 n.15

ēthos, character, 61

ētor, vital spirit in the heart, 252 n.21

eu (adv.), well; to eu, the doing-it-well, 61

euchē, a formal boast, 207. See also euchesthai

euchesthai, to boast, to pray, 129. See also euchē

euchomai elpomenos, "I claim my hope," "I hopefully pray," "I confidently boast," 138. See also euchesthai

eulogistoi gar, "since they are good at reasoning," 85

eunoia, good will, 239 n.12. See also noos

exarchein, to initiate, 229 n.2

geinato, (she) bore, gave birth to, 119. See also genos

geneē, breed, breeding, 242 n.4. See also genos

genos, breeding, 135. See also geneē, geinato

geras, a mark of status, 94, 111, 112; of the dead, 175

gooi, formal laments for the dead, 180

hamartia, error, 88, 90, 97, 240 n.17

harmonia, harmony, 233 n.35

hēgemones, leaders, 241 n.3

hēroēs (sing. hērōs), heroes, 99, 111, 241 n.3

hestēkei, "he takes his stand" (stative perfect), 226 n.15

hubris, outrageous behavior, 3, 136

hulakomōroi, foolish barkers, of dogs, 195

ideein, to see, 176, 254 n.32. See also istōr

iphthimos, mighty, potent, 226 n.18

istōr, judge or arbitrator, 240 n.15. See also ideein

kakia, vice, contrasted with hamartia (error), 190. See also hamartia

kata kosmon, according to order, in due order, 39

kata phusin, natural, 233 n.35. See also sumphuton

katharsis, purification, 52, 67–68, 89, 236 n.53, 236–37 n.54; discussion of, 67–68

kephalē, head, 261 n.75

kēres (sing. kēr), death-bringers, 134, 183–85, 198, 258–59 n.57

INDEX

Acharnians (Aristophanes), 59
Achelous (river), 217
Achilles. *See also* Hector; Odysseus; Patroclus
—breeding of (son of Peleus and Thetis), 6, 11–12, 17, 19, 93, 119, 212, 215, 250 n.15
—character of, 10–13, 17–18, 22–24, 27–29, 93–99, 104–8, 118, 197, 202–3, 211–18, 250 n.11; compared with Coriolanus, 104, 106; compared with Hector, 27–29, 202–3, 211, 222; compared with Sarpedon, 105; as poet, 36, 221–22; as rhetorician, 7, 10, 13
—critics' view of, 8–11, 24
—error of, 106–7
—fate of, 29, 34, 93, 134
—helmet of, 148
—horses of, 260 n. 69
—and other characters, 7–8; Agamemnon, 3, 13–17, 92–94, 194, 209–10, 222, 226 n.16, 228 n.25 (*see also* Achilles, story of); Ajax, 16–17; Andromache, 122, 169; Briseis, 17, 226 n.16, 242 n.7; the Greeks, 16–18, 221–22; Hector, 28–29, 155, 158–59, 194, 198–99, 211, 261 nn.75–76 (*see also* Achilles, story of); Hecuba, 198; the Myrmidons, 16, 197; Nestor, 206; Patroclus, 17–19, 36, 106–7, 118, 179, 203, 211, 215, 226 n.16, 261 n.75 (*see also* Achilles, story of); Peleus, 112, 182, 215 (*see also* Achilles, breeding of); Phoenix, 7, 17, 217; Priam, 119, 202–3, 215–18; Scamander (river), 251 n.15; Thetis, 18, 107 (*see also* Achilles, breeding of); Zeus, 22, 212–13, 216, 221

—in similes: like a dog, 199; like the dog star, 203; like a king receiving a stranger, 215; like a lion, 7, 192, 212
—story of, 20, 24, 27–28, 103–8, 203–4, 221–23; events of (in chronological order): calls the assembly, 12, 95; quarrels with Agamemnon, 3, 12–14, 92, 96, 103, 111; decides to kill Agamemnon, 103; is restrained by Athena, 3, 15, 77–78, 98, 103, 136, 213 (*see also* Hera): withdraws from his community, 15–17, 27, 103; appeals to Thetis, 3, 136–37; refuses Agamemnon's gifts, 3–11, 15–17, 103–6, 139, 252 n.23; vows not to fight until Hector reaches his own ships, 17–18, 106, 140; inquires about Machaon, 106; sends Patroclus into battle, 18, 106, 141; warns Patroclus not to go too far, 18, 106, 149; hears of Patroclus' death, 9–10, 18, 22, 107; determines to kill Hector, 18–19, 28–29, 107, 220; shouts from the wall, 150; receives new armor, 14; is reconciled with Agamemnon, 22, 107, 218; launches his *aristeia*, 19, 107, 141, 155; encounters Hector (inconclusively), 155; kills Lycaon, 8, 19, 77, 155, 168–69; kills Asteropaeus, 169, 250–51 n.15; contends with the river Scamander, 19, 214; kills Hector, 8, 141, 149, 159; despoils Hector, 8, 27, 107, 169, 203, 261 n.76; dreams of the dead Patroclus, 257 n.50; celebrates funeral of Patroclus, 108, 171, 181–82; celebrates funeral games of Patroclus, 108,